Spirited Practices

Spirituality and the helping professions

*Edited by Fran Gale, Natalie Bolzan,
and Dorothy McRae-McMahon*

Routledge
Taylor & Francis Group

LONDON AND NEW YORK

First published 2007 by Allen & Unwin

Published 2020 by Routledge
2 Park Square, Milton Park, Abingdon, Oxon OX14 4RN
605 Third Avenue, New York, NY 10017

Routledge is an imprint of the Taylor & Francis Group, an informa business

National Library of Australia
Cataloguing-in-Publication entry:

Spirited practices : spirituality and the helping
  professions.

Includes index.
ISBN 9781741750614 (pbk.).

1. Counseling - Religious aspects. 2. Counseling
psychology. I. McRae-McMahon, Dorothy, 1934- . II.
Bolzan, Natalie. III. Gale, Fran.

158.3

Set in 11/14 pt ACaslon Regular by Midland Typesetters, Australia

ISBN-13: 9781741750614 (pbk)

To the spirit of those who have inspired us

Olive Collett, Amy Bolzan, Sophie North, Julian of Norwich,
and for all who work to bring spirituality into their helping practice

Foreword

Spirituality and religion are among those phenomena that can be observed in all human cultures and throughout human history. Yet in the helping professions, whose shared objective is to promote human wellbeing, questions of spirituality and religion have so often been avoided. As many of the chapters in this volume note, the reasons for this can vary but most usually follow from two particular factors.

First, the very idea of a profession as we now understand it is a product of modernisation. The contemporary professions have developed within the historical processes of industrialisation, at the core of which lies a materialistic view of the world. This in turn has been a significant element in the secularisation of modern society. So, associated with this trend the idea of spirituality was either rendered illegitimate or at least confined to being a type of anthropological curiosity. The particular view of science that has predominated through this period has marginalised the spiritual, even, at times, denying the very idea. Some critical social and political analyses had the same impact, by equating all spiritual and religious experience and practices with particular oppressive historical forms.

Second, ethical practice in the helping professions is conscious of the power that the professional may exercise over the person seeking help. In seeking to avoid the imposition of the professional's own beliefs and values within the helping relationship, it became a matter of routine to avoid spiritual or religious matters. This tendency is also exacerbated by a lack of clarity between spirituality and religion. Especially for those who would wish to assert a materialist view of the world, or at least of their professional practice, the solution was to place the spiritual outside the sphere of interest of the helping professions.

Yet spirituality and religion continue to be crucially important aspects of life for so many helping professionals as well as for those who seek their help. One of the more interesting developments of recent times has been the re-emergence of attention to these phenomena, placing them back within the sphere of questions that may be raised publicly. Behind this shift we can see changes also among other branches of human inquiry, such as science and politics. For example, the assumption that has marked the last century, that science opposes belief, is being challenged increasingly and it is also becoming more plausible for politicians from all sides to express spiritual and religious ideas as the basis for their views. The sense that science and spirituality consti- tute a binary choice is being rethought in ways that make it possible for helping professionals to think critically and to be open to spirituality at the same time. It may well not be coincidental that the return to a more overt recognition of matters of spirituality and religion is happening at the same time that we also see a great increase of public interest in ethics, ecology and other challenges to crudely acquisitive materialism. For the helping professions a more conscious response to the spiritual and the religious in the lives of both professionals and service users makes visible something that has been covered over and gives a voice to a part of life about which we have been silent for so long.

The very diversity of this collection is its strength. This book brings together a wide range of practitioners and teachers in the helping profes- sions. There are many different styles of thinking and writing: some parts are speculative and others are didactic. It is multi-professional, with contributions across education, medicine, nursing, psychology, religious ministry and social work. It is multi-faith, including Aboriginal spirit- uality, Buddhism, Christianity, Islam, Judaism and Wicca. This diversity is its strength because it models a concept that lies at the heart of the various contributions, namely that we learn and grow through careful and open reflection and listening. It invites us to look honestly at ourselves and our own practices through learning about those from other professional and faith backgrounds. In that way it encourages anyone in a helping profession to think further about spirituality in practice.

Richard Hugman
Professor of Social Work, University of New South Wales
January 2007

Contents

Acknowledgments

Questions of spirituality and helping practice have been of interest to us over many years, but it was the influence and questioning of our students which resulted in this work. We would like to acknowledge our students' contribution to this book's existence and thank the many people, family, friends and colleagues who over the years have in diverse ways shaped its content.

We are deeply indebted to Karen Wilcox, whose editorial work and caring has been vital to the creation of *Spirited Practices*.

Thanks particularly to Angela, Dominic, Gabriella, Joel, Nat, Oli, and also Eileen Baldry, Ali Blogg, Nat Bolzan, Lena Bruselid, Manning Clark, Dymphna Clark, Julia Coleman, Ian Colley, Ann Deveson, Michael Dudley, Jan Fook, Carmen Gale, Ivan Gale, Winton Higgins, Lisa Hill, Adele Horin, Richard Howitt, Paul Ireland, Rachel Kohn, Andrew Leon, Louise Loxton, Sarah Mares, Viv Miller, Mick North, Julia Perry, Adam Possamai, Jenny Pry, Alan Rosen, Sue Smith, Liz Watson, Melinda Webb, Helena Weber, Tracy Wilcox and all our contributors.

We would also like to thank Elizabeth Weiss and Allen & Unwin for their confidence and support in publishing *Spirited Practices*.

Picture Acknowledgments

p. xx, *The Wounded Angel* c.1903, Oil on Canvas by Hugo Simberg. Courtesy Finnish National Gallery, reproduced with permission Finnish National Gallery.

p. 1 *Open Door* 2005, Ink on Paper by Sarah Mares, reproduced with permission of the artist.

p. 31 *Hindu God Ardha* c.2005, photograph by Alan Croker, reproduced with permission.

p. 69 *Waterbird, Alligator River, Northern Territory*, c.2005, photograph by Ali Blogg, reproduced with permission.

p. 101 *Lantern, Memorial Garden, Dunblane*, 2006 photograph by Mick North, reproduced with permission.

p. 133 *Lotus*, 2006, Ink on Paper by Sarah Mares, reproduced with permission of the artist.

p. 151 *The Walker, Port Macquarie* c.2005, photograph by Ali Blogg, reproduced with permission.

p. 187 *Daisies*, 2000, Acrylic on Canvas, by Lisa Hill reproduced with permission of the artist.

p. 221 *Two Women Dreaming*, 2002, Oil on Canvas, by Rene Campbell, Lynne Trindall, Mary Davison, Gloria Martin, Beverley Simon, Shirley Murphy, Leisha Brown, Dianne Lindley, Esmé Holmes, Barbra & Camara Asplett, Christine Mason and Leanne Mason, reproduced with permission of the artists.

p. 233 *Sand Writing, Port Macquarie*, c.2005 photograph by Ali Blogg, reproduced with permission.

About the editors

Fran Gale is Senior Research Fellow in the Social Justice Social Change Research Centre and lecturer at the University of Western Sydney. She is a political scientist and social worker who researches and writes in the areas of civic connectedness and marginalised groups, the theory/practice nexus, particularly socio-political theories and practices, human rights, and spirituality and social justice.

Natalie Bolzan is an associate professor in Social Work and Head of Program (Social Work) at the University of Western Sydney. Her research and writing focuses on exploring the ways marginalised groups challenge their marginalised status.

Dorothy McRae-McMahon has worked as National Director for Mission for the Uniting Church, as a staff member of the NSW Ecumenical Council and a parish minister with the Pitt Street Uniting Church. She is now retired and conducts workshops on spirituality; she helps with ministry in the Redfern/Waterloo area for the South Sydney Uniting Church Parish and acts as a panellist for the Faith column in the *Age*, Melbourne.

About the contributors

Darri Adamson utilises Tibetan Buddhist insights in her work as a registered nurse in the Coronary Care Unit of a major Sydney teaching hospital. She has an Arts degree with majors in History and French from the University of Sydney, a Certificate in Coronary Care, and a Graduate Diploma in Education.

Giles Barton is a nursing unit manager at Rivendell Child, Adolescent and Family Psychiatric services. He draws on Theravada Buddhist insights in his work with young people in the areas of aggression, self-harm, suicide prevention, early intervention in psychosis, and psycho-education.

Subhana Barzaghi draws on two different Buddhist traditions, Zen Buddhism and the Vipassana Insight tradition, in her work as a counsellor and therapist. Subhana is currently the spiritual director and resident teacher of the Sydney Zen Centre, and leads regular Zen sessions in Sydney and Melbourne. She is, as well, a teacher in the Vipassana Insight tradition. Subhana leads regular retreats in Zen Buddhist and Vipassana meditation throughout Australia, New Zealand and India.

Lyn Bender is a registered psychologist who has worked in community welfare and corporate organisations. Currently in private practice, she maintains her practice across community welfare and private sectors. She works with asylum seekers and has a strong commitment to human rights.

Elizabeth Benson-Stott is a psychologist who has worked in both the United States and Australia in the fields of clinical psychology and mental health, human resources, education, management and psychology. Elizabeth currently sits on several boards and tribunals in Queensland.

Veronica Brady is a Roman Catholic nun and an Honorary Senior Research Fellow at the University of Western Australia. She has published widely on Australian literature, culture and belief, on Aboriginal issues, women's issues and ecology.

Hilary Byrne-Armstrong is an adjunct senior research fellow in the School of Psychology, University of Western Sydney, and Director of Training and Research at the Institute of Executive Coaching, Sydney. She is committed to processes that build and tell stories of courage, hope and resilience.

Mark Carroll developed the BACE (Balancing Awareness, Community and Empowerment program) while working as a probation and parole officer. He incorporates his experience as an adult educator and yoga teacher in his work with ex-prisoners and parolees. For further information, or to become involved as a community volunteer, email markarmas1@yahoo.com or visit http://www.baceprogram.com.

Diana Coholic works as an assistant professor in the School of Social Work at Laurentian University in Sudbury, Ontario, Canada. She also maintains a small private psychotherapy practice. Presently, her research program is investigating the helpfulness of spiritually influenced social work group practice.

Gillian Coote teaches at the Sydney Zen Centre, having been a student of Robert Aitken Roshi since 1980. Since 1991 she has been coordinator of the Sydney branch of the Buddhist Peace Fellowship. She is currently working with a team of bush regenerators in Sydney's bushland reserves.

Margaret Crompton is a writer, editor, lecturer and consultant with particular interests in children's spiritual wellbeing and English literature. Margaret's experience includes social work with children and families, teaching English in Poland, lecturing in social work and literature.

Hanan Dover is a practising psychologist. She is president of both the Mission of Hope and the Australian Society of Islamic Psychology. Her passion is to rediscover the positive contribution religion can make in psychotherapy, and to apply it in practice.

Michael Dudley works as a psychiatrist at Sydney Children's Hospital and Prince of Wales Hospital, and is a senior lecturer in psychiatry at the University of New South Wales. He specialises in and researches suicide and self-harm among young people, and chairs Suicide Prevention Australia.

Douglas Ezzy is a senior lecturer in sociology at the University of Tasmania, Hobart, Australia. His research is driven by a fascination with how people find meaning and dignity in contemporary life. His publications include books and articles examining contemporary spirituality.

Julie Foster Smith is an Aboriginal Australian woman from the Kalkadunja peoples of far northwestern Queensland. Julie locates her sense of self as an intercultural traveller and educator who has lived in many geographical and societal locations.

Esmé Holmes has, since 1999, been coordinator of a funded project called The Two Women Dreaming, which has encouraged and enacted culturally appropriate practices for healing in Sydney. She is a trained psychotherapist in private practice with a particular expertise in working with creative arts for the healing of body, mind and spirit.

Joanna Macy is an eco-philosopher, a scholar of Buddhism, general systems theory and deep ecology. She is also a leading voice in movements for peace, justice and a safe environment. Her wide-ranging work addresses psychological and spiritual issues of the nuclear age, the cultivation of ecological awareness, and the fruitful resonance between Buddhist thought and contemporary science.

Nooria Mehraby grew up in Afghanistan, where she graduated in medicine. A refugee herself, she worked in various refugee camps. She now works as a counsellor/team leader for the Service for the Treatment and Rehabilitation of Torture and Trauma Survivors (STARTTS) in Sydney.

Yvonne Orley has an Indigenous Australian heritage. Her early life experiences on mission stations in New South Wales have prompted her life's passion for the promotion of empowerment. She is currently employed as Regional Manager of an in-home aged care agency which has a spiritual basis.

Shanti Raman is Area Community Paediatrician, Sydney West Area Health Service, and Research Fellow, NSW Institute of Psychiatry. She has sub-specialty training in public health. Her research and teaching interests include poverty and health, health of ethnic minority populations, and child development.

Lorraine Rose is a psychologist and analytic psychotherapist working in Sydney. She has a special interest in the process of emotional development from infancy and coordinates the Infant Observation component of the Infant Mental Health Program at the NSW Institute of Psychiatry.

Weis Shuiringa studied social work in the Netherlands before migrating to Australia in 1972. For the majority of her career she has worked in health settings in New South Wales. Currently she manages one of the services of the Benevolent Society.

Joseph Daniel Toltz is a cantor and director of *bikkur cholim* (pastoral care) with his local Jewish congregation. He is a hospital chaplain in Sydney, where he works with people encountering illness and death. Joseph is also Musical Director at Temple Emanuel, Woollahra.

Michael Wearing is a senior lecturer in social work at the University of New South Wales. He has a long-standing personal interest in issues of spirituality and faith, with special emphasis on traditions of Christian mysticism and Eastern religion and practice, especially Buddhism.

Karen Wilcox is a community worker and researcher who has worked primarily in services for women. Karen teaches politics and law in several Australian universities. She currently works for the Centre for the Study of Gendered Violence at the University of New South Wales.

Introduction
Spiritually sensitive helping practices

Fran Gale

Kim was attracted to social work as it seemed consistent with her spiritual commitment. Two years into her course, she was sitting in the university café in tears. Spirituality, she said, was given no space in the social work curriculum and, moreover, she believed it was not seen as legitimate in helping practice. She didn't 'belong' anywhere any more, Kim felt—neither at church nor at university. We talked about holistic practice and she challenged me—where was the literature on how helping practice integrated spirituality? Scouting around for such literature, particularly Australian literature, demonstrated a recent growth in academic material on helping professions such as psychology, nursing, social work and medicine including psychiatry (see, for example, Rice 2002; Lindsay 2002; D'Souza 2003; Hassad 2000; Tacey 2005; Rumbold 2003). It is still rare, however, for practitioners to have a presence in this literature although it is they who daily negotiate the complexities of integrating spirituality and helping practice. Moreover, little Australian work in this area addresses cross-disciplinary, multiple and non-Western spiritual traditions, despite the richness of traditions which inform spirituality in Australia and the uniquely Australian cultural contexts of those spiritualities.

Spirituality has not enjoyed a prominent position in the literature of the helping professions. Emphasis on 'rationality' and on the 'scientised' construction of knowledge in the development of the professions (Fook

2002: 4) led to a false dichotomy of rationality and spirituality, reflecting a dualistic and hierarchical conception at the heart of modern
Western thought, and privileging rationality (Grosz 1990). This
construction also reflected notions of progress and views of human
nature that represented humans as rational beings. Human beings could
and should look to human wisdom, scientifically validated, to solve
problems. Spirituality was of little significance.

Such views are now keenly challenged. Scientific materialism and
individualism have failed to meet enduring human needs for meaning
and connection. The modern embrace of scientific rationality, Jung
argues, has brought an illness of soul, a lack of meaning, which can only
be cured by a return to myth (understood as orienting paradigm, rather
than illusion) and symbol (see, for example, Jung 1961). As Clifford
Geertz reminds us, this is not just about individual meaning and
purpose. Religion and spirituality are fundamental to the wellbeing of
social groups. Geertz describes religion as 'a system of symbols which
acts to produce powerful, pervasive and long lasting . . . motivations in
groups of people' (Geertz 1972: 205).

Evidence also mounts for the importance of spirituality for prevention and intervention in situations of crisis, distress and mental and
physical illnesses (Koenig et al 2001). As the contributors to this
volume demonstrate, helping professionals report a growing number of
people bringing spiritual issues to the helping relationship, challenging
the exclusion of those issues from dominant professional discourse.
Many helping professionals find themselves ill-prepared to respond
to these new demands, which concern not only conventional religious
beliefs and practices but also new faith understandings emerging
from encounters with multiple and non-Western faith traditions. Such
developments emphasise the critical importance of spiritual awareness
in a human service context.

We particularly listen in this collection to practitioners who are
negotiating the challenges of dealing with spirituality in their practices,
focusing on situations in which helping professionals often find
themselves. The book is organised around the themes of disconnection, violence, loss, illness, stigma and discrimination, guilt, cycles of

hopelessness, transitions and resistance, with two or three essays from a variety of spiritual traditions addressing each of these areas.

Contributors range from grassroots workers to theorists to teachers to clergy, coming from a range of disciplines which may not otherwise have been grouped together (psychiatry, social work, nursing, theology, politics, psychology, literature, community work, paediatric medicine, sociology, criminology and education). Contributors' diverse religious and spiritual perspectives also reflect practices that have evolved from different cultural orientations now sitting side by side in a multicultural Australia. We do not aim to comprehensively review the growing body of academic literature in this area (see, for example, Kohn 2003: 120–38; Moss 2005); rather, we hope to open up further conversations between researchers, practitioners and interdisciplinary groups in the helping professions, and with those exploring or reconnecting with spirituality who may seek assistance from helping professionals.

Indigenous Australian spirituality, Christianity, Islam, Judaism, Hinduism, Wicca and Buddhism are some of the spiritual traditions which inform contributors' helping practices. New faith understandings, emerging from encounters with multiple and non-Western faith traditions, underpin other contributors' practices. For example, Indigenous psychologist Elizabeth Benson Stott discusses her use of insights from Indigenous Australian spirituality in work within the Christian faith tradition in her psychology practice; Mark Carroll, a probation and parole officer, integrates insights from a wide range of spiritual traditions in his work with ex-prisoners and parolees; and Michael Wearing shows how spirituality drawn from both Buddhism (primarily associated with Eastern religions) and Christianity (associated with the West) helps deal with human and social crises.

Developing a spiritually sensitive practice began, for many contributors, when they identified 'something missing', sometimes early in their professional training, sometimes a little later in their professional practice. Lyn Bender, for example, describes how she found both in her psychology training and then in her practice that 'something more' than the positivist paradigm underpinning her discipline of psychology was 'needed to aid the injured spirit'. For Hanan Dover, it is the secularisation of Western psychology that greatly limits its capacity to engage those of Islamic faith (see also Haque 2004). She describes a helping practice in which, as a Western-trained psychologist, she integrates Islamic belief and practices.

Yet for others, spirituality, while present, was not made explicit. Perhaps, as children's social worker Margaret Crompton found, it was transmitted through the qualities of her lecturers and colleagues. Diana Coholic and Lorraine Rose, in their respective social work and psycho-analytic practices, found that a spiritual dimension to their helping practice was revealed by those with whom they were working. For Coholic, as for some others, this identification came about at a time when spirituality was becoming increasingly important in her own journey. Echoing the experience of women in the awareness-raising groups of the early women's movement, Crompton writes that it is both liberating and energising to be able to discuss spirituality as a legitimate part of helping practice and to recognise that experience in this area is shared.

Raised awareness of the need for spiritually sensitive helping prac-tices points us to the task of transforming our helping practices. What does it mean for spiritual perspectives to be integrated into practices in the helping professions? What do such practices look like? The majority of contributors to this volume are engaged in creating 'spirited practices'. They reveal the considerable innovative practice taking place, much of which has not been in the public arena.

In 'naming' and relating their spiritually sensitive helping practices, the contributors offer patterns for transforming our own helping practices.

While signposting and raising questions about what spiritually sensitive practice offers, one question which all contributors deal with, either implicitly or explicitly, is: What is the change dynamic in spiritu-ally sensitive helping practice? (See also, for example, Carfagna 1990.) The spirituality of the worker, the spirituality of those seeking help and the spiritually sensitive relationship are all significant, with some aspects assuming more significance for some contributors than others. Weis Shuiringa tackles some thorny issues raised by these questions (particularly for a worker coming from a strongly defined Christian faith tradition), such as concerns about sharing faith directly with those who seek help, and dilemmas of faith arising for the worker when people's situations do not improve. For Yvonne Orley, an Indigenous counsellor working with Indigenous Australians, the crucial element for change lies in the nature of the relationship between workers, whatever their own spiritual beliefs, and Indigenous Australians seeking their help. Helping professionals, she argues, need to get in touch with their own spirituality in order to avoid a 'helping mentality' and 'missionising approach' in their relationship with Indigenous Australians. Practitioners, through 'careful nurturing of the soul', Michael Wearing adds, may bring greater discernment and warmth to their work, enabling the person(s) seeking help to make new beginnings in their lives.

Michael Dudley, from a medical perspective, illustrates with his own case examples the practitioner engaging with his patients' spirituality in their quest for wellbeing.

Darri Adamson and Giles Barton discuss how integrating Tibetan and Theravadan Buddhism, in their respective nursing practices in coronary care and in helping work with young people, makes a positive difference both for them as helping professionals and for their patients' wellbeing. Nooria Mehraby, working as a counsellor within the Islamic tradition, notes change occurring through strengthening and modifying beliefs, but also through the authority of the therapist, sheikh or spiritual leader.

A commonality emerging in many of the practices discussed is the use of symbolic actions and everyday objects, such as water, flowers, bowls, cloths, leaves, candles, stones, earth and fruit, as symbols in developing a ritual or ceremony as part of helping practices. In a chapter on the use of rituals in healing and helping practices, Dorothy McRae-McMahon notes that many people suffer from a lack of ritual in their lives and describes how healing rituals can assist those with and without formal religious or spiritual traditions. Joseph Toltz, in work as a Jewish chaplain; Subhana Barzaghi, Gillian Coote, as well as Joanna Macy, working in Buddhist traditions; Shanti Raman, in healing and helping in Hindu tradition; Julie Foster Smith, Esmé Holmes and Hilary

Byrne-Armstrong, in Indigenous Australian spirituality; Doug Ezzy, in Wicca spirituality; and Dorothy McRae-McMahon, in working with guilt within a Christian tradition, all discuss symbols and symbolic acts as powerful in a wide range of helping and healing contexts. Part of its healing power, writes McRae-McMahon, is that a ritual is 'almost always an occasion when someone or some people are gathered around our lives in a way which tells us that our life matters and that we are gathered into human community'. Rituals, and the everyday objects used in them in spiritual helping practices, portray symbolically a commonality perhaps hard to express in language, an interconnection between diverse spiritualities.

Casting off definitions of professionalism that exclude spirituality has been liberating for the contributors to this volume. It has afforded them opportunity for more authentic holistic helping practices, a point cogently made by paediatrician Shanti Raman in her chapter discussing helping and healing practice informed by insights from Hinduism.

However, could moves to include spirituality be regressive? Could this have unwelcome echoes, especially, for instance, for professions such as social work? Prior to its establishment as a secular profession, workers from Judeo-Christian religious philanthropic institutions not infrequently dispensed or imposed religious beliefs and values with their practice.

On a not entirely unconnected point, could it be used politically? The dominant welfare policy position of many modern Western governments, not least the Australian government, is of social order rather than social justice; of individual self-care, where the cause of social, and often individual, problems is frequently seen as lying in the decline of personal morality; and is associated with moves to privatise welfare into the hands of larger religious organisations which can shape moral character (Everingham 2001: 111). Could spirituality be inter-preted as playing into the hands of, or perhaps signalling acceptance of, this discourse?

On the contrary, as Veronica Brady argues, while our culture is concerned with profit and efficiency and orientated to self-absorption and self-care, there is nothing sentimental or irrelevant in the idea that we are obligated to care for and be responsible to and for one another. According to Brady, spirituality and spiritually informed helping practices open out largely neglected possibilities which are crucial for the survival of civil society and its continuing transformation. Joanna Macy writes about humans being challenged to put aside competitive individualism and to recognise their radical interconnectedness with each other and all beings through space and time for the survival of Earth. As people's fundamental values are challenged, spiritually sensitive practices will be increasingly important for helping practitioners. Spirituality fosters a sense of responsibility for and connection with others, Canda and Furman note. 'The self is no longer defined in egocentric ways but rather in relation to other people' (Canda & Furman 1999: 48). Spirituality thus has 'an outward looking dimension' (Moss 2005: 12).

Given the contributors' diverse approaches in spiritually sensitive helping practices, there is surprising agreement among them concerning a non-materialist position, which may sound a truism, but is profoundly significant in an age of consumerism and commercialisation of everyday life and relationships. Connection across space and time between all beings was a recurrent theme. Karen Wilcox, for example, in her work with victims of domestic violence, emphasises a spirituality rooted in compassion and connection; its role in negotiating working within, for instance, conservative religious traditions while maintaining and strengthening 'feminist priorities of safety and responsibility'. Connection, she argues, provides a drive and ambition for working for a non-violent world that is different from the ego-focused ambition often driving modern Western society.

Thus, the spirituality to which Brady, Macy, Wilcox and other contributors refer is defined differently from the spirituality of the early days of helping professions such as that of social work. It is inclusive and honours diverse religious and non-religious spiritual forms. Spirituality, in such practices, involves the search for a sense of life purpose, meaning and morally fulfilling relationships between oneself, other people, the universe and the ultimate reality, however that is understood (Canda & Furman 1999: 9).

According to Higgins, 'spirituality approaches the sense of tran-scendence in which the practitioner acquires a sense of his existence as part of a universal whole, a universal interconnectedness. Personal worldly welfare and survival move to the periphery. In this way, spirit-uality is tremendously subversive' (Higgins 2001: 5). Thus, spirituality can be positioned within a social justice framework (see also Moss 2005: 13).

This is not to naively gloss over differences, even around practices and beliefs of connection. However, interdependence is a motif through many of the contributions. For example, the Dalai Lama comments elsewhere that 'Buddhism does not accept . . . God as an almighty or as a creator . . . but at the same time, if God means truth or ultimate reality, there is a point of similarity to *shunyata*, or emptiness'. Shunyata, for Tibetans, is also the interrelatedness and interdependence of all living things and beings (Kamenetz 1995: 85). At a time in our history when the differences between religious and spiritual perspectives are being highlighted, these contributions show us that what we have in common with others is larger than what separates us.

Spirituality has always played a significant part in everyday life paths of community members, Berger (1999) and others contend, yet it has been made peripheral in professional discourse. Only after looking at Van Gogh's sketches of cypresses overnight did Alain de Botton, while on a visit to Provence, notice two large cypresses at the bottom of the garden, although he had sat in the same garden, in the same spot, the previous day. He comments that he only now saw them, noticing the particular way they moved in the wind (de Botton 2002). Seeing cypresses as Van Gogh had foregrounded them in his sketches enabled de Botton to notice and appreciate cypresses as features in the landscape itself. Our contributors, in foregrounding spirituality by sharing their spiritually sensitive helping practices, prompt us 'to notice what we have already seen' (de Botton 2002: 254).

References

Berger, P.L. 1999, 'The desecularization of the world', in Peter L. Berger (ed.), *The Impact of Religious Conviction on the Politics of the 21st Century*, Erdmans, Grand Rapids, pp. 1–19.

Canda, E. and Furman, L. 1999, *Spiritual Diversity in Social Work Practice: The Heart of Helping*, Free Press, New York.

Carfagna, R. 1990, 'A spirituality for the helping professions', *The Journal of Pastoral Care*, no. 44, pp. 61–5.

de Botton, A. 2002, *The Art of Travel*, Penguin Books, London.

D'Souza, R. 2003, 'Incorporating a spiritual history into a psychiatric assessment', *Australasian Psychiatry*, vol. 11, no. 1, pp. 12–15.

Everingham, C. 2001, 'Reconstituting community: Social justice, social order and the politics of community', *Australian Journal of Social Issues*, vol. 36, no. 2, pp. 105–25.

Fook, J. 2002, *Social Work: Critical Theory and Practice*, Sage, London.

Geertz, C. 1972, 'Religion as a cultural system', in W. Lessa and E. Vogt (eds), *Reader in Conparative Religion*, 2nd edn, Harper & Row, New York, pp. 204–16.

Grosz, E. 1990, 'Philosophy', in Sneja Gunew (ed.), *Feminist Knowledge: Critique and Construction*, Routledge, New York, pp. 85–6.

Haque, A. 2004, 'Psychology from an Islamic perspective: Contributions of early Muslim scholars and challenges to contemporary Muslim psychologists', *Journal of Religion and Health*, vol. 43, no. 4, pp. 357–77.

Hassad, C. 2000, 'Depression, dispirited or spiritually deprived?', *Medical Journal of Australia*, vol. 173, no. 10, pp. 545–7.

Higgins, W. 2001, *Spirituality, Religion and Politics*, Seminar paper (unpublished), School of Government and International Relations, Sydney University, 23 April.

Jung, C. 1961, *Psychological Reflections* (ed. Jolande Jacobi), Harper & Row, New York.

Kamenetz, R. 1995, *The Jew in the Lotus*, Harper, San Francisco.

Koenig, H.G., McCullough, M.E. and Larson D. 2001, *Handbook of Religion and Health*, Oxford University Press, New York.

Kohn, R. 2003, *The New Believers: Re-imagining God*, HarperCollins, Sydney.

Lindsay, R. 2002, *Recognising Spirituality: The Interface between Faith and Social Work*, University of Western Australia Press, Perth.

Moss, B. 2005, *Religion and Spirituality*, Russell House Publishing, Lyme Regis.

Rice, S. 2002, 'Magic happens: revisiting the spirituality and social work debate', *Australian Social Work*, vol. 55, no. 4, pp. 303–12.

Rumbold, B. 2003, 'Caring for the spirit: Lessons from working with the dying', *Medical Journal of Australia*, vol. 179, no. 6, pp. S11–S13.

Tacey, D.J. 2005, 'Spiritual perspectives on suicidal impulses in young adults', in R. Cox, B. Ervin-Cox and L. Hoffman (eds), *Spirituality and Psychological Health*, Colorado School of Professional Psychology Press, Colorado Springs, pp. 107–28.

Disconnection

1
Disconnection

Veronica Brady

Poetry often offers metaphorical insights that strike deeper than common sense. One of Israeli poet Yehudi Amichai's poems, for instance (quoted in Holloway 2001: vi), begins:

> From the place where we are right
> flowers will never grow.

Being sure of ourselves and of our practices, even our helping practices, is no guarantee that they are life-giving. In fact certainties often stifle compassion, thought and imagination, their essential sources. But these sources are often in short supply in our society today, with the result that many of us are feeling increasingly disillusioned, wondering where our hopes and energies have gone. If we are to survive as a decent and humane society, we need to interrogate current certainties that seem to care more for short-term profit and efficiency than for people in need. Enmeshed in the details and challenges of our work, it is time to renew our imagination and remind ourselves what a decent and humane society might look like.

A society which does not care for those who are less powerful or less fortunate, or even for those who are different, has forfeited the claim to be properly civilised. Yet, in our current culture, the larger world of the human mind and spirit, and the possibilities it opens out, possibilities beyond the mere business of money-making, money-having and money-spending, are largely neglected. Those of us who work for an increase in human dignity and hope for a better future for humankind are dismissed as 'do-gooders' or 'bleeding hearts'. Our concerns are seen as irrelevant and a distraction from the real business of increasing GNP and balancing budgets. History suggests, however, that, without a larger vision of the good life, tyranny flourishes and a people may perish.

Consider the danger signs around us: the growing violence and self-absorption, the indifference to the suffering of others, suspicion and fear of those different from ourselves and the implicit belief, in all of this, that might equals right: all suggesting an increasing, and indeed irrational, hard-heartedness in the way we imagine the world. Yet once in this country there was a strong belief, even at the level of government, in the idea of a 'fair go' for all, and support for values and policies which guaranteed the dignity, rights and responsibilities of every human being. Historian C.E.W. Bean commented, as World War II drew to a close, that this is 'a land where every boy and girl has a chance . . . not to struggle through life on a basic wage, but to develop to any greatness of which they are capable' (Turner 1968: 316). Today we seem to be losing connection with that tradition.

The reasons for this are understandable. There is a backward-looking strain in any culture, but especially in a culture like ours which is the product of imperial history. According to the Brazilian sociologist Luiz Carlos Susin, that history's hero figure is Ulysses, who left home to join in the war against Troy and travelled through strange places but was always determined to return home or, in the case of settler societies like our own, to turn these places into the equivalent of home (Susin 2000: 87), of building 'a new Britannia in another world' (Turner 1968: 12) as one of the early settlers put it. But that meant turning our backs on the strangeness of the land and on its First Peoples and their culture, locking ourselves into a 'closed circle around sameness' (Susin 2000: 87), believing that the values and certainties we brought with us were absolute and closing ourselves off from other possibilities.

This has helped to produce the 'imperial self' which Alexis de Tocqueville saw in its beginnings in the new United States of America in the 1830s but which is in vogue today:

> They owe nothing to anyone, they expect nothing from anyone: they acquire the habit of always considering themselves standing alone and are apt to think they have their whole destiny in their own hands . . . This [makes them] forget their ancestors . . . hides their descendants and separates them from their contemporaries, throwing them back forever upon themselves and threatening to confine them forever in the solitude of their own hearts (de Tocqueville 1956: 194).

In our case there is an added element, the 'sceptical and utilitarian spirit' of late nineteenth century English culture which, A.G. Stephens argued, 'values the present hour and refuses to sacrifice the present for any visionary future lacking a rational guarantee' (quoted in Turner 1968: x). But if we are to go against the current tide of so-called 'economic rationalism', as I suggest we need to do, it will demand a different vision, a readiness to accept the value of every human being precisely because she or he is a human being.

Our failure to do so helps to explain why 'spirited practices', inspired by this value, with quality—as distinct from what is immediately quantifiable and measurable—are unfashionable today. This disregard may be dangerous. The growing sense of alienation and meaninglessness, cynical attitudes to politicians and politics and the widespread breakdown of personal relationships and social trust evident today, suggest that social coherence is breaking down and that no amount of material prosperity can offer real relief from 'the heart pain, the world pain' (Conrad 1900: 241) afflicting us.

The good news, however, is that many people are looking elsewhere, searching for values beyond those of the 'present hour' and the merely pragmatic and utilitarian notions of reality, for richer relationships with others and with the natural world, for play and for creativity. True, this may seem to be, and sometimes is, merely an individual matter which mostly concerns people who are better educated. But a sense of values beyond the merely material is possible for anyone and offers a way out of the 'closed circle around sameness', an alternative to the *status quo* and a strong and abiding foundation for 'spirited practices'. It is not necessarily associated with institutional religion, or at least with the kind which is preoccupied with power: it is the basis, for instance, of the tradition of the fair go. But as I see it, genuine spirituality comes from a sense of the privilege and panic of our common humanity. As Shakespeare puts it in *The Tempest* (act IV, scene 1, lines 156–7):

> We are such stuff
> As dreams are made on, and our little life
> Is rounded with a sleep.

According to William James, the sense of privilege and panic is a 'primordial thing' which involves a 'total reaction to life in which one must reach down to that curious sense of the whole . . . cosmos as an everlasting presence, intimate or alien, terrible or amusing, lovable or odious, which in some degree everyone possesses' (James 1957: 35).

From the beginnings of settlement in this country there was a sense of something like this in the 'contemptuous grandeur' which Marcus Clarke saw in the land before which 'the trim utilitarian civilisation' which bred him shrank 'into insignificance' (Turner 1968: 102). In similar vein Joseph Furphy believed that there was a 'latent meaning' in the land at present but which it was our business 'faithfully and lovingly' to interpret (Barnes 1981: 65). Implicit here is an alternative to the model of Ulysses—the story of Abraham, called to travel beyond all known horizons in search of a promise, travelling in hope and trust, open and vulnerable to the approach of what is other (Susin 2000: 88).

This, I suggest, is the promise of a society 'committed to no usages of petrified injustice', as Furphy put it (Barnes 1981: 66), a society that would offer a new beginning to the poor and dispossessed. This vision found expression in the pioneering social legislation which made the significantly named new 'Commonwealth' of Australia the 'social laboratory of the world' (Barnes 1981: 94) and helped to create the welfare society that is now being dismantled. In contrast with the individualism which underpins present policies, its basis was a profound sense of community, of our common vulnerability, a sense that, to quote Furphy again, we 'are all walking along the shelving edge of a precipice; any one of us may go at any moment, or be dragged down by another' (Barnes 1981: 94), a view which represents a profound and compassionate sense of human community.

This is very different from the current preoccupation with success and power. But it is surely more in tune, not only with the experience of most of us, but also with reality as a whole. As Albert Einstein, for instance, described it:

> Human beings are part of the whole we call the Universe, a small region in time and space. We regard ourselves, our ideas and feelings, as separate and apart from all the rest. [This is] something like an optical illusion . . . a sort of prison [which] restricts us [so that] we put personal aspirations first and limit our affective life to a few people close to us. Our task should be to free ourselves from this prison, opening up our circle of compassion to embrace all living creatures and all of nature in its beauty (in Clayton 1975: 127).

In this context there is nothing 'sentimental' in the belief that we are obligated to care and be responsible to and for one another and that such an obligation is necessary for the survival of a decent society. Martin Buber understood this when he argued that 'the idea of responsibility [needs] to be brought back from the province of specialised ethics, of an ought that swings free in the air, into that of life. Genuine responsibility exists only where there is real responding' (Gaita 2004: 12).

Responsibility, then, is not just an individual matter but implies a mutual respect and sympathy which come from understanding who we are and where we belong in the larger scheme of things. Our present society has little sense of this understanding, caught up in the play of appearances which rests on 'the exaltation of signs based on the denial of the reality of things' (Baudrillard 1990: 69) and, I would add, denial of people, especially those who are different, disadvantaged or just plain unfashionable. I believe, however, that 'spirited practices' that derive from a sense of respect and responsibility to and for others and for the living world around us will bring us back in tune with reality, shifting 'the emotional centre of [our lives] towards loving and harmonious affections—yes, yes, rather than no, no', as William James has it (James 1957: 279). Flowers may then begin to grow in the hard ground of our times and we may begin to listen again to voices from the old house of the tradition of justice, compassion and hope.

References

Barnes, J. (ed.) 1981, *Joseph Furphy*, Portable Australian Authors series, University of Queensland Press, St Lucia.

Baudrillard, J. 1990, *Revenge of the Crystal: Selected Essays on the Modern Object and Its Destiny, 1968–1983*, Pluto Press, UK.

Clayton, D. 1975, *The Dark Night Sky: A Personal Adventure in Cosmology*, Quadrangle Books, New York.

Conrad, J. 1900, *Lord Jim*, Penguin Twentieth-Century Classics, 1998, Penguin.

De Tocqueville, A. 1956, *Democracy in America* (edited and abridged by R. Heffner), Mentor Books, New York.

Gaita, R. 2004, 'Breach of trust: Truth, morality and politics', *Quarterly Essay No. 16*, Black Inc., Melbourne.

Holloway, R. 2001, *Doubts and Loves: What is Left of Christianity*, Canongate Books, Edinburgh.

James, W. 1957, *Varieties of Religious Experience*, Random House Modern Library, New York.

Susin, L.C. 2000, 'A critique of the identity paradigm', *Concilium International Journal for Theology*, no. 2, pp. 78–90.

Turner, I. (ed.) 1968, *The Australian Dream*, Sun Books, Melbourne.

2
Helping practices within a strongly defined faith tradition

Weis Schuiringa

As I was developing my social work skills, I was often left feeling bewildered and powerless. 'How is it that people's lives can go so wrong?' 'If there is any justice out there why is it not happening here?' 'Why do bad things happen to good people?' 'Why do bad people keep on doing bad things?' Like many social workers, I felt the need to be able to put these musings somewhere and my tendency to put them in 'God's hands' seemed a good place in my developing practice. Not that I knew what God would do with them but, having introduced a spiritual domain, my load felt lighter. It enabled me to begin to integrate a spiritual dimension into my practice that developed over the years.

Strength-based perspective and spiritual practice

Social work practice is strongly founded on the belief that each person has the ability to change and develop and that, with appropriate facilitation and support, growth and change can happen. This position is strongly represented in the 'strengths-based' approach to service delivery, in interpersonal work as well as community development. The process of compassionately identifying and developing innate strengths and learned skills is believed to lead to growth and greater human fulfilment.

Social work has its roots in the humanistic tradition of human dignity and fulfilment, as well as in the Christian values of compassion and service. Social work and other helping professions are attractive to people searching for a career underpinned by their values. Humanistic values and Christian values overlap and staff can work side by side in their professional roles.

I graduated in social work in the Netherlands and have worked in several government and non-government agencies in the Netherlands and in Australia. I am a member of the Mennonite Church in the Netherlands, to which my family has belonged for generations. In Australia, since the late 1980s I have been closely involved with Quakers, the Religious Society of Friends.

My own spiritual understanding and the concepts of strength-based work overlap. This has not been a sequential development, but a slow process of personal and professional understanding.

The Quaker beliefs that 'there is that of God in everyone'[1] and that 'the good will rise', while seemingly bland, have been triggers for me to see past the tragedy of the moment, to recognise potential and recovery and to look at the wider context of somebody's life. These beliefs have put me in a better space to work in the helping professions, without seeing my clients as spiritually lacking or lost. I have often talked with my clients about their spirituality in my counselling practice, to assist them in making sense of their existence, to connect or reconnect with essential aspects in their lives.

Although what I have written here comes from a Christian belief framework, it could be potentially applied in Jewish, Muslim and related faith settings where workers accept that their beliefs are received directly from God and therefore bind them to certain courses of action.

Issues of helping practice within a strongly defined faith tradition

The faith-based worker in the helping professions can have a strong sense of being led, that God has called them to be on this career path. Problems can arise, however, when there is apparent tension between the career path and the religious path that God requires.

The Christian faith-based worker knows that the client or patient needs the worker's knowledge and skills. The worker also often believes that to be fully recovered, Jesus needs to be called in, to get this troubled life 'on God's track' and to be assured of eternal life in God's care, and may be convinced that they will play a key role in enabling God's plan for the client to take the path to salvation. Workers in the helping professions meet clients or patients whose troubles can cover all aspects of the human condition: from substance abuse to terminal illness, from mental illness to permanent physical disability, from child abuse and relationship problems to a life of crime. At times a worker can face a client or patient in whom all these troubles combine. Their client may also have no belief in being 'on God's track' or might have a non-Christian understanding of God.

When clients or patients come in contact with the helping professional there is a power imbalance in the relationship. The client or patient is acutely aware of their troubled predicament. They are often in an existential crisis, vulnerable, and possibly dependent on the worker for care, compassion and advocacy. When workers in the helping professions are confronted with tragic or destructive lives and discover that all the available interventions are seemingly ineffective they can, particularly as new graduates, feel highly stressed.

The Christian faith-based worker in this situation may confront additional challenging questions generated by their beliefs and expectations of themselves: 'How can I not share the great news and revelation of Christian salvation with my client or patient?' 'Why leave a job half done?' 'Why has this client or patient left without being converted?' 'Why is God forsaking me, the worker?' 'Why is this client or patient forsaking me, the worker?' 'How can I, the worker, deal with defeat, not having completed God's mission, not having brought this lost soul to God?' 'If only the "magic" ingredient could be added: turning the client's or patient's life to Jesus and accepting God's track.' The faith-based worker, faced with apparent failure, may even feel frustrated or hostile towards the client or patient who lacks faith or who relapses from a previous commitment to Jesus and God.

Such responses especially occur when the worker has a strongly defined faith and clear-cut religious beliefs that are held to come from God and are therefore regarded as binding. The worker believes that they are part of God's purpose and on God's path, and that faith will keep them on this path. Such a faith is supported by religious rituals, ways of speaking and a communal sense of purpose, and provides a great sense of belonging and personal purpose. Human trouble and suffering are understood, within this faith, as being part of God's purpose, and alleviation is achieved by being on God's path.

Faith-based agencies have often been the channels through which social work and welfare services have been provided. In the last 10 to 20 years there has been a trend for governments of all persuasions to outsource human services. Increasingly, the recipients of government funding to provide human services are Judeo-Christian and Muslim faith-based non-government organisations. This arrangement can be very attractive for workers with a strong faith, who will include those who believe that God has now led them to this faith-based place of work.

Christian-based organisations often recruit staff who have a current Christian church affiliation. Staff may be encouraged to participate actively in Bible readings, prayers and devotions. There may be conversations at lunchtimes about participation in churches, affirming for staff that they are among faith-based workers. Such organisations may have prayer meetings and clear protocols for 'sharing one's faith'. God's intercession may be called upon to turn a client or patient's life around. The worker himself or herself may devote time in prayer on behalf of clients or patients.

However, the challenges arising for workers in such a situation may be considerable. Although in a faith-based agency most workers are aware of their professional boundaries and will remain in their professional role and assist the client or patient to the best of their abilities, the boundary around expression of faith beliefs within the helping relationship may be less clear. With the best of intentions, the worker can be convinced that the essential course of intervention for the client or patient is to bring this person to Jesus and pray for God's intervention. If the client or patient has a religious belief that is similar to the worker's belief, the worker may feel obliged to pray with that person and perhaps not refer them to a pastoral care worker. Praying with clients may even be experienced as a pressure in some faith-based workplaces that are proactive in affirming the faith, perhaps especially when a church is financially or materially contributing to the service. This raises issues around questions of professional boundaries which need examining.

Moreover, in the sealed faith environment, the worker may become more comfortable working with clients or patients with whom there is a shared faith. Faith-based workers may be ambivalent about a client's or patient's ability to grow, change or find peace if this projected future lacks a commitment to a religious path similar to the worker's path. Prayer can be used to reassure the worker as much as the client or patient. Outside this familiar faith environment, staff may experience difficulty switching to a different, secular reality and working with clients or patients who may have a very different faith or little or no faith at all.

By contrast, in a secular workplace, an action such as praying with a client may lead to conflict, for it may be seen as a transgression of professional boundaries. Workers in the health care professions who have a strong faith can feel isolated in a secular workplace where there are few like-minded colleagues who speak their faith language and with whom they have shared experiences. Small enclaves can form, which may be unhelpful for team work. In a secular agency it may be difficult to discuss boundary issues raised by faith practices, such as prayer, within the helping relationship.

As well, it can be difficult for such workers, perhaps especially recent graduates, to raise these matters within their faith community. Workers expressing uncertainty or doubt, or wanting to review beliefs in the broader context of their professional experiences, may find that their faith community sees them as being in jeopardy and calls the strength of their faith into question. They may be 'prayed for' in the hope that they will stop questioning and get back on God's track of helping and providing service.

In both Christian-based and secular organisations, however, the question needs to be raised: How would clients or patients feel if they discovered that they had been prayed for by name? In our own time of need, many of us might not mind a little divine intervention, but do we

want to be recommended through prayer to the God of this particular
Christian faith or encouraged to find Jesus and place our life in His
Hands?

Genuinely engaging with such questions can leave a worker in a
divided world—caught between secular helping and believing in God's
power, dealing with the challenges of not being able to 'share their faith'
and working with clients and patients with a different or little or no
faith. Work places, faith-based or secular, may not have the resources
or the inclination to discuss the worker's frustrations and the validity of
God's track for clients or patients.

The chasm between faith-based motivation and the realities of
professional life may be so great that skilled and compassionate workers
may either withdraw from human services or continue in their professional role but leave their faith communities.

A response

Values such as compassion and service, human dignity and human
fulfilment are central in the helping professions.

Workers in the helping professions need to understand the boundaries between their personal religious beliefs and world-views and their
roles as professional helpers. It is important that workers can maintain
their own beliefs while at the same time being able to identify and
develop innate strength and learned skills in the client or patient who
has a different or no religious or spiritual belief.

If the client or patient's situation does not improve or it deterior-
ates, the worker and faith-based agency need to find a framework for
understanding and accepting this without attributing the unfolding of
life events to the lack of a solid faith. Rather than seeing a chasm
between sacred and secular, it may be possible for the worker and faith-
based agency to imagine a bridge that joins religious and secular ways of
knowing, and to see themselves as part of that bridge.

Knowing that 'there is that of God' in my client already means that
the client is not 'the other', who is outside of God's grace. I do not
discuss my belief with my clients but my belief assists me in relating to
my clients' 'Light' and to recognise the grace of God in my clients. My

clients are seekers of their own path and fulfilment and my role is to facilitate and support them.

Endnote

1. A well-known Australian Quaker described the Quaker belief as follows: 'If Quakers were challenged by the question, "What do you believe in?" I think that it would be safe to say that the majority would reply, "We believe in the Inner Light . . . the Inner Light can illumine our own spirits, enlighten our conscience and reveal to us what God's will is for us; this light can illumine every area of life and that therefore there are no such divisions as secular from sacred . . . we are all bearers of the Light which is universal and that therefore we believe in the worth-whileness of each person in the sight of God and of each other"' (William Oats [1990] quoted in *This We Can Say: Australian Quaker life, faith and thought 2003*, p. 67).

3

Spirituality and displaced persons

Lyn Bender

Love alone does not heal all—I learned this the hard way. Nonetheless, deep connection with another appears to work in almost miraculous ways.

The people I work with are adults who have suffered childhood trauma. This has included children of Holocaust survivors, children of Vietnam veterans, adults who have been sexually abused through the church, adults who have been wards of the state and, most recently, people in immigration detention. Many of these people were on a quest to find meaning and a clearer sense of self. The need to find meaning is common to many who have suffered trauma, and frequently leads them to seek help (Fontana & Rosenbeck 2005).

Unfortunately, many of the courses for training helping professionals fail to address the complexity of profound trauma, or even ordinary human pain. Something more seems to be needed to aid the injured spirit.

My own profession of psychology, for a variety of reasons, still appears to patrol its territory and to adhere to a positivist, research-based study realm. The espousing of (narrowly defined) evidence-based practice as an ideal leaves out a huge and legitimate realm of concern for the practice of psychology: that of the world and the actual experience of the person who presents urgently, in pain and in need.

The human dimension, the 'being with', is not easily fabricated or measured.

This human and spiritual dimension is integral to all healing, but for me this is not sentimentalised, schmaltzy, idealised or saccharine sweet. It can be the agony and the ecstasy of existence, in which you confront the most ghastly and the most admirable. My own history helped me towards the capacities of empathy and survival skills.

My Jewish Orthodox family upbringing was never big on the rewards of the afterlife. To be Jewish came to mean a focus on earthly existence. I imbibed an uneasy doubt about a God who, for many, was notably missing in action during the Holocaust. For a brief period, at age thirteen, I conversed with God as a kind of invisible friend but as I got older the concept of a Judeo-God faded easily. It did not seem necessary to have a deity in order to sustain a burning passion for life. *Simchas* (celebrations) were eagerly embraced as times of triumphant joy spent with families and friends. These were proof of survival, where the common toast was *L'Chaim!* (to life!).

The post-war Jewish community of my experience in Melbourne consisted overwhelmingly of people who had survived the Holocaust in Europe, had been hidden, or had fled the atrocities. All had lost family members. My father, who came from a town called Lowicz, south of Warsaw, and fellow townspeople who survived to come to Australia formed their own supportive group. They would sit in a circle on fold-up wooden chairs in the front bedroom of our largely unfurnished Elwood house, talking of their struggles, the past, their rage at the anti-Semites, and their hopes. There was no group leader, but they drew comfort and strength from this therapy. Alongside a deep mistrust of non-Jews there existed a passion for survival, not just of the individual, but of a people. Perhaps this transformed, 'mission like', into the ten years I focused on suicide prevention and care for those bereaved by suicide.

Driven by a largely unrecognised desire I sought to prevent untimely and tragic deaths in a vicarious quest to save my own lost history. While it ensured that I was conscientious, energised and empathic, it also drove me in a manner that was leading me to the brink of burnout. During one particularly stressful period, my supervisor gently challenged my compulsion: 'You can't save the six million'. At this point I went into therapy and over three years discovered and uncovered the layers of unconscious intensity that were permeating my work.

In my life and work I began to move beyond survival, towards the possibilities of a stronger, more hopeful engagement with life. My practice began to reflect this as I worked with people who were reconstructing meaning and not solely preoccupied with ambivalence about life and death (Valent 1998). Up until this point, I had not believed with conviction that fulfilment in life was possible. For me, snatched periods of joy were the rewards. I had tremendous reserves of hope but not much sense of attainment. In therapy I learned to believe that joy, love and enthusiasm could be sustained, and they became part of my experience.

Empathy may be defined as the capacity to recognise, comprehend and respond with compassionate behaviours to the situations of others. The seeds are sown in our own experiences. Empathy may start with, but moves beyond, a more self-absorbed identification with another. Study, supervision, personal therapy and my work with clients are the tutors who have helped me towards an intentional and fulfilling life. This translates into an increased capacity to assist others to this goal. The Holocaust experience of my family gave me a drive towards reparation. My practice expanded my own hope in the healing power of love and connection. I have learnt that I do not have to supply this love, only to encourage, witness and nurture its growth. One supervisor termed this 'being as a midwife to the process of birth'.

Practitioners need to find a way to connect with the person's life, past and present, but without homogenising it as 'just like mine'. I have not been through drug addiction nor lived in a cold institution, but there is common ground in my own emotional history. It seems to me essential for the therapist to recognise and come to terms with his or her own wounds, for empathy and survival skills are not all the practitioner needs in working with those who have been traumatised, especially when the trauma is ongoing. My work with a variety of clients has taught me the importance of limits and rigorous assessment.

As I listen to the stories, I search for my own connecting experiences. At times even the recognition of the gulf between our experiences can add mutual understanding. At times I must recognise that their experience is quite outside my own and must make an effort to comprehend it. When someone speaks of an emotion I can seek out some of my own times of rage, sadness, despair or self-doubt. The transformation of my own wounds and history is a pathway to a deeper connection to the experience of the people I seek to help.

Ultimately, my work with detainees in immigration detention, for whom daily life is still a struggle for survival, has given me hope in the potential for compassion in us all. There is a place for bearing witness, and it is possible to reduce human distress through listening and the telling of important stories.

As part of my private practice, I was contracted to work for six weeks at Woomera Detention Centre. For the period that I was employed at Woomera my challenge was working ethically and validly within the constraints of Department of Immigration, Multicultural and Indigenous Affairs' policy, and the immigration centre management.

In the first two weeks I witnessed daily acts of self-harm, heard account upon account of war, imprisonment, flight from danger, loss of family, guilt, shame and despair (Mares 2002). I developed a plan for my work that would honour the humanity of those I worked with, while also struggling to have their human rights respected.

I adopted a strategy with a five-point focus: first, the building of trust and the formation of working relationships; second, redefining goals for myself and the detainees (including the reframing of requested tasks from the management); third, advocacy and increasing community awareness; fourth, self-care and support. Finally, but inextricably threaded and woven into the fabric of practice, were ethics and integrity of spirit.

Mohammad from Afghanistan confronted me angrily as I walked through the compound, trying to attend to too many needs. 'Why you do not answer me?' he was shouting. 'Each day, ask for appointment. I not try kill myself like others, but you not answer. I want to tell you what is in my heart.' From that time I spoke daily with Mohammad. We sat in the dust and I heard how successive regimes had murdered his family. The Northern Alliance killed his father, the Russians his brother, the Taliban his wife and child. His mother died brokenhearted. He was a musician but he could not play again. He had failed to save his family. When he watered the garden outside the department's office he felt he was watering the graves of his loved ones, and this comforted him. We went to the property store together to retrieve the photo of his dead child. Mohammad believed he would be released, but was afraid to see the photo. We sat together looking at this photograph while he wept and talked. I held his hand. This touched my own experience. We truly shared these moments. He could have been my father weeping for his own lost family. I became like his mother, comforting him in his loss.

I remain eternally grateful that my moral compass was unequivocally set by my family's experience, that it gave me a firm basis for my ethical position. After listening to the stories of the detainees, I was in no doubt that the detention system was toxically abusive (particularly of children) and a violation of human rights (Singer & Gregg 2004). Throughout my childhood I had heard that 'the world turned a blind eye to the plight of Jewish refugees' (Neumann 2004). Now I was driven to reveal what I had seen and heard with these other refugees.

My resolve to advocate publicly, however, presented me with an ethical dilemma. Would I be compromising the detainees' wellbeing? Was I violating confidentiality?

Bidding farewell to the detainees was very difficult—I felt as though I was abandoning them, so on my last day I spoke to as many detainees as possible about my intention to plead their case. All were eager for me to be an advocate and to be a voice on their behalf. My continued advocacy was a silent promise I made to myself. I was aware how excited the detainees became when anyone went to bat for them in the media, for they had a great fear of being forgotten. This was not irrational, as many had been in detention for several years. When I was interviewed I spoke in a non-identifying way about them, except where identities were already highly publicised and my information offered an appropriate perspective.

Had I lost usually appropriate professional boundaries? The answer is another question. What boundaries are appropriate when a professional is confronted by unethical practice and human rights violations?

What if objecting exposed the detainees to punishment or disadvantage? Remaining silent seemed to be more harmful. I had witnessed Woomera's operations first hand and knew they were unjust.

I try, despite the difficulty of this, to listen to the testimonies of people who have suffered in many contexts.

Mohammad is now on a Temporary Protection Visa. In his good times he is ecstatic. In his black times he has cried out, 'Why did they make us temporary people?' He has a job and has tentatively started a relationship. I have helped him with his application for permanent residency. He played the harmonium and sang at my son's wedding.

'As I sat with the refugees the link between their plight and that of my own family's crystallised. There were moments when these people felt like my people' (Byrne 2005). Many times sitting and listening to people who were yearning for a normal life, I was struck with an awareness of what really matters. Many of us only learn this through great suffering and loss (Frankel 1985). I felt that the detainees had bestowed an enormous favour upon me. Their magnanimity towards my good fortune was bountiful. Each night I could leave the centre, while they remained incarcerated. They rarely expressed envy of this.

Keeping my promise to speak for the detainees liberated my own spirit. To continue to believe in the human capacity to regenerate and to act with love is a sustaining hope in my practice.

I must keep my heart and understanding engaged, even though it is tempting to try to forget the ills of the world. Keeping abreast of valuable research findings and theoretical constructs is essential and helpful to practice. While this is necessary it is not sufficient, for theory and research emphasise technique and ideas. They do not teach the student how to sit with or be with the person. Nor do they convey how to respond or manage the process.

My passion for this work has made me quite driven. My focus on healing has developed into a quiet rage at the holocausts that continue to be perpetrated around the world. Life itself may bring unavoidable loss—that is the existential lot of humanity. But so much distress is additional and unnecessary. It is visited upon us by neglect, injustice, ignorance, fear and war. These are the ongoing holocausts and that is why we all need to understand and learn the lessons of history. Truly moving on means never forgetting, always seeking not to repeat the horrors of the past. Luckily there are many working towards this transformation. It is the search for meaning which drives and unites so many of us, when 'them' and 'us' dissolve into 'all of us' and a sense of meaning is restored.

References

Byrne, M. 2005, 'Tales from the desert: People like us', *Griffith Review*, Winter 2005, pp. 177–94.

Fontana, A. and Rosenbeck, R. 2005, 'The role of loss in the pursuit of treatment for posttraumatic stress disorder', *Journal of Traumatic Stress*, Wiley Periodicals Inc., vol. 18, no. 2, pp. 133–6.

Frankel, V.E. 1985, *Man's Search for Meaning*, Pocket Books, Washington Square Press, New York.

Mares, P. 2002, *Borderline*, UNSW Press, Sydney.

Neumann, K. 2004, *Refuge Australia*, UNSW Press, Sydney.

Singer, P. and Gregg, T. 2004, *How Ethical is Australia?*, Black Inc., Melbourne.

Valent, P. 1998, *From Survival to Fulfillment Therapy*, Brunner/Mazel, Philadelphia.

4
Guilt

Dorothy Mcrae-McMahon

When I began my ministry, I assumed that if people from outside my congregation asked to speak with me, they would most probably be asking for financial help or wanting to share with me general stories of pain and grief. In fact, the most common problem which people from both outside and inside the church brought to me was their experience of guilt. Given the propensity of some parts of the Christian Church to invoke guilt in people, perhaps I should not have been surprised!

So, what is guilt?
Because I was so often relating to people whose lives were in some way incapacitated by guilt, I began to reflect on the nature of guilt. I saw that it has to do with a sense of having betrayed yourself or someone else and, in doing so, betraying your God—this last can take many forms and is sometimes not even able to be named explicitly. When it begins, it may be a perfectly healthy response to something you have done; if it persists, as it often does, it can become life-consuming and sometimes distorting of reality.

In some people, guilt can become an almost pathological self-hate, something which colours all of one's life in ways which are out of proportion to the situation involved. It can also be projected onto others, as though the guilt for things done by the person concerned can be expiated by punishing those who are perceived to be engaged in a similar 'sin'. This sort of projection of guilt is, in my experience, most often connected with perceived sexual sins.

Guilt can be a form of death within yourself. It tells you that you are not worth the respect that others receive. It can convince you that you are never truly loved because, if people knew who you really were, they would not love you. It can lie within your life, often hidden from others and sometimes yourself, but in either case like a barrier between yourself and the freedom to live.

There are some painful parts of life which, unless they become pathological, carry with them a creative edge. Grief, suffering, pain and tragedy, while never to be underestimated in their capacity to destroy, in my view almost always have possibilities lying within them for brave, struggling and special life. I don't think that guilt carries that possibility, however, unless we can own our shame, make reparation as far as possible, and move on.

The origins of guilt

Religions are often used as a reference point for the sustaining of guilt—regardless of the spiritual practice of the person concerned. Sometimes this reference point is from generations back but is still operating. People can hold in their memories attitudes and judgments of the church, some of which are quite outdated but which stand within their lives with significant power. I would have to say that institutional religion has probably never really faced the consequences of its pro-nouncements for people who are outside its membership, or within it, for that matter.

Sometimes the sense of guilt is enlarged by the holding of a punishing view of God, often alongside an over-high expectation of what a good human should be like. Of course, some parts of the religious community encourage such views—both directly and in-directly. If you teach people that they are loved by a God who has endured terrible suffering in order to make that love possible, it is all too easy to move into the idea that a faithful response is to try to be very, very good and earn that love. To fail is to betray this God and add to the suffering that this God carries. The person who fails carries a sense of guilt both for letting themselves down and for further wounding a vulnerable God.

This can be made more extreme by parents who give evidence of being wounded by the failures of their child. Most of us learn very early the difference between what our parents regard as a mistake and what they see as our letting them down personally. There is a terrible amount of room in the parent–child relationship for manipulations which invite us to feel as though we have been worse than our virtuous parents ever expected and that they will bear our shame forever, or at least for a long time. Many people have been controlled by this parenting strategy all their lives.

Community attitudes also teach us what is acceptable and what is not. All cultures have views on what are lesser and greater sins; sometimes they punish those who are known to commit the greater sins by rejection as well as through more direct punishment. This invites not only guilt but also guilty secrets.

Dealing with guilt

Obviously the nature of the guilt needs to be owned and named. This is, in itself, quite a large step for some people, especially if the cause of the guilt lies many years back in their lives. The environment in which people are most likely to feel safe to express and look at their guilt is one in which someone near to them has created a space in which all are assumed to be vulnerable, failing humans. In other words, where the person trusts that they are little worse than everyone else—just rejoining the human race, so to speak, instead of assuming that they are different and 'special' in their life journey.

Questions can be asked. 'Can you think of any of your friends or family members who do not make mistakes in life?' 'When you look at public figures and leaders, do you really think they never fail?' 'Is there some reason why you would be different from these other people?', for example.

Even if a person is not explicitly or implicitly religious, the way we perceive ourselves in relation to everyone else is a central part of our world-view and one which shapes our very spirit. Of course, a diminished view of ourselves can be there before the guilt-producing event which then simply confirms our low view of ourselves. Or it can be the catalyst for perceiving ourselves as 'outside' the good human community.

It is important to explore whether there is some 'authority' which directly or indirectly has made a judgment on the person. Is there a harsh God in there somewhere, or a harsh religious institution? At this stage it can be helpful to check whether that judgment is the orthodox position of the religion concerned and the accepted theology of the God involved. If the professional person is not in a position to explore the depths of theology or other spiritual practice and theory, it may be helpful to find another kindly and creative resource to offer to the client.

If the originally condemning religious institution is still that way inclined, a hard road often lies ahead if the client concerned still gives authority to that body. It can be assumed that, if a person is sharing her or his agony of heart, that person is at least subconsciously looking for a way through to freedom. Sometimes it is worth exploring with the person the way they see their god. Do they really see this god as the best form of parent or friend? What sort of god would they actually long for and love to have? Is this god less loving than they would be as a loving parent? If so, what sort of god would be like that? If people reach for the idea that they are dealing with the purity of God, in the Christian tradition it needs to be pointed out that the purity of God as revealed in Jesus is about absolute love, mercy and forgiveness, not judgment.

It is usually good to explore whether the person needs to have forgiveness in some shape or form from the authority which they are honouring—their religious or spiritual authority or their god? Sometimes if an authority has convinced a person of their guilt, that person will not feel forgiven unless by that same authority. On many occasions when people came to me, I noted that they had nothing to do with the church and yet they were coming to me to ask for forgiveness. When we reflected on that together, they would tell me that they wouldn't really feel forgiven unless the body that told them they had sinned used the same authority to release them from their guilt.

In my experience, if only because I know what damage a harsh religious institution can do, it is often a beginning point on the journey towards forgiveness to cooperate and make possible a formal 'confession' and act of forgiveness for the person concerned—this to be offered with all the authority of the more gracious part of the religious institution concerned. If I say that this is a beginning point, it is because I observe that the hardest authority to claim is that of the right to forgive yourself. Often, until a person can come to that, they will be less than free to move forward in their life.

Claiming the power to forgive yourself

It is good to reflect on whether holding on to guilt, that is, refusing to forgive yourself or to be forgiven, in any way enhances future life or brings recompense for the wrong done. Has the person been punished enough, wounded enough, and thus needs cherishing after a harsh journey? Is there a place or person that could help with what is now healing so that creative life can be resumed?

The healthy response to the shame of human mistakes is to move into grieving rather than guilt. The grieving may take many forms and can be chosen by the person concerned. This is a grieving for the loss of who we thought we could be; it is good to map out a way of entering that grieving and then laying it down, like a burial followed by an affirming of life. It can also be seen as a healing—a healing of the wounding of oneself, both in the action which we regret and in the guilt which we have carried for too long. If the person concerned feels that a ritual to claim healing and forgiveness would be appropriate, it is often helpful to do this with a few close friends around the person concerned.

Below is one way of doing that in a non-religious way. Obviously it can be adapted with religious references and language if appropriate.

A ritual for healing of guilt

You will need
A bowl of salt water
Wine (or fruit juice) and glasses for everyone present, with a special glass for the person to keep

Opening

We are gathered here as human beings,
celebrating the beauty of that
and also knowing that none of us is perfect.
Forgiveness is necessary for all of us
and we are able to offer it
as a powerful and creative gift for each other
and, on this day, to our special friend.
We are here to affirm that,
no matter what has been done, or not done,
love still waits for us again.
We need not be destroyed by the failures in our lives.
We are free to claim here that grace is always possible
and that healing will come as the beginning of a new day.

Music

The grieving journey

Let us recall the journey of grieving
the day of regret when these feet left
what felt like a safe road and stepped into
a shadowy space in life:
(The confession is made—the story told)

Let us taste the tears of pain in this journey, now shared with us:
*(the bowl of water is passed around, people dip a finger in the bowl and
taste, and the pain is honoured in silence)*

Reading or poem

Silent reflection

The assurance of kindness

There is a greater kindness than our own
at the time of failure.
It waits for us in the love and understanding of others,
if only we will receive that
and let it be the beginning of our re-creation.
The love which lies in the universe
is grander and wider than we can ever imagine
because it is born of humble companions who walk the same way
and a generous spirit within all things.

On behalf of those who care for you,
we, your friends, offer to you unconditional forgiveness.
We offer it now and we offer it for your new future.
All that we ask is that you receive it from us
and live as though you are one of us—an ordinary stumbling human being
and one who can begin again from this moment on.

The forgiveness
(Name), are you prepared to receive this forgiveness which we offer to you?
Even as you struggle to believe that forgiveness is possible,
are you open to the grace in this moment
and in the days to come?
The person responds

The affirmation
The friends of the person gather around
(Name), we your friends announce to you that you are forgiven.
We will remind you of that when you forget it.
We will help you to believe again
that you are no more human than we are
and that this joins us with the reality of all humankind.
We will journey on with you
into all the ambiguities of daily life.
We will call you into freedom,
wholeness and humanness,
for that is the true hope of all of us.

The gift
We will share with you a cup of celebration.
(Wine is shared and a toast is given)
We give you the glass which we have filled with wine/juice for you
to take with you as a reminder of this moment.

The sending out
Let us all go in peace to share the integrity of honest human life
and all that it brings in both pain and joy.

Illness/health

5
Healing in Hinduism
Shanti Raman

Hinduism has long been involved in constructing explanatory systems for psychic and physical distress, and evolving techniques for its alleviation. Hindu thinking is all about a therapeutic approach, where every aspect of daily life (animate and inanimate) can be considered sacred and may be used in healing (for example, stones, ash, roots, leaves). If the act of healing is offered up to God/the absolute/Krishna (as it is invariably done), then all that is asked for as an offering from the devotee is a leaf, a flower, a fruit (*Bhagavad Gita*, ch. 9, v. 26):

> Whoever makes an offering to Me with devotion, be it a leaf, flower, fruit or water—that devout offering made by a pure-hearted person, I accept with joy.[1]

My very earliest memories of growing up in India contain glimpses of ordinary everyday and extraordinary healing practices. Exploring some of these memories actually help explain how Hindu thought has pervaded my own much later path in the healing arena.

In the realm of the extraordinary, I was struck by a paralysis when I was not quite three years old. This either occurred coincidentally or was directly caused by a virulent poliomyelitis epidemic in the hot, dusty, central Indian town we lived in then. I was taken to the district hospital, where my parents were told to expect me to have an ongoing disability of the kind that polio brings. Within two days, at the end of an intense period of fasting, prayer and 'laying on' of the hands on my mother's part, I was walking, indeed running again. Needless to say, this episode will form part of the folklore of the family for generations to come, and whether it is transmitted as a *miracle*, an atypical manifestation of poliomyelitis or a bit of both, will depend on the teller and the recipient(s). Since my childhood was an essentially healthy one, there were very few visits to an allopathic physician for acute health concerns. There were certainly medical doctors my family knew who also practised Ayurveda. Interestingly, they were only consulted when it was clear that Western medicine would not make a difference, such as recuperation from acute viral hepatitis. I remember the thrill of seeing a prescription written in both Sanskrit (for the ayurvedic herbs) and in English (for Western medicine).

In this chapter I attempt to reconcile the personal and the public journeys that Hindus make in the context of healing and I suggest that Hindu healing, successfully internalised but made publicly available, can be a personal and a shared journey towards salvation.

There are many learned arguments back and forth about whether there exists a distinct Hindu world-view. These arguments about philosophies, various ways of thinking, practising and *being* Hindu, are precisely what define my Hinduism. Hinduism is about diversity in all its imprecise brilliance, it is about every conceivable path to attain oneness with the absolute; through devotion (*bhakti*), work/action (*karma*), seeking knowledge (*gyana*), meditation, yoga, dancing, chanting, healing, living in the world, withdrawing from the world.

These fuzzy boundaries and indistinct definition provide a home to many seekers and agnostics. For the Hindu practitioner there can be an almost joyous sense of the anarchic underlying and supporting their beliefs and practices. To the practising (or non-practising) Hindu, 'philosophical reasoning', 'religious sentiment' and 'theological reasoning' may all meld into one. A Hindu can thus be fiercely agnostic or deeply and piously devoted to one (or many) God figure(s). In Hindu thinking the ultimate aim of existence is *moksa* or *mukti*. These terms have been variously and inadequately taken to mean self-realisation, transcendence, salvation, release from worldly involvement or, perhaps more simplistically, as liberation from human pain and suffering.

> In its fullness mokṣa is the state in which all distinctions between subject and object have been transcended, a direct experience of the fundamental unity of a human being with the infinite (Kakar 1981).

As Lord Krishna extorts Arjuna in the *Bhagavad Gita* (Tapasyananda 1984):

> Engage yourself in action with the mind steadfast in Yoga. Abandon attachments, and be unperturbed in success and failure. This unperturbed sameness in all conditions is Yoga (ch. 2, v. 48),

a simple goal and message for the everyday practitioner but immeasurably difficult to carry out.

Healing and helping

The sheer number and diversity of Hindu practitioners in the business of healing can make a stranger to the culture feel that healing, in its manifold aspects, is a central individual and cultural preoccupation (Kakar 1982). There are the traditional *vaids* of Ayurveda, some of whom practise Western medicine simultaneously.[2] In addition, there are palmists, astrologers, herbalists, diviners, sorcerers and a variety of shamans whose therapeutic endeavours combine elements from Indian astrology, medicine, alchemy and folk traditions. Then there are the ubiquitous gurus, swamis, *babas* and *bhagwans* who trace their lineage to the mystical-spiritual traditions of Hinduism. They specialise in what would be called in the West 'soul health', the restoration of mental and spiritual wellbeing, or a state of equilibrium (ibid). The diverse activities of Hindu healers (loosely defined) share a certain family resemblance in that the role of the sacred is prominent. It is the sacred that links the guru concerned with the malaise of the spirit to the shaman treating illness due to the machinations of the spirit.

A central etiological idea is that illness occurs through actions that follow lapses of 'judgment'. This judgment (*prajñā*) is a composite of three mental faculties: intelligence, willpower and memory. Erroneous mental processes and/or misuse of the senses lead to sickness. Another equally significant etiological idea is the operation of *karma*. The good or bad deeds during a previous embodiment show up in the present as good or bad luck, added to the further karma one creates in the present lifetime. Demonic interference and possession are also viewed as valid causes of illnesses.

Ayurveda recommends a wide range of therapeutic techniques, including herbal drugs, massage, exercise, diet, simple psychotherapy and surgery. Of particular interest are philosophical passages contained in several ayurvedic texts including the path towards mokṣa (or liberation) and an eightfold path of yoga aimed at developing memory (Larson 1993). So Ayurveda, with its systematised diagnostic and therapeutic procedures, nevertheless allows in, indeed depends upon, both the sacred and the metaphysical. In Ayurveda the person is conceived of simultaneously living in and partaking of different orders of being: physical, psychological, social and metaphysical.

This then is the theme that pervades Hindu healing and helping; a restoration of balance, of equanimity and ultimately liberation from the bonds of material existence. Again from the *Bhagavad Gita* (ch. 6, v. 17):

> For one who is temperate in food and recreation, who is detached and self-restrained in work, who is regulated in sleep and in vigil—Yoga brings about the cessation of the travails of Samsara [the bonds of human and material life].

Experiencing Hindu healing in India

The primacy of the 'therapeutic' in India is reflected in many facets of Indian culture, including its myriad gods and goddesses and the profusion of myths and legends that surround them. There is a god for every psychic season, a myth for every hidden anxiety, a deity for every physical ailment (including smallpox).

Growing up in a Hindu household in India means that you have constant contact with healers of varying hues and pedigrees and with those seeking healing. I have vivid memories of visiting shrines and temples where a range of shamans, mystics, gurus and beings possessed by (benign) spirits practised their extraordinary healing. One particularly famous temple to a goddess in Kerala had a regular 40-day program of healing for those 'possessed' by malign spirits. This generally consisted of a fairly exhausting regimen of exercise, diet, massage, prayer and a physically injurious exorcism ritual at the end that often resulted in a cure. Our ritual Friday night visits to this temple always included being exposed to 20 to 30 women and men (more women than men) in a floridly psychotic state, although we described it as being in a 'trance' or being 'possessed'. Many were later seen in a more 'normal' state, presumably after their exorcism ritual.

A more personal and painful childhood experience of gurus/faith healers and their power over families concerned one of my favourite uncles. A previously fit, healthy and God-fearing teetotaller, he was only 32 when diagnosed with rapidly progressing oesophageal cancer. He had the requisite therapy at a leading tertiary hospital in South India, including radical surgery, radiotherapy and chemotherapy. Given less than a year to live, his family turned in desperation to a guru or swami (a man internationally known for his miracles) and placed all their faith in this person. At their last visit to the swami's ashram, the family had a special audience with the holy man. They were reassured 'he will live', and they were given a special holy ash (*vibhuti*) with which to anoint him. My uncle died very soon afterwards. For years I could neither understand nor forgive my uncle's family for accepting naively the swami's words; even less did I understand their continuing devotion to him. With the wisdom of mid-life, I recognise now what my uncle's family implicitly understood then. His life on earth was not in question, it was restoration of balance and preparation for mokṣa that was implied. The holy ash would act in the capacity of a laying on of hands, with the added value of being blessed by the swami.

Healing and Hinduism in contemporary Western practice
If the above discussion about Hinduism implies that healers, doctors, nurses and/or therapists who are consciously practising Hindus

somehow practise their craft differently from their non-Hindu peers, nothing could be further from the truth. Hindu practitioners are no more or less likely to employ complementary therapy, no more or less likely to be disturbed by the prospect of death and dying, no more or less likely to question their patients or clients about their spiritual beliefs. However, those with Hindu beliefs, whether they believe in one, many or no gods, may be far more comfortable incorporating diversity. I suspect they would tacitly acknowledge that patients who came to them for a therapeutic encounter, particularly if they were themselves Hindu, would have many alternative sources of healing. Some would actively encourage their patients to seek other forms of therapy including Ayurveda, homeopathy, Hindu massage or a spiritual guru. They would understand the very profound healing effect that a simple offering such as *vibhuti* (sacred ash), *chandanam* (sacred sandalwood paste), holy water from the Ganges or a healing touch could have. This tradition of viewing every encounter or intervention as being touched *by* or *in* the divine is quintessentially Hindu, where there is little distinction between the sacred and the secular.

More important than notions of health and wellbeing are the dual notions of auspiciousness (*śubha*) and purity (*śuddha*). Auspiciousness— that which brings about a pervasive, established domestic value of collective and comprehensive wellbeing (Madan 1987)—is an over-whelming pursuit for the Hindu. For both the healer/helper and those seeking help, finding the most auspicious time to do the intervention/ procedure may be as important as the procedure itself. The term *śuddha* invokes images of fullness or completeness in the specific sense of perfection. Thus it refers to the most desired state of being for the human body (Madan 1987).

Finally, death can be seen as the ultimate liberation, at the cognitive level, where its significance is seen in an encompassing cosmo-moral scheme of life. Death gains a particular social import in Hindu life because the ultimate and critical sign of having lived a good life may be available only in the manner in which a person attains death.

Case study 1

Mrs A was a middle-class Indian woman in her early fifties living in a major Australian city. Her husband was a well-known academic. She herself worked in administration in the public service. The couple had lived in Australia for the last 20 years. She was diagnosed with advanced (grade 3) breast cancer, with spread to the lymph nodes. Being a devout Hindu and having been previously healthy, with no known risk factors, Mrs A rejected any further treatment following her lumpectomy. She said she was ready to meet her end, having discharged her earthly duties (the couple had two adult children), and preferred to do it with dignity. Within the next few months, with metastatic spread of the cancer, Mrs A suffered severe pain and resultant depression. In the last month of her life, her suffering was so intense that she begged medical staff to put her on aggressive treat-ment and treat her pain. Mrs A died of an intercurrent infection, having just commenced chemotherapy. Her family was angry with the medical and healing professions *and* with her for not being able to bridge the cultural and religious gaps.

The main elements of a 'good death' are the (auspicious) place, the (auspicious) time and the physical state of the person at the time of death. The best place to die would be in one's own home or in a holy place. One would strive to die at an astrologically appropriate time. And most important of all, one should die in full consciousness of the event, with one's mind fixed on the Divine Spirit. A person who departs thus, having fulfilled their worldly obligations and 'chosen' the exact moment of their death, is said to have attained the 'good way of going' (Madan 1987).

Many Hindus will have a regular biomedical practitioner as well as a spiritual guru, a vaid, special religious (auspicious) powders and unguents. Moreover, practising Hindus follow their own calendar of festivities and auspicious events, which includes several rituals with special diets, fasts and feasts. The time of day, week and month that a health or helping intervention is planned can take on greater meaning if it is understood in the context of this separate calendar.

Case study 2

L was a 10-year-old Indian girl who was diagnosed with a form of leukaemia with a poor prognosis. She was a bright, happy girl, living with her brother and parents in a suburb in Australia. The family was extremely religious and well known in the Indian community for their active participation in religious and cultural events. Over the next two years, L was in and out of hospital and was enrolled in aggressive chemotherapy and radiotherapy. The family kept up and intensified their religious and spiritual practices, involving their daughter in prayer and discussion about Hindu philosophical issues, including living and dying. Despite and perhaps because of the aggressive treatment, L died from an overwhelming infection and complications. Over the three days before her death, the family had organised a constant vigil, with friends, priests and spiritual advisers reciting vedic hymns and prayers and performing rituals. L died in peace, fully aware of her death, but bright and not despairing. The family even today are grateful for how the hospital staff accommodated and encouraged their various requests for prayers and rituals, even if these sometimes interfered with strict infection control procedures.

Both case studies involve middle-class Hindu families coping with serious, even terminal illness in a Western system of care. While there are no easy answers and no right way, in the second case the family could incorporate their Hindu notions of spiritual healing into the care plan.

Hindu practitioners, already respectful of diverse healing traditions, may come into their own in contemporary society. Today many kinds of healing practices jostle for a space in the marketplace, including diets, yoga, meditation, biofeedback, iridology, primal screaming and re-birthing. The latest scientific opinion also suggests that longevity comes with eating the right breakfast, regular exercise, not eating between meals, not smoking or drinking excessively (a little bit is encouraged) and having eight hours of sleep a day; then we are squarely in the realm of Ayurveda!

The personal and the public, from personal healing to social healing
Recognising the oneness in all human (indeed, all) beings does in a sense promote the concept of social healing.

And he who sees all beings in his own self and his own self in all beings, he does not feel any hatred/revulsion because of this view. What delusion and what sorrow can be to him who has seen the oneness? (*Upanishads*)

The struggle for me is about how to reconcile the very strong Hindu focus on liberating/realising oneself (which is an intensely personal or individual journey) with the need to actively engage with the community therapeutically or in terms of activism/advocacy (which is a very public role).

Hinduism, like other Eastern spiritual practices, tends to emphasise the individual's path to liberation, with multiple well-lit and signposted roads to reaching the absolute (none of them easy!). These are personally very liberating but may not lead to any public or community action. The personal therapeutic encounter can be easily incorporated into Hindu thinking, where a restoration of balance or, if that is not possible, striving towards an equilibrium is a goal. But moving from personal healing to 'social healing' is more complex.

Ramana Maharishi, a 20th century Indian seer, interprets the essential teachings from the *Upanishads* thus: 'Service to the world should be done with the thought that the world is a manifestation of God'. This teaching certainly informs my work with refugees, asylum seekers and the Indigenous population in Australia. While there are no specific markers in the Hindu philosophical tradition for innovative social action, I interpret passages like these as providing a sort of personal road map. A lonely path, in that it is *my* path and not a shared journey, but a path trodden by many before me and, doubtless, many to follow. Interpreting *Karma Yoga* (the path of communion through action) in its broadest sense to me provides the only possible pathway. Again in the *Bhagavad Gita* (2004), Krishna spells out:

He who, controlling all sense organs [by the power of will] and being non-attached, lives a life of communion through dedicated action—such a person excels . . . In this world all actions, unless they are done as an offering to God, become causes of bondage.

Reconciling the personal journey towards healing and the public, social act of healing is a challenge, and I suspect not just for Hindu practitioners. If the healing act, for individuals or society, is offered as karma, then it opens a spiritual path in healing that accepts both levels of practice.

Hinduism can also broaden the healing domain considerably by simply celebrating (not just tolerating) the myriad paths to the whole. My hope is that Hindu thinking in the healing and helping professions, successfully internalised, but made publicly available, can be a personal and a shared journey towards salvation: a life of communion through dedicated action.

OM SHANTIH, SHANTIH, SHANTIH[3]

Endnotes

1. *Bhagavad Gita*: patram, pushpam phalam, toyum, yomeh bhaktya pravar-tate.
2. Traditional Ayurvedic healers (vaids) are still in great demand in India and in the West. Many vaids are also biomedical doctors and practise truly complementary medicine.
3. 'Peace beyond all understanding'.

References

Bhagavad Gita, 2004 translation by Eknath Easwaran, Shambhala, Boston.
Kakar, S. 1981, *The Inner World: A Psycho-analytic Study of Childhood and Society in India*, 2nd edn, Oxford University Press, New Delhi.
Kakar, S. 1982, *Shamans, Mystics and Doctors: A Psychological Inquiry into India and its Healing Traditions*, Unwin Paperbacks, Sydney.
Larson, G.J. 1993, 'Ayurveda and the Hindu philosophical systems', in Thomas P. Kasulis, Roger T. Ames and Wimal Dissanayake (eds), *Self as Body in Asian Theory and Practice*, SUNY, New York.
Madan, T.N. 1987, *Non-Renunciation: Themes and Interpretations of Hindu Culture*, Oxford University Press, New Delhi.
Maharishi, Ramana, <http://www.poonja.com/Ramana.htm>
Tapasyananda, Swami 1984, *Shrimad Bhagavad Gita: The Scripture of Mankind*, Shri Ramakrishna Math, Madras.
Upanishads, <http://www.yoga-age.com/upanishads/isha.html>

6
Aboriginal healing Dreaming and Western medicine

Esmé Holmes and Hilary Byrne-Armstrong

I knew it would be different, and I would be different if I sat and waited.

The idea of waiting contradicted what the worker had been trained to do.

This was a foreign concept and she could not do it.

A large drug and alcohol facility, based in Sydney, had attempted to connect with the Indigenous community at La Perouse. After three months of attempts to make a service available to the community, the worker concerned felt very frustrated because nobody had come for counselling. An Aboriginal health worker suggested that perhaps if she sat with the frustration and waited, she might find a different way to connect and that might bring people to see her. The worker, however, felt she was wasting her time, that she should get back to the hospital where there was so much work to do.

Later, while I was working as a psychotherapist at the centre, the local Aboriginal Lands Council at La Perouse invited us to set up a collaborative health project. The project's aims were twofold:

- To establish a health link between the centre and the Aboriginal community of La Perouse, by opening a space, in collaboration with the community, between Aboriginal healing Dreaming and Western medicine, for ways of doing wellness.

• To develop understandings for culturally appropriate protocols and processes that would enable a bridge to be built between Aboriginal healing Dreaming and Western medicine (and with a view to, later, increasing access to health services).

Although well intentioned, the mainstream health system struggles with finding a way in which the cultural and spiritual health needs of Aboriginal Australia can fit with essentially Western methods of health care. The middle space (Byrne-Armstrong & Melser 2004) is the space between different knowledges, where tensions about difference, stereo-typing and power can be aired and talked through. In this context, the seemingly irreconcilable differences between Western medicine and Aboriginal spiritual healing practices are shared, sat with and reflected upon while finding new spaces to understand the perspective of the other.

My role in the middle space has been as a conduit between the community and the centre through our project, known as 'Two Women Dreaming'.

I am strongly aware of many influences, including my own mixed cultural heritage of Maori and European, but most of all it was my Maori family who walked with me during this time with the Indigen-ous community. As Bowers (2004) writes, 'The Indigenous wisdoms of the world carry ancient technologies of connection, of working with unconscious awareness, with ritual space, and honouring the wisdom of the environment around us' (p. 114). The presence of these ancestors guided me through cultural ways of knowing, not knowing and respect. Over the last 30 years other practices that have given meaning to my life are meditation and holistic healing with sound, song and energy. This was the reflection of my own healing journey as I walked with the community in healing.

WAITING, WATCHING AND DEEP LISTENING
As the Indigenous community and the staff of the centre walked together in the spirit of healing, the foundations to our relationship were established through waiting, watching and deep listening.

Waiting: the lawn-mowing room

As I arrived at the community one morning, the breath of the Bay (Botany Bay) danced through my veins and every pore of my body. I remembered words from the Goanna Band in 1982, 'standing on rock, standing on sacred ground', as the ocean lapped the ancient shore of 'solid rock' that is Australia. I slowly made my way to the huge old English mansion at the centre of the community and wandered around. I wondered about the history of the house. Some told me this was the land of the Eora nation and the Dhuriwal people. I stepped softly around, unsure of protocol, where I should walk and where I should not—a mere visitor to the land in the midst of the sacred ground of the ancestors and all those present. I felt my feet heavy. Someone approached me and offered to do the introductions to the different departments at the bay—a horticultural program, an employment program. This seemed to be a way, I came to know, that things come to those who wait. There was no sense of place, no room to work. Someone asked, 'Where will you be?' I answered, 'Walking around.' The reply was, 'Ah, walk-about.' Then the lawn-mowing man offered me his office, which he used only sometimes.

The lawn-mowing room I like very much; it is bright and light, a yellow room. The history of the house was told to me: it was once a boys' home. Next door was a small storeroom, the size of a walk-in pantry. One of the women told me that this was where some of the children took their own lives. There was a small hole in the door. I felt an overwhelming sense of sadness. I stood quietly and then moved away. I could sit in the yellow room and wait, trusting something would happen . . . sit and wait, wait and sit. Moments would arrive, fill the gaps then disappear—not of my making—as though in the waiting and searching for a reference, any ways of familiar knowing collapsed into something like a twilight zone, a type of fluid suspension opening spaces beyond barriers.

For myself this was waiting, listening with the ears on the heart with all senses including intuition and feeling.

Watching: the blue-tongue lizard

It was a sunny morning at Yarra Bay. A Sydney radio station had announced that a whale was coming into nearby Botany Bay. The bay was full of excitement. I had just arrived at Yarra Bay House[1] and was on my way upstairs to the bright yellow lawn-mowing room where I had been sitting and waiting for some weeks in the hope that community members would chat to me. Gradually I had made a few friends. That morning I'd noticed that few of my new friends were around. I took myself into the room and sat down. I gazed out the window at the ocean waves rolling into the bay. People were milling around waiting anxiously for Alex the whale to dock. Someone rushed past and yelled up at the window, 'Es, look at the black cockatoos . . . they haven't been in the bay for years.' Parrots and finches were flying in and out of the windows of the house. Then a young boy rushed in asking, 'Have you got a shoe-box?'

It seemed so out of context. 'A shoe-box?' I thought to myself. 'Why would he think I would have one? How strange!'

I answered, 'Ah, no.'

'Do you mind if I look around in here?'

'No, of course not, but I haven't seen any shoe-boxes.'

He went to the back of the room. It was a small room. 'Yeah, here's one . . . he nearly got caught in the snippers.'

'What the hell is he talking about? Something else I don't understand . . . I'm not getting it,' I thought to myself. I stood up, turned my gaze away from the window to face him and said, 'What do you mean, what nearly got caught in the snippers?'

'This blue-tongue.'

I looked down at his hand. The silvery white belly of a blue-tongue lizard—all of 30 centimetres long—took my breath away. Throughout our conversation the boy had been standing in front of me and I hadn't seen what was right in front of my eyes, the lizard in his hand! Whose window had I been looking out of?

How can we walk through a day and not see what is right in front of our eyes? The irony of this moment was that what had seemed out of context had actually linked me into the moment and enabled me to see what I had been missing. This was what I had been looking for—a pathway to connect me to the immediate environment. Rather than being stuck within a frame of reference I had brought with me into a landscape where it didn't belong, I had to be open to other ways of doing and being. The community members later referred to this experience as my initiation into the community. Initiation, of a different way of seeing and listening—seeing and listening to the space between—the interconnectedness. This experience prompted me to consider my own ways of being, seeing and healing that I was bringing into the community with me.

Deep listening: the clinic

After some time of sharing our different and similar ways of doing wellness we were able to identify culturally appropriate activities as vehicles for the many ways of healing that held meaning *for us*, including a carers' group, women's healing retreats, and a weekly health clinic at La Perouse.

At the clinic, one Monday, Billy told me in a soft voice that he was going into 'another one'. In another second he was having a grand mal, a major epileptic seizure, the third in a row. The ambulance was called and I went with him to the local hospital while I tried to reach his family on the mobile. He was given valium and an oxygen mask and fell into and out of sleep. After some time he was assessed for admission. He whispered to me, 'I don't like these places.' I remembered reading something the Yolngu people of the Northern Territory say, that when you go to hospital you die twice, once from the sickness and again from the fear of hospital (Trudgen 2000). I stayed with him. A young doctor eventually saw us. He began his diagnosis, his manner efficient and strident.

'You drink a bit, do you? Listen, mate, the drinking isn't helping these fits.'

Billy did not reply. He asked me to take him home.

I intervened. I told the doctor that Billy had designed the entrance doors to the hospital. He didn't seem to hear me as he went on talking loudly, engrossed in the task. Suddenly there was a silence, a pause. The doctor looked at me as if to say, 'What was that?'

'The glass doors,' Billy said.

'He did?' the doctor turned to me for verification. I nodded.

'Did you? On your own?'

'Just me,' said Billy.

The doctor's voice became softer, his manner more relaxed and warming.

'You're from La Perouse—I used to go fishing out there.'

He talked to Billy by name, asking questions about the painting, listening carefully to the responses and interspersing them with questions about Billy's health. We all relaxed. My comment had woken him up. Both he and Billy could begin listening to each other. This experience resounded deeply within me as we were all brought into the one moment of awareness.

Aboriginal writers (Ungunmeer 1988, cited in Atkinson 2002: 107) refer to the practice of listening deeply as 'a deep contemplative process of listening to one another in reciprocal relationships'. The doctor was initially focused on his task and his conversation style reflected this. Billy became even more afraid. But when connection was made, the relationship changed. The discovery of shared knowledge—first the hospital door and then fishing at La Perouse—forged a connection that in the long run affected the outcome of the health intervention, that is, determined whether Billy would stay or leave the hospital with fear. This also invited the young doctor to consider a new way of listening.

For myself this was listening with all the senses, including intuition and feeling. It was these practices or ways of being by those around me in the community that also seduced me into the position of waiting, watching and deep listening.

The metaphor we used of Two Women Dreaming was a basic principle of Aboriginal spirituality and wellbeing, namely, interconnectedness. In 2002 we painted the story of Two Women Dreaming at one of our community women's healing retreats. The two rivers in our painting depict the cultures of Aboriginal healing Dreaming and Western medicine walking side by side as they share the ways that the two healings can complement each other and then come together in the ocean. The red-bellied snake gave us a visit while we gathered at the sacred rock, so she had to be included—she is shown protecting her eggs. The eggs symbolise members of the group and the La Perouse Aboriginal community. At the top, the two spirits are shown as they guide each culture in the ongoing dialogue on healing.

THE GROUND BETWEEN TWO CULTURES

The middle space: Two Women Dreaming

Two Women Dreaming is now in its fifth year. Activities and outcomes have included the re-opening of a clinic, weekly circles, tri-annual healing retreats and re-incorporation of telling story through song, dance, history, painting. There are also monthly meetings, intercultural dialogues and the re-introduction of Aboriginal healing practices. While these are the threads that make the weft and the warp of the fabric of spirituality and wellbeing, the pivotal axis linking all these activities is conducted through a circle solely for the expression of spirituality, called Keeping the Spirit Strong. The community is now in the process of becoming an incorporated association, the Two Women Dreaming Association for Wellbeing.

The Two Women Dreaming collaborative project has not only given breadth and depth to my own experiences but has challenged any romantic notions that one can adopt of Aboriginal ways and spirituality. The words of Aboriginal social activist Leila Watson ring loud: 'If you've come to liberate me forget it, if you've come because your liberation is wound up with mine then welcome.'

Endnote
1. The house is situated to one side of the mission at Yarra Bay, not far from where James Cook landed and exchanged beads for Aboriginal land. In 1882 the house was first used as a cable house, with a varied history to follow as a girls' home and later a boys' home.

References
Atkinson, J. 2002, *Trauma Trails: Recreating Songlines. The Transgenerational Effects of Trauma in Indigenous Communities*, Spinifex Press, Melbourne, Australia.
Bhabha, H. 1994, *The Location of Culture*, Routledge, New York and London.

Bowers, R. 2004, 'Our stories, our medicine—Exploring holistic therapy integrating body wellness, mindfulness and spirituality: An Indigenous perspective on healing, change, counselling, and the social and political contexts of an emerging discipline', *Australian Counselling Association Journal*, vol. 4, no. 4, pp. 114–17.

Byrne-Armstrong, H. & Melser, P. 2004, '"Policing" ethics: Critical action research and the middle space', *Mainstream Psychology in the Spotlight*, *International Journal of Critical Psychology*, Issue 11, Lawrence & Wishart, London, pp. 150–67.

Trudgen, R. 2000, *Why Warriors Lay Down and Die*, Aboriginal Resource & Development Inc., Darwin.

7
Illness

Joseph Daniel Toltz

The entire world is a very narrow bridge,
The most important thing is not to be afraid.
(R. Nachman of Breslov, *Likutey Moharan* II: 48)

Rabbi Akiva walked into the house, swept and sprinkled the ground before the sick man. He had gone to visit the house of a disciple who had fallen sick; no one else had visited this man. After the man had recovered he thanked Akiva, saying that it was his visit that made him well (*Talmud Nedarim* 39b).

Performing the *mitzvah* (religious obligation) of *bikkur cholim*, which literally means 'visiting the sick', is an obligation placed on all Jews. One of the morning prayers that we recite every day from the Mishna (a redaction of Rabbinical Oral Law) says, 'These are the obligations without measure, for which the reward is without measure: honouring father and mother, practising acts of loving kindness, hospitality to strangers, visiting the sick . . .'. Akiva expressed this strongly, saying to his other disciples, 'One who does not visit the sick is like a shedder of blood' (*Talmud Nedarim* 39b). The word *bikkur* means more than just visit—it includes going to all places where sick people reside, and performing any deeds that aid the comfort of those who are ill or dying.

For the past 10 years I have worked as a visiting Jewish chaplain to various hospitals in Sydney. This has been most often at St Vincent's

Hospital in Darlinghurst, a Catholic hospital where I did training in hospital chaplaincy through enrolment in the Clinical Certificate of Pastoral Education (CPE) course in the Department of Pastoral Care. It was with some trepidation that I began the course, being the first Jewish person to undertake this training in New South Wales.

The CPE was one of the most amazing, personally challenging and rewarding courses of education I have undertaken. Many encounters have been with non-Jewish patients. After chaplaincy to those with kidney and liver problems, I requested a transfer to the Sacred Heart Hospice, to work with dying patients. My deliberate move was to confront fears around death and dying. Working with atheists, fundamentalist Christians and those of other faiths shattered many preconceptions, causing me to re-examine my own inbuilt prejudices. Most of all, learning the power of listening and suspending judgment has been one of the most rewarding and useful skills I have developed, applicable to every life situation.

Basic philosophical differences between the Christian and Jewish approaches to pastoral care are quite great, and working in the context of Christian theology challenged me at times. The inspiration that comes out of pastoral care theology from a Christian standpoint is an emulation of the compassion of Jesus, and much of the thought and theology that went into the post-patient analysis part of the course (verbatims and group sessions) was centred on this theology. Such a model does not resonate with a Jewish pastoral care worker, so with the guidance of my Rabbinical debriefers I went to various Jewish textbooks to seek a Jewish model of pastoral care that would be a counterpoint to the Christian model I was encountering. One of the most useful in terms of practical advice was by an Orthodox author, Rabbi Aaron Levine, who wrote the manual *How to Perform the Great Mitzvah of Bikkur Cholim, Visiting the Sick* (1987).

The Jewish approach: bikkur cholim
Like all Jewish law, bikkur cholim emanates from the Torah—the first specific mention is that of God visiting Abraham after he performs the ritual of circumcision on himself, his son Ishmael and all the men of his

household (*Genesis* 18:1). The Talmudic interpretation of this is that 'Just as God visited the sick, so, too, you should visit the sick' (*Talmud Bavli*, Sota 14a).

Judaism doesn't have a notion of pastoral care as such. However, many valuable references are contained within the Talmud about the action of visiting the sick, and practical advice abounds in the literature concerning the limits and rules around approaching this mitzvah. The visitor should not visit late at night or early in the morning, and although relatives and friends can visit the *choleh* (sick person) immediately, for others it is more customary to visit after three days. Jewish tradition encourages frequent visits: the sage Raba (*Talmud Nedarim* 39b–41b) says, 'One must visit even a hundred times a day, so long as the visitor does not trouble the sick person'. We are taught that it is permitted to visit on the Sabbath and it is, in fact, a great service to do so. During a visit, one must help the person, making sure that his or her needs are being attended to. There is a controversy about visiting an enemy who falls sick; there are prohibitions against engaging in behaviour that will endanger one's life (for example, visiting highly contagious patients); one should not visit a patient if the conversation might be injurious to their health; and one should be mindful of the patient's own sense of modesty, not visiting when they have an embarrassing affliction.

Judaism is a life-oriented religion and the mission of bikkur cholim is not to counsel the patient into acceptance of the illness. The visitor is expected to reach out to the sick person, to express concern and offer encouragement that urges the striving towards recovery. In general, Judaism views the speculation about God's motives for bringing suffering upon an individual negatively. Such speculation is inappropriate and not directed toward healing. In the *Book of Job*, Job's friends tell him he should examine his past to determine the nature of his current afflictions, but we know that Job is a righteous man. Our many rabbinical interpretations of the texts explore, and more often discard, the notion of God chastising those whom God loves (*yissurim shel ahavah*) for the sake of making them stronger. Judaism has a good number of philosophical views concerning illness, but a visit to a choleh is not an appropriate time to discuss them.

Prayer is an essential component of the obligation of bikkur cholim.
One should pray in the presence of the patient or elsewhere. Prayers
may be in the vernacular or the more traditional Hebrew. The *Shulchan
Aruch* stresses that prayers for the sick should request healing for all who
are ill. Our tradition also speaks of the *Shechinah* (the Feminine Divine
presence) hovering over the bed of a sick person, protecting the soul of
that person and encouraging healing. With this in mind, the *Shulchan
Aruch* instructs us to sit in front of the sick person, rather than on their
bed. The notion of the Feminine Divine presence is detailed in many
Kabbalistic texts. Outside of these texts, the Shechinah is mentioned
most strongly in the context of *Shabbat* (the Sabbath), where we usher
the presence of the Shechinah into the synagogue on a Friday night,
bringing the Jewish people and the Divine Feminine together in a state
of wholeness, of wellness and completion, that exists only during the
period of Shabbat. Touch is also an important component of healing
in Judaism—deriving again from the Talmud, this time from Rabbi
Yochanan, who said to his ill friend, Rabbi Elazar, 'Give me your hand'
(*Berachot* 5b).

Integration

One of the most challenging aspects of receiving this wonderfully rich
and codified tradition was to try and integrate it in the pastoral care
techniques I was learning. Without the benefit of a clearly defined
theology as motivation, I had to develop a personal ministry, a belief
system grounded in my Judaism but taking into account the strengths
and demands of CPE. Reinterpreting my tradition was a first task.

The rigorous course process involved the delicate taking apart and
reconstruction of our constructed identities as hospital visitors; from the
beginning, the quality of empathy was accentuated as one of the prime
goals of pastoral interaction. The prohibitions against visiting late at
night or early in the day inform the visitor to be sensitive and thought-
ful of the weakness or strength of the choleh. When visiting people who
are gravely ill, I am acutely aware of not tapping their strength too
greatly. The encouragement of frequent visits and visiting on the
Sabbath goes towards a notion of caring for the individual through this

work. Expressing concern that the patient is being well cared for can be a slippery slope—very often patients can be unaware of the nuances of their illnesses and the health-care professionals surrounding them may unwittingly leave them out of the information loop. Such situations must be handled with the utmost sensitivity.

The prohibitions against visiting enemies, contagious patients or those to whom a conversation might be injurious again go straight to the heart of the matter—having empathy for the choleh. Often in my rounds I may be unaware of the full state of health of the individual, and therefore my visit may transgress one of these prohibitions. It is incumbent on me to develop a rapid response in these situations, picking up important information before I enter the room. If the person is in isolation or in an intensive care unit it is exceptionally important to realise that medical care is the primary concern in such situations and bikkur cholim may not be an appropriate action at that time. A notice on a patient's door such as 'wash your hands before entering this room' does not only warn us against bringing infection into the room, it may warn us about the serious nature of the patient's health—physical and, following on from this, mental and spiritual. Just as Judaism cares about the choleh, it cares about the visitor's health as well. The empathic response builds up an awareness of the relationship between self and other: I may never understand what you are going through, but through conversation and dialogue I can come towards your viewpoint, at the same time that you come towards mine. The pastoral care role can be integrated into the bikkur cholim model with great effect.

There are specific conventions of prayer in the situation of bikkur cholim: the recitation of specific psalms designed for healing became a great feature of my learning process. The psalms also bridge a common ground between Judaism and Christianity, and during my studies I found particular inspiration in a book edited by Rabbi Simkha Y. Weintraub, *Healing of Soul, Healing of Body: Spiritual Leaders Unfold the Strength and Solace in Psalms* (1994). Here rabbis from many different traditions (Reform, Conservative, Reconstructionist and Orthodox) come together to discuss the potent power of the message of healing contained in specific psalms. Two very useful psalms during periods of health crisis are Psalm 121 (*Essa Enai el Heharim*: I turn my eyes to the mountains, from whence cometh my help?) and Psalm 30 (*Mizmor Shir Chanukat Habayit*: I sing to you, Lord, who lifted me up).

These two psalms were an important starting point for visits to a patient with a terminal illness, a man whom I had been visiting regularly for many years. The patient was a respected physician who had given much to his community and family. He was at various different places of emotion during our visits and each time we were able to find a psalm that connected with his feelings. At first our prayers were focused almost exclusively on hope: hope for healing and recovery and, particularly, hope for a scientific solution to the health problem. Time passed and it became apparent that even after radical therapies, physical healing would not come to his frail body. We turned to spiritual healing, reconciliation between himself and his Creator. Various psalms contributed to resolving many issues—anger, frustration, a sense of hopelessness and powerlessness. Some psalms talk of cries of despair in the face of overwhelming odds (Psalm 137: *Al N'harot Bavel*: By the rivers of Bavel, there we sat down); others speak of forgiveness and reconciliation (Psalm 130: *Mima'amakim k'raticha Hashem*—Out of the depths I have cried to Thee, O Lord) while others simply praise God as inspiration for humanity (Psalm 146: *Halleluyah, Halleli nafshi et Hashem*: Praise the Lord, oh my soul). We both came to a point of acceptance and I tried, as best I could, to assist his family to that same point when he lapsed into unconsciousness. Even then, in his unconsciousness state, his family wanted me to sing various psalms, strongly believing in his ability to hear and be comforted by them.

Each time we came together I prayed for his recovery, as is our tradition—Judaism teaches us that we always pray for recovery, even at times of despair and hopelessness. The prayer invokes our ancestors, Abraham and Sarah, Isaac and Rebecca, Jacob, Leah and Rachel, who were blessed by God. Just as they were blessed, so too we pray for perfect healing for all of those who are sick in the community; each time we prayed this, we also invoked my friend's name. Our prayer is for both physical and spiritual healing. This formulaic pattern gives great comfort to patients, as it is all-embracing in its outlook. Finally, when my friend was nearing the end of his life, we recited the *Vidui* prayer, the final confession, on his behalf as he was unable to speak at that point. This prayer begins with a plea for healing, moving into an acceptance of the process of dying, and finally ending with the acclamation of God's oneness, God's sovereignty and God's eternal care. Assisting my friend and his family through this final passage of life, seeing him breathe his last breath and feeling the presence of his soul in the room was one of the most transformative experiences of my life. The memory of this and countless other profound hospital encounters sustains my work and informs all that I do, culturally, creatively and spiritually.

Walking into a hospital room is a confronting and challenging experience—for the visitor, for the patient, for the health-care professionals. It is, however, one of the most rewarding experiences when approached with care and forethought.

From the Talmudic story of Rabbi Akiva, we gain a measure of the worth and value of this work and an understanding that bikkur cholim does indeed make a difference to the wellness of the choleh, as well as affecting the visitor in a profound manner.

Visiting the sick, bikkur cholim, pastoral care, whatever we choose to call it, brings us closer together as humankind and is an active work of *tikkun olam*, repairing our broken world.

References

Levine, A. 1987, *How to Perform the Great Mitzvah of Bikkur Cholim, Visiting the Sick*, Zichron Meir Publications, Ontario.

Rabbi Simkha Y. Weintraub, S.Y. 1994, *Healing of Soul, Healing of Body: Spiritual Leaders Unfold the Strength and Solace in Psalms*, Jewish Lights Publishing, Woodstock.

Talmud Bavli, Sota 14a, <http://www.jewishgates.com/file.asp>

Talmud Berachot 5b, <http://www.jewishgates.com/file.asp>

Talmud Nedarim 39b–41b, <http://www.jewishgates.com/file.asp>

Acknowledgments

The CPE course was pioneered at St Vincent's Hospital by the late Sister Margaret Lee RSC. I particularly want to acknowledge the support and understanding of Jenny Washington and Monica Dwyer from the CPE, my classmates, Anglican chaplain the Reverend John Hawkins, as well as Jewish input from Rabbi Jeffrey Kamins, Rabbi Brian Fox and Rabbi Dr Jeffrey Cohen.

8

Mental health and young people

Michael Dudley

(with acknowledgments to Dorothy McRae-McMahon)

Among the things that Amy, a 16-year-old Aboriginal woman from a remote community, nominates that keep her alive and wanting the best for her baby are her grandmother's company and her grandmother telling her about 'the Lord'.

Amy lives with her 18-year-old Aboriginal boyfriend in town, but also at times with her mother and grandmother at the Aboriginal housing cooperative. She has a problem with depression, heavy alcohol and cannabis abuse and life-threatening suicide attempts, involving overdoses and near-miss hangings. Two young male acquaintances have died this way in the past three months in her community, which is struggling to respond. Amy is terrified of abandonment by her boyfriend. Amy falls pregnant, her boyfriend is reportedly intimate with other girls and she dumps him and goes on 'a bender'. Amy resolves to keep the baby and decides to stay off all alcohol and to continue prescribed medications that keep her emotionally stable. This resolve is broken, on a couple of occasions, by her boyfriend's reappearance. Amy's mother was separated from her own mother when young—as one of the 'stolen generations'—and used to drink heavily. However, she is now employed as a bush nurse and gets Amy to appointments with her female mental health counsellor, who visits weekly, and organises her antenatal attendances at the nearest regional centre.

Amy's grandmother's long search for her own daughter and her integration of Christian and Aboriginal 'ways' has sustained her and made her a leader in her community. The mental health counsellor encourages contact between the three generations of women, and offers to see the three women together to understand what measures can support Amy and her baby. Amy also nominates as important a planned 'return to country' with other Aboriginal women: she believes this will help her understand her spiritual and cultural heritage more clearly, as it is a journey aimed to help young women to learn lost 'women's business'.

Spirituality, recognised as central to mental health from ancient times, has remained so in many non-Western and Indigenous traditions, while this knowledge has been substantially lost in the West in recent centuries. Modern Western psychiatry is a secular discipline that applies scientific methodologies to clinical questions and hence to solving complex human (socio-cultural, moral, spiritual) problems. Recently, however, the 'deep-freeze' between religion/spirituality and the mental health disciplines has begun to thaw. A growing body of quality research indicates that what we tell ourselves about our life and its ultimate significance is central both to our health and wellbeing and to the prevention and management of physical and psychological disorders.

Spirituality is important in my work as a child and adolescent psychiatrist. At a personal level, it informs the reasons why I work in this area, the perspectives I take and the kind of work practice I have with depressed and suicidal adolescents. However, consideration of spirituality is (and should be) an integral part of every mental health professional's role. I try to understand my patients' lived experiences, strengths, culture and beliefs in shaping their responses to illness and intervention, and I know the importance of my fully engaging with these if I am to respond successfully.

Spirituality is central to the questions of meaning, value and belief that we face together yet it is seldom in the foreground of discussions with clients and colleagues. There are many definitions of spirituality. One, that is both succinct and inclusive, refers to the deepest human longings: for wholeness, connection and transformation, for providing a sense of purpose and agency, for the sense of the sacredness of life and sacred presence that often anchors these (Tacey 2004). It also often signals a sense of what is ethical and just and a vision for the betterment of the world (Elkins et al 1988). Individualism, consumerism and fractured social bonds have been claimed to contribute to rising depression and suicide rates (Eckersley & Dear 2002). Continuing high suicide rates among young adult males, especially in Indigenous and rural communities and culturally diverse groups, suggest an urgent need for (among other measures) cross-cultural dialogue and exploration of spirituality in mental health promotion, service delivery and research.

As Australia has changed demographically there has arisen a wide diversity of cultural and language groups and their spiritualities, which are potential resources for everyday clinical situations. Non-traditional forms of spiritual expression (including Eastern, non-Anglo-Saxon, feminist and Indigenous spiritualities) receive increasing attention.

A standard part of any mental health enquiry concerns young people's views about what is most important to them and what gives their life purpose and meaning. I ask about whether spiritual belief is important in their life and in coping and, if so, whether it is important in their current troubles and whether they belong to a spiritual or religious group or organisation. In approaching clinical assessments, I assume that, although the spiritual domain may sometimes have a mixed significance, it is usually health promoting, and it is always important to enquire about.

Case study 1

Hassan, the 16-year-old son of a consular official and his wife from a central Asian state, is afflicted with a rare and disabling movement disorder following encephalitis. The parents are separated and he and his 9-year-old sister live with their mother, but see their father regularly. In hospital, the neurologists call the psychiatry team because they think Hassan is depressed and that this impedes his willingness to accept further medical intervention. Although he has difficulties keeping still, Hassan makes a major effort to answer the psychiatry team's questions. He hopes for a medical breakthrough, and tells us that God makes him very strong. He has good school friends and his teachers are supportive. He prays five times a day. Hassan asks us why he is afflicted with this condition. His mother privately tells us that her son feels bad because he thinks that God may be punishing him. Hassan requests to see the Muslim chaplain, who prays with him and tells him his illness is not divine punishment, but something for medical science to deal with. The chaplain alerts the treating team to Hassan's belief that his illness and distress caused his parents' marriage to break up and that he is not able to look after his mother. Clearly the medical outcome, if adverse, will pose further spiritual challenges for Hassan and the treating team.

If a young person, such as Hassan, nominates a spiritual orientation or framework, I try to explore how this fits with their self-concept, aspirations and values. The protective effects of religion for young people's mental health have been argued for by recent reports (US Commission for Children at Risk 2003). Although religious or spiritual practices are sometimes associated with negative health effects, well-designed population-based studies find that religion and spirituality are sources of strength and wellbeing rather than evidence of psychopathology (Koenig et al 2001).

The reasons for the overall positive effects of religion/spirituality are moot. They may promote better relationships, healthier lifestyle or reduced substance misuse. Perhaps the belief in God's care, in the final triumph of justice, that adverse events have meaning and a message is protective, reducing hostility and promoting optimism, hope, wellbeing, self-esteem and, perhaps paradoxically, an inner sense of directedness (Koenig et al 2001: 99–101, 213–20).

I am particularly interested in how a spiritual framework may help young people to cope with stress and depression. The young person's family's stories and religious practices may be important in helping to define this.

Case study 2
Naomi is 15. When her Jewish Israeli parents separated five years before, a court order decreed that she would migrate to Australia with her mother, who would pay costs for her to return to her father and her younger brother in Israel twice a year for at least two weeks. When Naomi turned 16, she would decide whom she would live with and where. Her father, a businessman and one-time politician who lost his

seat in the last Israeli elections, puts continual pressure on her to return to live with him. Her mother has suffered from anxiety and depression since the break-up. Both her mother's and her father's parents are Holocaust survivors (their parents and extended families being mostly annihilated). Naomi excels at her Jewish high school, has numerous friends to whom she is fiercely loyal, avidly reads Jewish mystic literature and political writings, attends synagogue with her mother and hopes to become a rabbi. (Although there are no women rabbis yet within Orthodoxy, she does not see this as a barrier.) She has been learning about the Holocaust at school and debates her ideas with friends and teachers. Naomi loves Israel and Australia and both her parents and can't decide where she wants to live. She is anxious, depressed, losing sleep and less hopeful because of this dilemma. Counselling involves acknowledging her distress that she cannot please both parents, supporting her in not deciding now and communicating this to them, and considering how to manage her low mood and insomnia. It emerges that her high self-expectations hinge on a feeling of responsibility—that she must do something with her life, given her intimate knowledge of life and death—and feeling she must be a leader for her people in a threatening world. Naomi is encouraged in her quest, but we discuss with her and her school how to reduce some of her expectations, especially around deadlines. The therapy is deepened by various Jewish stories and tales that her mother's mother has given her, stories that take up themes of grief, loss and perseverance, and also by Naomi and her mother talking about her family's history.

As part of a young person's developing critical faculties, religious organisations and beliefs are re-evaluated, and religious practices may be intensified, abandoned or transformed during the period of their coming of age and searching for a place to belong.

For young people, and for health professionals working with them, spiritual development is at least potentially as significant as other areas of development. Spiritual development mirrors family relationships in different language: it concerns young people's needs for secure attachment, the need to know that they are not alone, the need for consistent, safe limits, and their need for stable personal identity and place in a created, spiritual order (Josephson & Dell 2004).

Case study 3
Ewen, a young man of 18 from a church-going family, suffers from Asperger's syndrome (involving a significant impairment in social relationships and a restricted pattern of interest in activities). He was counselled, with his older brother and mother, for several years in relation to organising schoolwork, difficulty with friendships and conflict and violent threats at home, arising from battles with his mother which seemed based on his sustained difficulty understanding others' needs. Nevertheless, he gained university entry and started psychology as part of a general arts course. After some months' absence from counselling, Ewen returned to report that he had been depressed and not sleeping. This problem occurred after he had withdrawn from his local church, where he had been invited to take a youth leadership role. Since he publicly disputed some of his church's unquestioning biblical teaching and theological positions, even sometimes during services, he ran into trouble. He was asked to meet with the minister, when his challenging of church doctrine was branded disruptive, and he was relieved of leadership responsibilities. Ewen felt bad. He felt that church people were giving him the 'cold shoulder'. He has now moved to a different church, which allows him to be a leader but also to ask more questions about belief. He is no longer depressed.

This young man's significant pre-existent difficulties may have proved too challenging for, and alienated him from, his church community. On the face of it, there may have been a significant shortfall in pastoral care in his case. The case illustrates Ewen's religious maturation going hand in hand with emerging maturation in terms of communication abilities and ethical behaviour.

Depression, young people and spirituality
There are many reasons for choosing to consider spirituality in relation to youth depression in particular, although space and focus preclude detailed analysis of the latter. Depression usually begins in childhood or adolescence. It is frequent among young people, occurs in most cultures, presents in diverse ways and coincides with various other mental health disorders (which means that it is greatly under-recognised and under-treated).

In some faith traditions, being depressed or mentally ill may result in stigma: if faith is meant to safeguard against these problems, their emergence may be seen to prove a lack of faith. Religious practices are sometimes used to replace traditional mental health care. Mental health problems may also be more prevalent for those whose spirituality is 'extrinsic', that is, which operates as a means to an end (Koenig et al 2001: 127)—for example, neoliberal consumer spiritualities which promise worldly success. While the frequency of negative effects of religion is still unknown (Koenig et al 2001: 77), related studies are largely isolated case reports and highly selected case series, rather than population-based systematic research studies.

Conditions such as the 'dark night of the soul' and 'melancholy', and their connection with spiritual growth, have been recognised within Judeo-Christian traditions for centuries (an extensive literature review is beyond our scope here). For some, however, being depressed may originate in closed religious traditions, where personal development and autonomy are identified with selfishness, and doubts or questions with lack of faith or a challenge to authority. Religious groups may disparage, ridicule or ostracise such members, or may indoctrinate, isolate and alienate them from their families and communities. Some spiritual frameworks, for example cults and Satanism, may be particularly associated with negative mental health effects. Depression may also arise from failure to reconcile contradictions inherent in different world-views (for example, religious and secular or differing religious perspectives).

By contrast, many studies show that frequent involvement in religious community activity is, for the most part, associated with a reduced incidence of depression and suicide. Intrinsically religious people (whose practice is an end in itself rather than a means to other ends) have lower depression and suicide rates and speedier remission from depression (McCullough & Larson 1999; Koenig et al 2001: 129–30).

Spirituality is now attracting intense interest after decades of suspicion and neglect, as practitioners and researchers increasingly appreciate its positive significance. The change of climate between religion/spirituality and mental health disciplines has been liberating for many mental health professionals. The West's recognition that spirituality, culture, the sciences and medicine share considerable common ground has been central to the rise of religious and spiritual therapies. Many Western-trained clinicians are now using spiritual techniques such as meditation and mindfulness and adding them to mainstream therapies (Kabat-Zinn 2005; D'Souza 2003).

The involvement of clergy in a process of healing is illustrated in the following case of complicated bereavement.

Case study 4

Kylie is 15 and suffers from depression. Her mother is itinerant and drug addicted. Her father, an ex-jockey and motor car racer, reared her. He drank heavily and died two years earlier of cancer. He was never violent or abusive to her, but nor did he tell her that he was dying. Kylie was his principal carer, and very attached to him. She has been in the care of a family friend since. She stopped her daily cannabis use at her boyfriend's insistence and became overwhelmed by her dead father's voice telling her to join him. After she wrapped cords around her neck she was hospitalised and judged to be at high suicide risk. She was treated with antidepressants, antipsychotics and supportive therapy. As her father's voice became less intimidating, Kylie talked about missing him and about what she would do with his ashes. She had attended a Christian Sunday school and believed in and prayed to God. Though her belief did not prohibit suicide, as she became less agitated she relinquished the idea of suicide to rejoin her father.

Kylie found contact with the hospital chaplain helpful. It affirmed her belief in God and that her father and she were both safe in God's care. A staff member suggested that some form of healing ritual or ceremony might be of use to her. The participating mental health professionals concurred and the chaplain agreed to undertake it. A skilled liturgist, in consultation with the chaplain and key team members, used various items and symbols from Kylie's life and the different voices she heard (her own, her father's and others) in a ritual to represent and affirm a new reality for her. Her father's ashes and his photo were placed on the ground inside a wide circle of cloth. A bowl of water placed within the circle symbolised the waters of weeping and fear. The Bible placed within the circle was used as a sign of the authority of the love of God that would take the place of the destructive voice in her life. As Kylie gave expression to her own voice and her father's voice, she poured more water from a jug into the bowl, which the participants then passed to one another to taste, affirming solidarity with her grief and pain. She placed objects associated with her father's memory within the circle. While she did not bury her father's ashes during this ceremony, keeping this until she could join with his relatives in another city to do so, she reported that it had been a positive event.

The ceremony placed Kylie within a circle of concern. It sought to help her to find a 'safe place', to acknowledge and share her grief, to emphasise her liberation from harm and to anchor and affirm her in her new life. It avoided treating her as though she was inhabited by a 'demonic' problem external to herself, thus running the risk of taking the solution out of her hands and further fragmenting her sense of self. The ceremony instead aimed to help her to integrate different parts of herself. The event did not mark the end of Kylie's troubles, for she has continued to have problems with depression, cannabis use and social connections, but she has continued to work, with renewed courage, on getting her life in order.

In relation to suicidal ideas and attempts, I indicate that I will do anything possible to ensure that the young person is safe and that I work with them and those who care about them to ensure this. Along with other protective factors, I enquire about whether any spiritual or religious reasons make suicide unacceptable to them, and seek to bolster these reasons if they are in evidence.

These four examples indicate various ways in which spirituality may be important for young people presenting with mental health problems, with particular reference to depression, and how it may be used in therapeutic interventions with individuals from a number of faith traditions. Spirituality may be used to help young people cope with stress through such means as solving problems, identifying and challenging beliefs that maintain depression, acknowledging and working with grief, and handling interpersonal challenges (for example, sustaining personal networks and minimising conflict).

More research is required to understand the phenomenon of spirituality among young people and how they may use it in situations of stress or mental illness, while much is still unknown about the religious or spiritual beliefs of mental health professionals. Although these may be important in sustaining practitioners and supplementing their therapeutic repertoires, little is known about their impact on patients.

Spirituality is the meeting point of many paths, has demonstrable mental health benefits and is capable of protecting and connecting young people in their quest for a viable life in an increasingly consumer-driven society. Spirituality is not a panacea, however, and should always be considered critically. Though genuine spirituality cannot be prescribed, and is not a Medicare benefits item, aspects of it (such as meditation) are being adapted for use with young people in clinical settings with promising results. Given their clients' wishes to talk about spirituality, mental health professionals need to overcome the current limitations of Western medicine and of their own cultural frameworks, signalling by their questions that this area can also be part of the conversation.

References

D'Souza, R. 2003, 'Incorporating a spiritual history into a psychiatric assessment', *Australasian Psychiatry*, vol. 11, no. 1, pp. 12–15.

Eckersley, R. and Dear, K. 2002, 'Cultural correlates of youth suicide', *Social Science and Medicine*, vol. 55, no. 11, pp. 1891–904.

Elkins, D.N., Hedstrom, L.J., Hughes, L.L., Leaf, J.A. and Saunders, C. 1988, 'Towards a humanistic-phenomenological spirituality', *Journal of Humanistic Psychology*, no. 28, pp. 5–18.

Josephson, A.M. and Dell, M.L. 2004, 'Religion and spirituality in child and adolescent psychiatry: A new frontier', *Child and Adolescent Psychiatric Clinics of North America*, vol. 13, no. 1, pp. 1–16.

Kabat-Zinn, J. 2005, *Full Catastrophe Living*, Delta, New York.

Koenig, H.G., McCullough, M.E. and Larson D. 2001, *Handbook of Religion and Health*, Oxford University Press, New York.

McCullough, M. and Larson, D. 1999, 'Religion and depression: A review of the literature', *Twin Research*, vol. 2, no. 2, pp. 126–36.

Tacey D. 2004, *The Spirituality Revolution: The Emergence of Contemporary Spirituality*, Brunner-Routledge, New York.

US Commission for Children at Risk 2003, *Hardwired to connect: the new scientific case for authoritative communities*, United States Commission for Children at Risk, 2003, <http://www.americanvalues.org/html/hardwired.html>

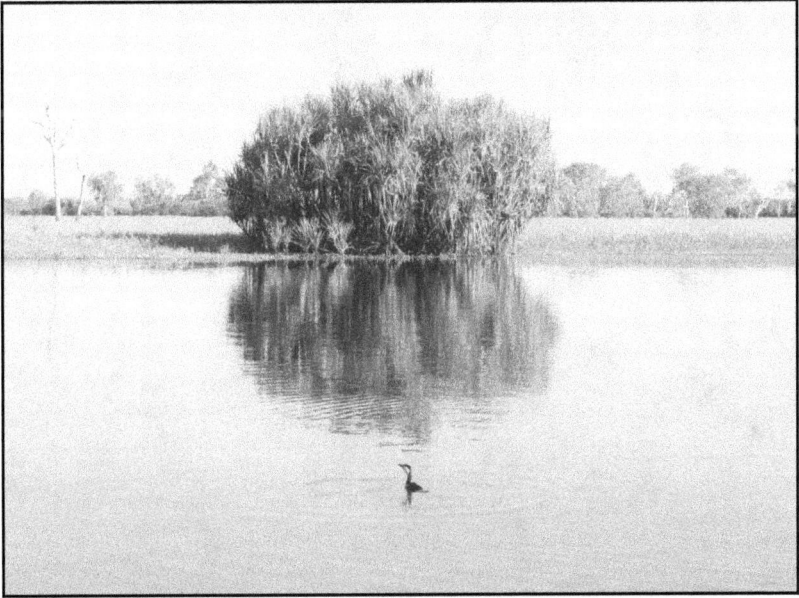

Loss and Death

9

Loss and death in Islam

Nooria Mehraby

To Allah we belong, and to Him is our return (Qur'an: 2: 155–7).

While much attention has been paid to recovery from grief within the context of Western cultural values, this chapter reflects on the way loss is dealt with when counselling Islamic clients. Counselling and spiritual direction as therapy has an ancient tradition in Islam. Here I discuss how Islamic beliefs and traditions provide essential frameworks of meaning for those who face loss and grief, especially clients whose distress stems from, or is exacerbated by, their relationship with God (Allah).

A Muslim practises the religion of Islam; the word Islam means 'peaceful submission to God's will'. In accepting grief and loss, the relatives of a deceased person are urged to be patient (*sabr*) and accept Allah's decree. People who have patience in accepting Allah's decree will be given a reward from Him.

I have no reward other than Paradise for my believing servant who is patient when I take away one of his beloved from among his companions of the world (Qur'an: 63).

In a hadith (one of the sayings and customs of the prophet Mohammed, peace be upon Him) the prophet says:

whatever trouble, illness, anxiety, grief, pain and sorrow afflicts a
Muslim, even if it is the pricking of a thorn, Allah removes some of his
sins because of it (Bukhari, date unknown).

Muslims believe that all suffering, life, death, joy and happiness derive
from Allah and that Allah is the one who gives strength to survive:

> Be sure we shall test you with something of fear and hunger, some loss in
> goods, lives and the fruits of your toil, but give glad tiding to those who
> patiently persevere. Who say, when afflicted with calamity: To Allah we
> belong, and to Him is our return. They are those on whom descend
> blessings from their Lord and mercy, and they are the ones that receive
> guidance (Qur'an: 2: 155–7).

These beliefs are usually sources of comfort and strength that aid the
healing process.

As a person's religious belief and traditions are a dynamic part of
their personality and life viewpoint, these need to be considered in the
treatment of Muslim clients.

Muslims are most likely to seek assistance from family, close
friends, a community member or a trusted Imam or scholar. While a
Muslim therapist will be closer to the client's reality, many Islamic
clients accept non-Muslim therapists, generally of the same gender as
themselves. Those who seek assistance from mainstream therapists will
require a culturally appropriate intervention from someone who understands the beliefs and teachings of Islam.

Muslim communities are too often labelled in Western countries as
terrorist, rigid, aggressive, militant, uncivilised or closed-minded. A
non-Muslim therapist thus needs to be, and to be seen to be, impartial,
open-minded, and for the client. A non-judgmental attitude will
reassure and enable Muslim clients to talk about difficult matters,
including depression, anxiety, stress, loss and grief, post traumatic stress
or suicidal ideation.

A counsellor working with Muslim clients will support their religious
beliefs, strengthen their faith, correct their thoughts and beliefs (cognitive
re-structuring) and help them change their behaviours. 'Counselling' and

'psychotherapy' within Islamic belief has an ancient tradition of changing the behaviour of clients by cognitive and behavioural psycho-spiritual methods that rely extensively on the righteous and exalted personality of the therapist, sheikh or spiritual leader (Badri 1996). Counselling is not an activity for a few specialised professionals, but is the responsibility of every Muslim and a main tenet of Islamic studies.

Loss and grief

Verily in remembrance of Allah, do hearts find rest (Qur'an: 13: 27–8).

Muslims believe that death is essentially an interface between the life of this world and the next. While death is inevitable, Allah appoints its time. Since death is not final but the first step to eternal life (Mission of Hope 2005), for the majority of Muslims grief is illogical. However, it is still unhealthy to skip over the tragedy and feeling of loss too rapidly (Maqsood 2002).

Individuals are encouraged to talk about and remember their loved ones and recall the good deeds of their lives. When the Prophet Muhammad re-visited the grave of his mother many years after her death, he cried and encouraged others to weep (the Prophet's mother died when he was six years of age) (Maqsood 2002).

Although wailing and tearing one's clothes are still common among some Muslims, Islam discourages such conduct (Khattab 1998). Khattab states that in Islam it is permitted to weep softly before someone dies, at the time of death, and afterwards. A few words may be said when crying over a deceased person, but these words should be true, unaccompanied by wailing and expressions of dissatisfaction with God's decree. For instance, when the Prophet's son Ibrahim died, the Prophet said, 'We are very sad for your death, O Ibrahim.' This does not indicate any discontent or complaint against God (Khattab 1998). Various respected hadiths describe the Prophet crying on several occasions when one of his loved ones died. Although the period of outward mourning lasts no more than three days, grieving may never fully end (Mehraby 2003).

Funerals are very important, offering an opportunity to grieve, pay respect to the deceased and express faith in God. However, Islam disapproves of expensive funerals or gravestones, or making a shrine of grief. Such shrines can often generate feelings of guilt, or create financial burdens for the bereaved who cannot afford them (Mehraby 2003).

Islamic rules concerning death vary from country to country, and between denominations such as Sunni and Shi'ite. Some derive from variations in national, ethnic, tribal and folk cultures (Lapidus 1996). Generally, when Muslims die, they are buried as soon as possible. Burial represents the human being's return to the most elemental state, since the Creator formed humans from earthly materials. Therefore, cremation, preservation, interment in above-ground mausoleums or other methods are not permitted. Prompt burial may help lessen the mourning. The deceased person's body is ritually washed, wrapped in plain white linen and placed in a simple wooden coffin (if one is necessary) facing Mecca. Prior to burial a special congregational worship service is offered and prayers are made for Allah's mercy upon the dead person. The deceased's affairs may be handled via a will or testament, and the Qur'an specifies means for distributing the inheritance to the spouse, children and relatives (Council on Islamic Education).

There are different kinds of loss such as sudden death, miscarriage, stillbirth, abortion and suicide. For refugee survivors of torture and trauma, loss of children, spouse, homeland, social status, career and customary lifestyle lead to different kinds of mourning, requiring different responses.

Maqsood (2002) states that bereavement is a traumatic experience and mourners may be comforted by knowing that their reactions and feelings are almost universal, and not sinful. Shock, disbelief, denial, anger, guilt, bargaining, depression and acceptance are common responses to loss. Maqsood advises that not only are Muslims allowed to express these feelings, but also that it is damaging to suppress them. The loss must be acknowledged, the emotions freed, new skills may need to be developed and emotional energy channelled into new life.

Islam acknowledges in particular the hardship of losing a child. When a child dies, fellow Muslims should help, comfort and support the parents, advising them in the best Islamic manner (Abdullah 1999). There are special rewards from Allah for parents whose children die. 'The Prophet always insisted that children who died before their parents went as forerunners for their parents in the life Hereafter, and would serve as "protection" against Hell-fire' (Maqsood 2002). In the case of sudden infant death, parents should be allowed full opportunity to grieve and be assured that their innocent soul is safe with Allah. Similarly, grieving over a miscarriage or a stillborn baby should not be downplayed. It should be recognised that the parents have sustained a real death.

Abortion is not permitted in Islam unless the mother's life is at risk; such cases are highly sensitive and the mother's guilt feelings are very real. She may be unable to forgive herself or feel that God will never forgive her. Women who do not mourn the loss may experience great unresolved grief (Maqsood 2002).

According to Islamic law, when a Muslim woman loses her husband, she must not re-marry until four months and ten days have passed (exceeding the three days of grieving for other loved ones). This *iddah* (waiting period) allows a woman to mourn, and also to determine whether she is pregnant with her deceased husband's child, for this will affect issues of inheritance and related matters. Although modern DNA technology could ascertain parental identity in the case of women who marry before this time, the waiting period honours the late husband and maintains the dignity of the marriage bond (Council on Islamic Education).

Although a similar waiting period is not required for a man to re-marry, a Muslim man is also allowed to mourn the death of his wife. The Prophet himself never forgot his love for his beloved wife Khadijah, even years after her death (Maqsood 2002).

Suicide is strictly forbidden in Islam: 'Do not throw yourselves with your own hand into destruction' or (an alternative translation) 'Do not commit suicide, as God is merciful to you' (Qur'an: 4: 29). Self-harm and other self-destructive behaviours are also prohibited. Allah creates every soul and life and no one has the right to take their own or anyone else's life. Many Muslims consider those who die by suicide as turning their back on Islam, with the result that suicide is a most difficult bereavement crisis for any family to face because shame, guilt and anger predominate. Bereavement therapy after suicide should be generous, empathic and challenge distorted thinking. It is crucial that the bereaved person accepts that the suicide was not preventable and that the bereaved family is not at fault or held responsible. The family can pray to God for mercy and for the forgiveness of the deceased (Mehraby 2005).

Although Muslims may not easily discuss personal and family matters with a stranger, concerns about shame and stigma may mean they are more likely to discuss sensitive issues such as suicide and abortion bereavement with a non-Muslim therapist. A strong emphasis on confidentiality will enable them to trust the therapist and explore the depth of their suffering.

It is incorrect to assume that no suicides can be forgiven. The World Health Organisation estimates that mental disorders are associated with more than 90 per cent of all suicides (World Health Organisation 2002). The hadith states that the actions of a person acting out of a disturbed mind cannot be held against the person. Allah can forgive and the promise Allah gave to the Prophet should be remembered: 'If a person has in the heart the goodness to the weight of one atom, and has said, there is no God but Me, he/she shall come out of Hell-fire' (Qur'an: 21: 47). Allah, not his servants, is the only one who can decide what is wrong or right, to forgive or punish.

Working with the bereaved from the Islamic faith

He guides to Himself those who turn to Him in penitence, those who believe and whose heart has rest in the remembrance of Allah (Qur'an: 13: 27–8).

Muslims are advised to increase their devotion to Allah in times of distress, depression, loss and grief. Generally, in assisting bereaved Muslims the three main principles are:

* This life is temporary before eternal life begins.
* Only God determines the time of death.
* There are actions to continue to benefit the departed after death.

A collective grief system supports the bereaved family through frequent visits, food offerings, congregational prayer, reciting the Qur'an and strengthening their faith by returning them to Allah. The use of religious parables, the life story of the Prophet Muhammad with his multiple losses, and hadith and sura from the Qur'an are all beneficial (Mehraby 2003). A death is always announced by reminder of Allah's will.

The bereaved are also advised to pray for God's mercy and forgiveness for their sins and mistakes: 'And I have said: seek forgiveness from your Lord. He was ever forgiving' (Qur'an: 71: 10).

Badri (1996) states that Muslim clients experience most guilt regarding their relationship with Allah. Many have committed, or think they have committed, some serious sin. Feelings of guilt and regret are accompanied by anxiety and fear of Allah's punishment, in this present world and Hereafter. Many have been raised with a strong faith in Allah, but an exaggerated sense of His punishment; God's love and mercy are diminished in their relationship with Him. As the following case study illustrates, some Muslims might consider their continuing grief as a sin punishable by God. Such clients may improve with a safe environment that guarantees confidentiality, and interventions, such as cognitive restructuring, that focus on strongly emphasising God's mercy and forgiveness rather than punishment.

Case study

Mr A, a 52-year-old Afghan refugee, lost 61 close relatives including his mother, fiancée, brothers, sisters, uncles, cousins and other members of his family during the war in Afghanistan against the Soviet Union. His father also died when he was five years old. Mr A was his family's sole survivor. He was referred to the Service for the Treatment and Rehabilitation of Torture and Trauma Survivors because of chronic and complicated grief, survivor guilt, depression, anxiety and post traumatic stress.

Mr A was distressed and agitated, and cried throughout counselling sessions. In addition to survivor guilt, he believed God would punish him for not accepting God's decree and for his impatience. He still grieved even after many years.

A safe and trusting environment was provided for Mr A where his reactions were normalised and feelings validated. The Prophet Muhammad's life story, the enormous number of family members that he lost, and his remembrance of his mother and his wife Khadijah years after their deaths, was narrated to Mr A. God's mercy and forgiveness were re-emphasised.

Mr A processed his massive losses, developing his beliefs about God's love and forgiveness, and disputing his beliefs about punishment and revenge. He was supported in this and encouraged to increase remembrances of God in times of distress. He was encouraged gently towards accepting God's decree, his future reward from Allah for his deep suffering and multiple losses, the reward his relatives receive as *shahid*, or martyrs, whose resting place is Paradise, and the present gifts of his survival and life. He was given the opportunity to grieve, and his symptoms were deemed not only appropriate, but vital for him in order to remember those he loved. Over four years of therapeutic contact, Mr A gradually began to change.

Mental health professionals have recognised the role of cultural and religious values in psychotherapy with Muslim clients: indeed, religion's significant role in everyday Islamic culture makes counselling without engaging with such values difficult. Culturally sensitive psychotherapy requires as the core of the therapeutic relationship an understanding and adaptation of Islamic principles. The therapist must respect and accept the client's culture, demonstrating that therapy is not confrontation with culture and family, but an attempt to help the client within their culture.

Since the concept of counselling for Muslim clients involves direction, advice and emotional and material support, clients may expect the therapist to symbolise authority, and to take over and care for them. The therapist can lessen the client's burdens by encouraging talk about loved ones and exploring the painful reality of their death.

Prayer is traditionally considered one of the best ways to heal distress and deal with losses. Group prayer, especially Friday congregational prayer, and fasting contribute to the sense of identity and belonging, overcoming isolation (Mehraby 2005). Performing regular prayer five times a day also exercises the body, combining physiotherapy with meditation and relaxation (Mehraby 2002).

In life situations when nothing can be done except through observing patience, trust in God can reduce feelings of excessive responsibility and enable constructive methods to deal with, and perhaps overcome, the situation. Only God knows our ultimate destiny. The Muslim therefore feels reassured that trust is well placed and that God will not forsake him or her.

Islamic beliefs and traditions, like Christian and Judaic ones, provide essential frameworks of meaning for the grieving individual, particularly when their unresolved grief stems from or is exacerbated by their relationship with God. Exploring these beliefs, traditions and cultural norms within therapy can facilitate access to the client's world of meaning and thus help them to respond to the application of Western psychological interventions such as cognitive restructuring.

Ultimately, by sitting silently and praying one connects with the true self, which is intrinsically connected to Allah. This enables the individual to accept the self and the pain because one does not exist in isolation, but rather as a part of the total wholeness in relation to Allah.

From Allah we come and to Allah we shall return (Qur'an: 2: 155–7).

Amen.

References
Abdullah, R. (1999) 'Overcoming trials and tribulations', in *Advice from the Qur'an and the Sunnah*, 2nd edn, Ta-Ha Publishers Ltd, London.
Al-Assai (2000), *Al-Junun: Mental Illness in the Islamic World*, International University Press, Inc., USA.
Badri, M.B. (1996), 'Counselling and psychotherapy from an Islamic perspective', *Al-Shajarah: Journal of the International Institute of Islamic Thought and Civilization* (ISTAC), vol. 1, no. 182, pp. 159–91.
Bukhari, S. (date unknown), *The Hadith (Sayings) of Muhammid*, Volume 7, Book 70, <http://www.balaams-ass.com/alhaj/bukhari.htm>
Council on Islamic Education, <http://www.cie.org>
Khattab, N. 1998, *From Islamic Psychology, Patience and Gratitude*, Ta-Ha Publishers Ltd, London.

Lapidus, I.M. 1996, 'The meaning of death in Islam', in H.M. Spiro, M.G.M. Curnen and L.P. Wandal (eds), *Facing Death*, Yale University Press, New Haven and London.

Maqsood, R.W. 2002, *After Death Life! Thoughts to Alleviate the Grief of all Muslims Facing Death and Bereavement*, 4th edn, Good Word Books Ltd, New Delhi.

Mehraby, N. 2002, 'Counselling Afghanistan torture and trauma survivors', *Psychotherapy in Australia*, vol. 8, no. 3, pp. 12–18.

Mehraby, N. 2003, 'Psychotherapy with Islamic clients facing loss and grief', *Psychotherapy in Australia*, vol. 9, no. 2, pp. 30–4.

Mehraby, N. 2005, 'Suicide: Its pathway, perception and prevention amongst Muslims', *Psychotherapy in Australia*, vol. 9, no. 2, pp. 20–6.

Mission of Hope 2005, *Muslims in Australia: A Health and Community Worker's Guide*, Islamic Social Services Association, <http://www.missionofhope.org.au>

Qur'an 1999, *The Noble Qur'an: English Translation of the Meaning and Commentary*, Madinah Munawwarah, translated by M.T. Al-Hilali and M.M. Khan, Dar-us-Salam Publications, Saudi Arabia.

World Health Organisation 2002, <http://www5.int/mental-health>

I dedicate this chapter to my late grandmother, mother and sister, all of whom I have lost recently. While I am mourning their loss, their love, memories and thoughts gave me the inspiration to write this chapter.

Nooria Mehraby wishes to thank David Findlay and Peter Davis for their assistance in reviewing this chapter.

10
Working with children

Margaret Crompton

To Margaret Howe, 1920–2006, with love, respect and gratitude.

Attending to children's wellbeing in social and health care encompasses every aspect of life—cognitive, emotional, physical, social and spiritual. Article 27 of the United Nations Convention on the Rights of the Child (United Nations 1989) requires recognition of 'the right of every child to a standard of living adequate for the child's physical, mental, *spiritual*, moral and social development' (my emphasis).

Since practitioners have a duty to ensure nurture of children's spiritual wellbeing, they need to be aware of both their own and other people's beliefs about spirituality and religion. As an example, this chapter briefly surveys influences on my own practice, especially writing and teaching about spiritual wellbeing, and illustrates aspects of Quaker faith and practice in relation to interactions with children.

Respecting Children (1980), my first textbook, was written from 20 years' experience of work with children as student, practising social worker, adviser, university lecturer and writer. The title encapsulates the belief which underlies and pervades my work, which is that all work with, for and about children—that is, *in respect of* children—demonstrates *respect for* every individual child. I had been a Quaker (member of the Religious Society of Friends) for about two years and the book reflected Quaker concerns.

Writing this chapter, 25 years later, I realise that my own Quaker beliefs flow from and reinforce the ways in which I have always approached social work and the development of ideas about spiritual wellbeing. Essentially, I have been influenced not by deliberate, dogmatic teaching but by everyday, every-minute communication from inner conviction expressed through words and actions, whether personal or practice focused.

My Liberal Anglican upbringing (in the United Kingdom) led to social work training after a degree in English Literature. At Bristol University two of my tutors were Quaker; neither spoke of their religious beliefs but their faith was integral to their teaching and informal contact with students. I lived in an Anglican convent hostel; as with my tutors, it was the essence of the nun-warden which stays with me, a presence of peacefulness, understanding and firm comfort.

As assistant warden of a residential settlement in the East End of London, I left the church whose liturgy seemed to have no relevance to daily work among disadvantaged people, particularly poor children, disturbed adults and elderly Jewish immigrants from Eastern Europe from whom I learned about the radiance of the spirit undimmed by past dispossession and present disability, and I learned that care, respect and affection are not bounded by nationality or religion.

Social work training (London School of Economics) focused partly on *The Casework Relationship* by Felix Biestek (1957), a Jesuit priest, a book which addressed the whole person. From D.W. Winnicott (a famous child psychiatrist from whom we were privileged to receive lectures) I learned about wholeness, communication, concepts of health and challenge and, although he might not have used the term, the spirit of the child (for example, Winnicott 1965). I have always endeavoured to honour and pass on the spirit of his teaching and practice. As a young child care officer I was guided by a practitioner whose clear Baptist principles underlay the courageous, loving integrity of her work.

Anglican, Baptist, Quaker, Jew, Roman Catholic—thus people from a range of religious traditions influenced me as a young student and social worker. Later, teaching and writing offered opportunities to learn from others who worship in, for example, Buddhist, Christian, Hindu, Islamic, Jewish, Rastafarian, Sikh and Zoroastrian traditions. I have learnt that whether or not the individual is committed to a religious or philosophical tradition, denomination and detail of belief and observance are irrelevant; the essence is in the spirit and the spirit is in the every-minute, everyday communication of individual people deeply focused on the wellbeing of others. This is expressed through the advice of George Fox (the first Quaker) to 'walk cheerfully over the world, answering that of God in everyone' (Fox 1656). On the first page of *Respecting Children*, I say it is 'a declaration of my belief in that of God in every child'; every child is a separate individual of personal worth, capable of giving and receiving love, trusting and being trustworthy, accepting responsibility for responses, choices and actions.

I have been privileged to represent what I have learned from my teachers, including many children, in writing, conferences and consultations about communication and, since 1992, about spiritual wellbeing in the context of social and health care, including a government agency in the United Kingdom which commissioned an innovative training pack for social workers on *Children, Spirituality and Religion* (Crompton 1997). At every meeting and conference, participants express relief and delight that topics formerly ignored, or even prohibited, can be discussed and ideas and experience shared. Words like 'liberated' are used and much energy generated. One practitioner confided happily, 'We're doing it already!'—that is, attending to spiritual wellbeing in the course of everyday interactions. Topics have included ideas about spiritual qualities, needs and experiences, developing a 'language of spirituality with which we all feel comfortable' and creative methods of working with, for example, art, music, play and stories.

Respect for other people's beliefs and traditions is fundamental to the practice of social work. The central question is: 'How can you or your service apply ideas about spiritual wellbeing to everyday practice or develop ideas about spiritual wellbeing in everyday practice?' The basic method is sharing (see Crompton 1998, 2001, 2004).

Spiritual wellbeing

In the United Kingdom, many social work and other health and welfare agencies were established by charitable foundations with religious connections. As the state took over many formerly voluntary functions and responsibilities, these religious connections could attract suspicion from secular administrators and practitioners, including anxieties about abuse, exploitation and proselytising.

Since the early 1990s, discussions about spiritual wellbeing have focused on the whole life of the child, not on denominational dogma or details of belief. This derives partly from concern to respect the many religious beliefs and observances which enrich the multi-ethnic nature of British society. For many people, spiritual wellbeing is inseparable from religious belief and observance. Some regard 'spirit' and 'soul' as synonymous, both meaning the aspect of the person which expresses and responds to a deity and survives physical dissolution. Others are convinced of a spiritual aspect to life but are not adherents of any religious tradition: the phrase 'secular spirituality' might be useful and has important resonance for practice in an overwhelmingly materialistic culture (Crompton 2001: 6). Sensitivities towards such matters should inform any discussion of spiritual wellbeing and practice.

Spiritual wellbeing is inseparable from cognitive, emotional, physical and social wellbeing. If one aspect is neglected or harmed, the whole person may be impaired. Spiritual distress can result from or underlie more visible signs and behaviour. A social work colleague described an unloved girl as '"dis-spirited": she rarely smiled, and spent most of her energy in trying to attract attention from her rejecting family. She "had no spirit, a shell, no life or verve"'. He defined spirituality as '"positive movement, light, involvement, and emotional congruence", but work with the family was constantly blocked' (Crompton 1998: 31, 61–5). Another practitioner related 'his spirit was crushed' by the body language of children 'dragged down, slumping, their exuberance crushed' (Crompton 1998: 31, 65–73). Children who can be described thus are losing not only spiritual wellbeing but the whole of childhood.

Asked, for this chapter, to link grief and loss with the themes of spirituality and working with children, I realise that most, perhaps all, such work is concerned with loss. Even the happiest childhood is characterised by change and therefore loss. Birth requires the end of womb comfort, weaning separates baby from breast, developing autonomy costs dependency and protection. In Sunday school we sang, 'There's a Friend for little children/Above the bright blue sky'—but who would be my protecting Friend when I ceased to be a little child?

Many children lack not only the comfort of belief in a heavenly Friend but also the protection of loving, reliable, everyday earthly friends and carers. Practice in social and health care focuses on enabling and encouraging children whose lives include challenge and needs beyond the resources of family and community to engage with loss, gain strength, and incorporate difficulty and disadvantage into positive, fulfilled lives. Although children's rights are often emphasised, equally important are responsibilities, including the ability to make well-informed choices, to develop wise trust and realistic relationships.

My own faith is not one which holds the position that everything will be all right, that problems are solved, obstacles removed and prayers answered like miraculously granted wishes. Rather, I believe that the ability and resources to face challenge and difficulty, disadvantage and even disaster come through intra-personal strength and inter-personal relationships. I do not define 'God' but I characterise my concept of the divine as 'spirit', entirely encompassing and entirely immanent. This informs the concept of every-minute, everyday spiritual wellbeing, which is expressed through:

- intra-personal—for example, creativity, imagination, senses of awe, mystery, enquiry and wonder, worship, sense of self, taking responsibility for own responses and actions, endurance, courage;
- inter-personal—for example, love, relationship, wise trust, responding to and taking responsibility for other people;
- out-looking—awareness of, sense of connection with, and concern for things such as the Earth, animals, issues beyond personal relationships.

A practising Quaker

In a vivid fictional evocation of childhood, 10-year-old Emily was 'thinking vaguely about some bees and a fairy queen, when it suddenly flashed into her mind that she was *she*'. Exploration of her newly discovered self leads to 'another consideration: who was God? . . . wasn't she perhaps God herself?' (Hughes 1929, ch. 6).

To a Quaker the (or an) answer to Emily's question is 'yes', for our fundamental belief is expressed by the words of George Fox (written in prison in 1656) to 'walk cheerfully over the world answering that of God in everyone'. Emily—and everyone else—embodies the divine. A boy asked a Hindu priest, 'Have you seen Vishnu?' The priest responded, 'Yes, for I have seen you.' Adherents of other faiths express beliefs in different ways. People who do not believe in a deity may use secular vocabulary, recognising the spiritual in the whole (Crompton 2004).

A sense of identity is integral to development, to wholeness, and is easily eroded or even lost under stress or during crisis. Barnardo's (an agency whose aim is expressed as 'Giving children back their future') entitled a book about children's spiritual wellbeing *Who am I?*, identifying a central focus of social and health care (Crompton 2001). While the spirit cannot, I believe, be destroyed, inhibition of any aspect of life impairs spiritual wellbeing. By really respecting and attending to children, practitioners help their spirits to gain strength, enabling them to engage with and use feelings and experiences, however apparently 'negative' these might appear to other people.

This is illustrated by 10-year-old 'Mark', whom I was engaged to help prepare for placement in, it was hoped, a long-term foster home. His family had been irrevocably dispersed after a sexual assault on his sister, although Mark and his other siblings had not been involved. His skilled and devoted regular social worker was overburdened with crisis work and administration. My task was to help him develop a sense of himself since his life and family had been fragmented, and he had already moved several times.

When we visited important places from his lost past, including former addresses and the maternity hospital, he told me vivid stories. But a special field had disappeared, buried under a car park—symbolising his experience of loss. Mark was devastated, asking: 'Margaret, why do things have to change?' I still feel his bewildered sadness and the opening of his spirit to me. I had no answer. We walked in silence.

Later, sitting quietly over lunch, I narrated the story of our morning together while Mark drew the lost place of his memories. I hoped to help him develop a new way of remembering, integrating present and past and adding the memory of that special day and its discoveries. We both learned about change, loss, sadness and communication.

With Mark I responded always to 'that of God' and walked with him as cheerfully as I could. I helped him to engage with the facts and truth of his life, often painful and bewilderingly beyond his control. I tried to help him learn what he could control, and to develop through imagination and creativity a sense of himself. We discovered together that he was a fine artist: every week he dictated some event from his life (present or past) which I later typed for him to illustrate, creating a living life-story book. He honoured me by calling our regular date 'Margaret Day'.

Frustration and loss once distracted my attention from him when finance was suddenly withdrawn. My distress reached Mark and he closed a meeting prematurely: 'Can I go now?' We eventually achieved a positive parting in his favourite café. I still find endings difficult but learnt from Mark to be more aware of the impact of even unspoken feelings (Crompton 2002, 2004).

My work was not consciously 'Quakerly'; I never *thought* of 'that of God', for this approach is integrated, not explicit. I would explore such a concept overtly only if the child initiated discussion. But I am also ready to engage in discussion if a child wishes. I remember conversing with a boy who declared his belief in the Devil, for example. 'That of God', as expressive of inner strength and life-fullness, is essential to healing and wholeness, no matter how 'God' and 'spirit' are understood. That of God within the practitioner, in George Fox's terms, 'answers cheerfully' that of God in the other. True meeting and communication occur only when the whole self is engaged.

Working with Mark illustrates another fundamental aspect of Quaker belief—commitment to seeking and facing truth, not hiding behind half-truths or lies to avoid pain and distress. The greatest loss may lead to growth if faced with courage; the practitioner may need to be as brave as the child.

While Mark's loss did not include death, bereavement through death is not uncommon in childhood. When 'Frank' developed incurable cancer the consultant advised 'Jean' not to tell their son 'Roy'. I was dismayed but had no power to intervene. Frank grew rapidly weaker at home but still no one explained to Roy.

One day a priest removed Roy's beloved birthday present, an Alsatian puppy which had grown too boisterous for the dying man in a small house. When Roy returned from school, his dog had disappeared. Soon afterwards Frank died in the night. Roy was sent to school, in ignorance. When he returned his father, like his dog, had gone for ever. As a neighbour I couldn't interfere with his mother's wishes. Jean became increasingly and chronically depressed. When she too died, Roy went away to live with previously unknown relations, losing parents, home, friends, dog, school—everything. Roy expressed nothing, remaining stolid, pleasant, placid, apparently unsurprised and unmoved. Because he expressed no feelings, it was assumed he had none to express. Listening into silence is often more important than responding to words.

Over 30 years later I still regret that I failed to help Jean and Frank engage with Roy in the family tragedy in which he was inextricably involved. Fear and denial lost both parents and child the opportunity to share memories and anxieties, to express grief and love, to say goodbye and to give the boy a chance to grow. Jean's desperate decline derived from both Frank's fatal illness and a history of secrets and deceptions, dragged into light by this crisis. Every aspect of wellbeing was impaired for every member of the family by the inability to face and share truth. This was compounded by practitioners, including medical staff and clergy (Crompton 1990: 27).

In contrast, practitioners in an agency focusing on bereavement helped 11-year-old Danny engage with feelings about his mother's death. He said, 'We scattered my mum's ashes at her favourite beach. In one of the caves . . . special yellow flowers grow. I think these are my mummy.' This beautiful symbol of life helped him to express sadness and think about good times still available to him in memory (with thanks to Barnardo's, Belfast).

Whatever practitioners' own beliefs about death and the possible destination of the soul, the task is to respond to, and help expression of, the feelings, fears and anxieties of clients.

In concert with seeking truth, Quakers endeavour to promote peace and prevent violence; pacifism is not merely avoidance of fighting. 'Friends' in England in 1660 were exhorted 'to seek peace . . . seeking the good and welfare and doing that which tends to the peace of all' (The Peace Testimony 1660). Over 200 years later, New Zealand Friends wrote: 'The places to begin acquiring skills and maturity and generosity to avoid or to resolve conflicts are in our own homes, our personal relationships, our schools, our workplaces, and wherever decisions are made' (Religious Society of Friends in New Zealand 1987).

This endeavour has deep implications for social and health care. Violence includes abuse, discrimination, prejudice—any failure in respect. Although violence against children sometimes leads to loss of life, all too common is loss of confidence, health, home, relationship, trust—the loss of childhood. Seeking peace includes respecting 'that of God' in perpetrators who may themselves be children or impaired through earlier experience. Respect does not imply collusion, however, and perpetrators can be expected, and helped, to change.

The most important medium of communication for Quakers is silence. During our regular predominantly silent Meeting for Worship we try to still our thoughts, to be open to the Spirit and to attend respectfully to spoken ministry. We regard all meetings, including those for discussion and business, as worship; this extends to all interactions, whether or not with Quakers.

Silence and emphasis on attending and listening have implications for communication in social and health care. A friend recently noted how people listen inside their heads to what they plan to say next, rather than attending to the speaker. In contrast is the stillness and silence felt in times of deep concentration on 'the other' or 'thou', when 'my' next words flow true and right without inner rehearsal it is because 'I' have gone with you into the place of true communication; 'that of God'.

Being comfortable with silence helps me to still my mind in professional encounters, to focus on the other person, to listen deeply, to respond appropriately, to wait and not to rush into speech if no one else is talking. It also enables response if a child speaks directly about 'that of God' in whatever form or language. 'I like you,' said one girl, 'because you take me seriously.'

With Mark I usually achieved that inner silence, concentration and meeting, failing when I submitted to my own feelings. Roy's silence was an eloquent communication—but no one was listening. All children should be taken seriously.

Attending to children's spiritual wellbeing is an essential, fundamental element of social and health care practice. It requires that you know yourself, be yourself, and meet every child with love, respect and gratitude.

References

Biestek, F. 1957, *The Casework Relationship*, Loyola University Press, Chicago.
Bradford, J. 1995, *Caring for the Whole Child: A Holistic Approach to Spirituality*, The Children's Society, London.
Coles, R. 1990, *The Spiritual Life of Children*, Houghton Mifflin, Boston.
Crompton, M. 1980, *Respecting Children: Social Work with Young People*, Edward Arnold, London.
Crompton, M. 1990, *Attending to Children: Direct Work in Social and Health Care*, Edward Arnold, London.
Crompton, M. 1992, *Children and Counselling*, Edward Arnold, London.
Crompton, M. 1997, *Children, Spirituality and Religion: A Training Pack for Social Workers*, Central Council for Education and Training in Social Work, London.
Crompton, M. 1998, *Children, Spirituality, Religion and Social Work*, Ashgate, Aldershot.
Crompton, M. 2001, *Who am I? Promoting Children's Spiritual Well-being in Everyday Life: A Guide for All who Care for Children*, Barnardo's, Barkingside, UK, <http://www.barnardo's.org.uk>
Crompton, M. 2002, 'Individual work with children', in K. Wilson and A. James (eds), *The Child Protection Handbook*, 2nd edn, Balliere Tindall, London.
Crompton, M. 2004, 'Spiritual well-being; When I was a child . . .', script in *Conference Report*, H. Dunn (ed.), Barnardo's, Belfast (unpublished), pp. 14–31, <http://www.barnardo's.org.uk>

Crompton, M. 2005, 'Spiritual wellbeing in care practice', in J. Miller (ed.), *Care Practice for S/NVQ 3*, Hodder Arnold, London, pp. 266–71.

Crompton, M. and Jackson, R. 2004, *Spiritual Well-being of Adults with Down Syndrome*, The Down Syndrome Educational Trust, Southsea, UK, <http://www.downsed.org>, enquiries to <enquiries@downsed.org>

Fox, G. 1656, <http://www.strecorsoc.org/gfox/title.html>

Hay, D. with Nye, R. 2006, *The Spirit of the Child*, 2nd edn, Jennifer Kingsley, London.

Hughes, R. 1929, *A High Wind in Jamaica*, Harper, London.

Miller, J. (ed.) 2005, *Care Practice for S/NVQ 3*, Hodder Arnold, London.

The Peace Testimony 1660, *A Declaration From The Harmless And Innocent People Of God, Called Quakers, Presented to the King upon the 21st day of the 11th Month, 1660*, <http://www.rgvquakers.org/peace.html>

Religious Society of Friends in New Zealand 1987, *Peace*, Yearly Meeting Statement, <http://quaker.org.nz/whoweare/ymstatements.htm#jump1> [25 April 06].

United Nations 1989, Convention on the Rights of the Child, Office of the High Commissioner for Human Rights, <http://www.unhchr.ch/html/menu3/b/k2crc.htm>

Winnicott, D.W. 1965, *The Family and Individual Development*, Tavistock, London.

Margaret Crompton has written, contributed to conferences (with her husband John) and acted as consultant to groups developing practice reflecting these ideas.

11

Buddhism, mental illness and loss

Giles Barton

Open the door of your heart and soften to whatever is in the present moment, with acceptance rather than blame, anger or criticism; let go of trying to change or escape the circumstances, Theravadan monk and meditation teacher Ajahn Brahm encourages. From this point the confusion of our minds and the overwhelming emotions that arise can begin to be understood and calmed. There is no escape from these painful states; we take them with us wherever we go, and the constant effort of trying to escape them only leads to further suffering.

Frequently young people admitted to the unit on which I work are or become suicidal, believing that by killing the body they will be at peace. But from the Buddhist perspective the suffering is in the mind, not the body, and suffering remains with the mind as it takes rebirth in its next existence, in much the same way that we can experience vivid nightmares when the body is at rest. The anxieties that create the nightmare are independent of the body. For many young people their suffering is so great and so persistent that they are no longer able to see any way out other than suicide.

Young people who experience a mental illness can also believe they have failed at life, that they are worthless, a burden to others and, perhaps, even not worthy of love. During one group discussion, one girl was very quiet; when it came to her turn she said she couldn't talk to her parents any more because she had let them down and they deserved better than to have a 'retard' to look after. Strong feelings of shame and guilt can haunt the young person with a mental illness and trick them into believing they have a permanently 'bad self' inside.

It is because of this sense of being unworthy, empty and lacking in anything good that I believe the whole experience of mental illness for a young person is a spiritual loss. It is spiritual loss because they have lost connection with others, lost faith in who they are, lost meaning in their lives and have ended up feeling like outsiders, either undeserving of, or abandoned by, life. Most importantly, I believe it is young people's loss of a sense of goodness in their selves and the accompanying spiritual distress (feeling disconnected, empty of purpose, abandoned, unworthy, angry, defeated and hopeless) which puts them at greater risk of suicide.

Loss itself is not always bad: for young people to successfully negotiate their adolescence they must let go of or lose the dependency of their childhood so they may become independent adults. Many young people adjust and enter into young adulthood with a good sense of self and continuing hopes for the future, but for others there are a number of ongoing difficulties. In this chapter I would like to present my experience of young people with mental illness and how my spiritual practice of meditation and Theravadan Buddhism, as taught to me in the Thai Forest tradition, has shaped the way I approach young people in my job.

The guiding principle of the form of Theravadan Buddhism that I follow is that by calming and purifying the mind, and thus developing wholesomeness in thought and action, peacefulness develops; from a mind free from agitation, the wisdom arises that leads to the end of unhappiness, for the benefit of oneself and others.

Suffering in Buddhism

One of the teachings in Buddhism I have found helpful in meditation practice is that of the two arrows of suffering. The first arrow we may not be able to avoid, such as injury or illness and other situations not to our liking. But the second arrow, of mental suffering, comes from within. This second arrow consists of those reactions in thoughts and feelings that increase the pain of the first arrow. In young people this second arrow usually comprises their feelings of distress and the thoughts that fuel them. These thoughts include such beliefs as 'I'm not good enough'; 'my life is over'; 'no one will want to know me'; 'I have no future'; 'it's all too hard'; 'life's crap and so am I'.

Another aspect of this second arrow is the blame and judgment of themselves for the situation they are in, believing their illness to be a reflection of their true worth. Young people often have the idea that they won't be acceptable until they are as good as, if not better than, they were before their illness. People who feel undeserving of acceptance become stuck, continually putting themselves down and seeing their own efforts as inadequate. Too often I have heard young clients say they should be discharged so someone more deserving of our help can be admitted.

In meditation removing the arrow of mental suffering is achieved by being open and accepting what you find as you sit to meditate, not by finding fault with the situation and wishing for something better to come along. Although it is a natural response to want to get away from what seems unbearable, if the young person's resentment, sense of failure and hopelessness is too great they may seek to escape through alcohol, illicit drugs, self-harm and or suicidal impulses. I try to encourage people to let go of trying to escape that way. Meditation is learning to take responsibility for what is happening in one's heart and mind in the present moment and working with that. In even simpler terms, meditation is about learning to sit still and be at peace even when one is feeling restless, anxious, angry, sad or confused. It is not about cutting off such emotions so that one feels untouchable.

In trying to motivate young people to begin the process of coping with their negative emotions it is necessary to engage or connect with them. I can then create a base from which to begin to challenge their negative perceptions of themselves and what is possible for them. This can be achieved when they are able to re-connect with a sense of goodness. When our young clients see themselves as having some sort of ability and something to offer others, their hope and resilience begins to build.

One young man used to like calling out, 'Here comes Baldy, here comes Baldy', when I was walking past. I challenged him by saying, 'Is that the best you can come up with? I'd have thought someone as smart as you could come up with something much better.' He went quiet for a couple of days, but at the end of the week he came into the nurses' office and said, 'Ah, the bald and the beautiful, mostly the bald', which made us both laugh. Another client likes to call out, 'Giles working hard? Or hardly working?', to which I reply, 'Hardly working.' Laughter, I find, is a wonderful way of sharing and connecting.

Other patterns of thinking that I am familiar with in young people present a challenge in encouraging them to try to cope. These include the view that they have no future: the belief that nothing will change for them, that their current way of being is all there is, connects to the misleading belief that they have a permanently bad self inside. If they can experience the opposite, such as acceptance, success and enjoyment, then what they think is possible for them expands.

The experience of mental illness has a traumatic impact on a young person. They may lose their connection with their peers and their school. They are often no longer able to do things, such as sport or study, that they may have been good at, and which gave a sense of meaning or purpose to their lives. They become increasingly dependent on parents or mental health workers to look after them, and their sense of self is left in tatters with their hopes for their future diminished.

One young girl was really struggling one day, having difficulty studying and feeling stuck and just sad. I said, 'It's not a crime to feel bad and it won't last.' The next day she arrived bright-eyed and smiling, saying that the more she had thought about how it won't last the better she had begun to feel, until she felt better. So I said, 'You feel good?' 'Yes,' she said. 'It's OK,' I replied, 'it won't last.' She laughed and called me a bastard, but then we discussed how feelings always come and go. What we discussed was how it is not possible to feel one way all the time, good or bad, so it helps not to take either mood too seriously. Rather, knowing what it is that you're feeling and how to look after yourself when you're not a hundred per cent leads to less panic and distress and gives more of a sense of being able to manage. This girl gained a lot of relief from letting go of the expectation that she had to feel great all the time and that anything less was a failure.

Re-connecting to goodness

All human beings share in the potential to free themselves from pain, sorrow and grief, not by running away from such feelings but by understanding their inner world; this was what the Buddha saw at the end of the night of his enlightenment. During meditation as I strive for wisdom, I aim to be without expectations, to be aware and present with what is happening and to nurture qualities such as kindness, patience, generosity and perseverance. It is that inspiration of the Buddha and the qualities mentioned that I try to bring to working with young people, and which I hope contribute to their re-connecting with their own goodness. In working with young people with a mental illness, it is important to give the message that they are accepted and worthy just as they are, since the need for treatment can imply that they are not okay, that there is something wrong and unacceptable about them.

Further generosity is important in giving such young persons permission to feel the way they do. If there is permission to feel bad then they also have permission to 'just be' or even to feel better. As a helping professional it is important to realise that if a young person on the ward is angry, sad or anxious it is usually because they have a good reason to feel that way. This can be understood as the first step in helping the young person to see that feelings can be managed. The next might be taking the time to give acknowledgment or appreciation of all the efforts they make, no matter how small. I remember one girl groaning at me after being thanked for helping a new patient settle in, but after I explained that it was only fair to thank her for doing something good since she was always told when she did something wrong, she was able to accept the acknowledgment. Allowing/providing room for young people to give their opinions, to say what they think and to make decisions, is a very necessary part of helping them to re-connect with their strengths and take back some of their independence. Most important is being generous with one's time and one's availability. The willingness to spend time with a young person in what might seem insignificant moments is much more powerful in giving them messages of acceptance and worth than any number of words.

The Buddha himself pointed out that sickness, old age and death are great teachers about life, and that they come to us all in many forms and without discrimination. As one of the goals I have is to stop the young person identifying with his or her illness as a reflection of their personality, it is important to clarify what illness is and isn't. One approach is to normalise their illness and make it less personal, or less of a personal judgment on them, to get the message across that their illness is not personal in the sense of being a judgment and that it is not a punishment they deserve for being a 'bad' person. People get all types of illnesses, some harder to bear than others, but they are a reflection of life, not of personality.

Focus on the here and now

For a young person who has lost belief in his or her abilities, being able to achieve some success in the present can be very restorative. It takes a fair bit of ego strength to be able to look back on the past and make sense of it or come to an understanding that allows one to move on. When possible, focusing on the present decreases expectations, so that problems can become more manageable and goals more achievable. If the present becomes more bearable or even enjoyable the future can seem less frightening, and they begin to re-awaken to their potential.

Nearly all adolescents hate feeling negative emotions because these feelings can run their life and they can't get away from them. Furthermore, confusion sets in around the idea that to feel bad must mean one is bad, that such feelings are a reflection of one's true self. The best approach I have found to dealing with this is, as Ajahn Brahm encourages, to open the door of one's heart and accept whatever is found, whatever faults or failings, and to give permission for the door of one's heart to be open to love both from others and one's self.

I asked one young man I worked with to carry out some homework. Every morning, just after he got up, I wanted him to look gently in the mirror and say just once, 'The door of my heart is open to myself just as I am; may I be well, happy and peaceful.' The next day he returned looking calmer and happier but explained that he had found it extremely difficult to do the homework as it made him want to cry. He could see how difficult it was for him to accept kindness and how used to judging and blaming himself he was. The choice for him was no longer about being 'crazy' or not, but whether he was going to continue to punish himself through judgment and blame and hold on to the belief that he was essentially worthless and hopeless. His difficulty in offering kindness to himself showed him that he was holding himself back. He realised he did not have to accept thinking and feeling 'bad' or 'crazy'. The hard part is in developing kindness and having patience for oneself.

The second arrow arises because of hatred of what one is trying to avoid or escape. But when one begins to stop hating, there is less need to try to escape. Opening the door of your heart allows this to begin to take place.

The only true miracle is the miracle of human transformation, the Buddha stated.

There can be miracles but they take place slowly over time. One of the great teachings that has been shared with me is that of opening the door of your heart, because it goes right to your negative beliefs and perceptions. As an object of meditation it is: 'the door of my heart is open to myself just as I am; no matter what my faults or failures the door of my heart is open to me'. When trying to help young people under-stand, I ask them what they would do if someone were talking to their best friend in a harsh way. To follow this up, I ask what stops them from being their own best friend, since they need someone on their side if no one else is around. Lastly there is the need for patience and perseverance, because the young person who is recovering from a mental illness needs time and, no matter how skilful we are, nothing is guaranteed.

Suicide is an ever-present danger for young people recovering from mental illness. For some, their suffering is so great and persistent that they feel unable to continue living. I close with a poem by Alex Crawford. Alex was a delight to work with and I had felt optimistic when he left our service that he was going to go on and be okay—but he ultimately decided to suicide. For his mother the hardest thing to accept was that this was his decision because he felt his life was never going to get any better and the future he saw for himself was bleak. Alex for me represents the danger when young people have lost faith in themselves, connection with others, meaning and purpose in their lives.

AGAIN AND AGAIN
When you stop hearing the music, it's just a tune playing in your head
When what you see is just a reminder of how fucked up you are
But it's not even a picture anymore
When a thought is an attempt or a paranoid reflex
When a feeling has evolved from your own false world
It all goes in and bounces around bruising your soul and mind
When you don't know how to let anything out
And what comes out is a wishful act
And beauty gets tinted with the smell of shame, confusion, self-hatred
Stuck here between death and birth, like prison in your own mind
Where squirming inside moves so fast it becomes a blur
And looks just like frozen nothingness coloured with pain
And that's what my blank emotionless face screams
When I look at the ground when I walk past you
A stranger with my face head down.
           Alex Crawford (courtesy of John and Bronwyn Crawford)

I would like to acknowledge Ajahn Brahm, Abbot of Bodhinyana Monastery, Western Australia, Ajahn Sucitto and Ajahn Sujato for their kindness, compassion and wisdom.

Reference
Chödrön, P. 1991, *The Wisdom of No Escape*, Shambhala, Boston.

Violence

12
Working against domestic violence

Karen Wilcox

In professional work it is often tempting to disconnect one's spiritual self from one's professional self, particularly when working in areas of human service practice where practice paradigms are necessarily secular, and where spirituality may not be recognised. In my own faith journey, however, I have learnt the value of recognising the embeddedness of my spirituality in my approach to work in women's services.

Over the past fifteen years, one of the central aspects of my working life has been engagement with the struggle against domestic violence. I have worked in a range of women's services where I have been involved in providing direct support and group work, as well as in policy-making, community education, advocacy, law reform and worker training.

A spiritually informed professional practice has allowed me to engage with, and make sense of, the often difficult issues that emerge in human service work. Through my spiritual journey, and in the course of my essentially political work against violence, I have become aware of the need to engender a connective understanding of the experiences of women in culturally diverse communities.

Working with women who are in abusive relationships poses particular challenges for social and community workers, especially women workers, whose own experience of male violence, either directly or through close contacts, can challenge the boundaries and hierarchies created by secular, professional approaches to social and community work. Confronted with these complexities, my work has led me to examine my own spiritual journey. Domestic violence work, in its confrontation with violence, cruelty and loss, often shapes the spirituality of workers (Bell et al 2005). Through my experience, and in knowing and working with abuse survivors, I have been able to glimpse the amazing capacity of the human spirit to endure hardship and sustain life. For this reason, many domestic violence workers, myself included, have grappled with broader questions and the search for meaning in the face of women's suffering and struggle, which we both see and may endure ourselves.

My own spirituality is a kind of 'hybrid' Christianity drawn from the radical and scriptural elements of Catholic and other Christian faith traditions which have inspired me to tap into the vast and diverse storehouse of Christian thinking across time. My Catholic cultural and faith tradition also embraces a commitment to praxis: to practical action informed not only by one's personal politics, but also by a desire to relate expressively with the Creator through a love-based commitment to justice and freedom, and a compassion-centred discipleship. When aspects of the social structure or status quo are contrary to this commitment, Christians are called upon to follow the example of Jesus, and act in ways that could be considered counter-cultural. My personal politics, based on a belief in the oppressive nature of gender (as well as class and race), has connected with my spirituality in shaping a work practice against domestic violence.

Just as my work has been imbued with principles deriving from my spiritual journey, so too has my spiritual journey been enhanced by the political awareness that has arisen from my work and my life experiences. At times it is difficult for me to separate the spiritual aspects of my work from the political insights that define my world-view (similarly, see Flinders 1993). In this way, work and practice entwine like a helix, as parallel yet interconnecting strands of my life journey. This intertwining of spirituality and work has brought me to a more questioning and critical approach to work with domestic violence.

The essence of my spiritually informed professional practice is contained in four central spiritual dynamics: a belief in the fundamental oneness of human beings, compassion, acceptance, and a sense of spirituality as a place of rest. These four elements have bound the strands of my faith and work, and will be explored here in turn.

Intertwining spirituality and practice: four elements
1 The oneness of human beings
Central to my work has been a desire to practice *connectively*; this has emerged from my spiritual journey, which impels me to seek out and connect with the 'other'. In Christian spirituality, this desire stems from a belief in the connectedness of humanity in the goodness of creation—the oneness of human beings with each other through the Creator Yahweh and the Saviour Christ. Supporting this is the only *command* of Jesus in the Christian Bible—to love your neighbour, *as yourself* (John 15).[1] For Christians, the 'neighbour' specifically includes those who are constructed, through social prejudice or discrimination, as the 'other' (Luke 10).[2]

In this way, Christian spirituality compels acceptance of, and connection with, the other; this in turn has political implications, directing us to be aware of and join in the struggle against the other's suffering as part of our life work. Being a 'doer of the word' for political Christians (James 1)[3] can mean taking on struggle, and finding strength in connection—providing a drive and ambition for working for a new, non-violent world that is different from the ego-focused ambition that drives modern Western-dominated societies.

An awareness of how disconnecting oneself from the other can lead to oppression has led me to consider ways in which my work may have inadvertently constructed hierarchies, as mainstream-culture human service work may do, by its very nature. In thinking through the need for acceptance of the oneness of women in the struggle against domestic violence, I have become uncomfortable with some workplace 'givens'. For example, the dominant paradigm in community work, and the language that articulates this within women's services, can be seen as creating disconnection. Thus, the notion of women as 'clients' creates a distance from workers, rather than connectedness, leading to an artificial boundary between and hierarchy among women. Indeed, human service work can inadvertently construct many subtle divisions, whether by professional, knowledge-based hierarchies or by boundary-preserving strategies, such as impractical referrals to pass on responsibility to other services. For example, Sharon, a woman who had left a very dangerous perpetrator and was continually on the run from him, came to me in exasperation and exhaustion, having been advised by a worker that she needed to pack up her children (and life) yet again to maintain safety, without the worker getting involved in the practical-ities of this move. The worker had, in preserving her professional boundary, exacerbated Sharon's hardship. This observation, coupled with a sense of my spiritual unity and commitment to spiritual praxis, caused me to challenge the implications of the distancing implicit in my previous practice. As Brazilian social scientist/educator Paulo Freire has noted, rather than *transfer* knowledge and skills in the course of work, one must speak 'with' rather than 'to' the oppressed, thereby developing a non-oppressive practice (Freire 1975: 26).[4] My spiritual journey has led me to reflect on the need for a practice of working *with*, rather than *for*, women experiencing violence. Spiritually inspired praxis has led me to see women with whom I work not as my clients, but rather fellow-travellers in a common humanity and struggle against violence.

I have approached my practice with an assumption that unity can be found in recognition of our collective experiences of male violence, as women.[5] The strength, courage and connection with their spiritual selves that I have observed in women who have endured and persevered has bolstered my own courage and faith during wavering moments and 'dark nights of the soul'. With an awareness of women's connection, my social justice work and feminist politics, as well as my spiritual journey, have been moved along a little further—beyond my own personal issues and the concerns that emerge from my own life.

2 Compassion

My spirituality, grounded in the fundamental oneness and connection of human beings, has brought me to a practice that attempts to live out a spiritually informed compassion. Indeed, the notion of compassion is a key doctrine in many spiritualities. For me, compassion is not the lukewarm virtuousness and piety towards an objectified 'poor' that can sometimes be associated with Christian practice.[6] Rather, a belief in the unity and oneness of creation gives rise to what Christian writer Matthew Fox has called a 'spirituality named compassion' (1979). This entails a focus on the inherent goodness (and Godliness) of creation, and of all living things. An acceptance of this engenders an approach to living illuminated by connectedness, as I have mentioned, and compassion.

Compassion spirituality has influenced my approach to practice. Combined with my discomfort with conceptual hierarchy, it has helped me to deal with the paradoxes and complexities of suffering, brokenness, forgiveness and hope in domestic violence work. For example, it has helped me to deal with the difficult paradox whereby women escaping violence are abusive to or neglectful of their own children. Rather than approaching the suffering of children with violent fathers as a competing *need* in opposition to the needs of their mothers (even where it is the mother's own response to suffering that is the cause of harm), compassion and connection guides another path, acknowledging the truth of suffering experienced simultaneously. In this way it is possible to protect a child from suffering, *even if* that involves a child protection notification regarding actions by their mother, while at the same time compassionately connecting and working with her against the violence which she has experienced. A compassionate approach belies the construction of domestic violence work into competing needs and claims for support. In seeing the possibility of movement from chaos to cosmos, or creation, in Christian creation spirituality (Fox 1981), the dichotomies, which on face value emerge from the differing pains and struggles of individuals, can be reconciled.

Compassion spirituality has proven particularly important to me in my working against domestic violence as it also provides a focus for a non-violent approach to human struggle. Many spiritual frameworks, including my own, embrace principles of non-violence.[7]

For me, commitment to non-violence has galvanised my drive to work *against* violence, but to do so while processing the personal judgment and anger that it may engender. This is made possible through a commitment to compassion. In Flinders' examination of her own spiritual/political journey, she notes her move from blame and her rejection of violence-inspired strategies against the oppression of women. In this way, feminists' anger with the violent expression of male power, through spiritual growth, can be transformed into practical, yet fundamentally radical practice (she discusses Gandhi at length in this context) (Flinders 1998). Compassionately and connectively, we are able to work against male oppression without gender separatism.

3 Spirituality and acceptance

Another important aspect of a spiritually informed practice for me has been a recognition and acceptance of the spirituality of women with whom I have worked, regardless of any differences between us. Acceptance of other's spirituality or religion is another outcome of creation-centred spirituality: 'for it is precisely creation, the gifts of exis-tence itself and the sustainers of that common existence, that all peoples and all faiths share in common . . . an overflow of the relationship we experience with all that is' (Fox 1981: 16).

For some domestic violence workers who have developed feminist-inspired 'interventions', there may be difficulties in accepting the spirituality of women who are from faith communities that the worker may consider to be conservative in their approaches to gender. In my work I have learned from women who have experienced the prejudices and hidden processes that create this discrimination, be they Muslim women wearing traditional coverings, or fundamentalist Christian women reconciling their experience of violence with the notion of male household 'headship'. Such judgments by workers can leave women without appropriate help. Domestic violence support work may be particularly difficult in instances where women are from religious and cultural traditions considered conservative in their doctrines.

I once worked, for example, with a fundamentalist Christian woman who had not followed through with an AVO (restraining/ protection order) application, primarily because she was concerned about the mental health implications for her husband, whom she loved.[8] Other workers she had approached had written off any potential for her to receive protection, considering withdrawal of applications to be typical of the gender politics of fundamentalist Christians. However, in exploring her concerns, including the details of her husband's psychiatric illness, it was possible to devise an effective AVO which would protect her. A woman who is not keen to take out an AVO may have compelling reasons which could be addressed through modification of the order, were this choice not seen as typical of a particular religion.

Acknowledging women's spirituality enables engagement with the actual concerns confronting women and with the beliefs, circumstances and religious support people have in their lives, while maintaining the key domestic violence principles of safety and male (perpetrator) responsibility. Deborah's experience is illustrative in this regard. Her violent husband had told her that she would be sent to eternal hell because of the 'sin' of leaving her abusive relationship. He would frequently talk about this to their children during contact visits, which was particularly damaging to the children's emotional wellbeing. I learned through Deborah that I would need to work *with* these beliefs, rather than merely dismiss them. In doing this, I learned from Deborah's faith and could better support her through her difficulties— including compiling information for the Family Court that incorporated the spiritual aspects of this psychological abuse. Deborah learned to separate her husband's use of spiritual issues in his control repertoire from the doctrines of her faith without having to engage with the validity or otherwise of those doctrines. She was able to disconnect from his doctrinal 'judgments' and view them as the emotional abuse they were—the use of spirituality as another form of abuse. Even when some of the church elders supported the abuser, Deborah was supported in her own understanding of her faith and could recognise their position as 'third party' abuse. She was able to talk to other elders who, once informed of the dangers faced by her family and the ineffectiveness of reconciliation in limiting those dangers, provided support and spiritual guidance without undermining her safety and her children's wellbeing.

It is possible and desirable to develop a response to domestic violence that is not only tolerant, but incorporates the spiritualities of women.[9] By working within particular traditions, and with support from people from those traditions, feminist priorities of safety and responsibility can be maintained and strengthened, emphasising that these priorities are in the best interests of the family involved. From there, religious workers and counsellors might forge a respectful support relationship together in the context of networking and conversation with those from other spiritual traditions.

4 Spirituality as a place of rest

A spiritual life can also provide a real and effective antidote to burnout. Social and community workers are engaged continually with suffering, loss and grief, and courage in the face of burden can be difficult to maintain.

As a domestic violence worker, I have frequently been overwhelmed with feelings of anger and outrage—at the abuse and its ongoing manifestations through the family court, child support and legal system. By weaving connections with those with whom I have worked, I have found sustenance and inspiration. Spirituality provides the grounds and the means for hope. In work with the worst manifestations of oppression, be it race, as in Gandhi's analysis, class, as in Freire's,[10] or gender, hope is essential for keeping going. Freire notes that hope is an essential element of our sense of being. He continues, noting that '[h]opelessness is but hope that has lost its bearings' (Freire et al 1996: 8).

How can hope be restored and find its bearings? Here the connection of faith and politics is clear. As Freire suggests, the hope must be critical, politically aware, not blind to the oppression that has shifted its bearings. Through my spirituality, hope has become grounded—providing both a place of rest and 'holding up' (Isaiah 49)[11] as well as practices that have provided respite and relief. The Christian tradition (in common with many other spiritualities) has a meditative thread; through 'letting go' the self which contemplative, mystical and meditative spirituality fosters, I have been able to realign my need for hope with its 'bearings'. In addition, spirituality supports the 'fighting spirit' required for the sustenance of hope.

Endnotes

1. The Holy Bible, Jerusalem Edition, *The Gospel According to John*, chapter 15.
2. ibid, *The Gospel According to Luke*, chapter 10.
3. ibid, *The Letter of James*, chapter 10.
4. Liberation Theology has been controversially associated with violence, but in essence the acceptance of the challenge to move from individualism to collective responsibility for social justice remains inspiring. See for example Gutierrez 1988. For an evangelical Christian perspective on the social justice imperative of Christianity see also Sider 1993, pp. 177–8.
5. Which is not the same as claiming an essential *sameness*, or identical experiences.
6. Fox sees assumed piety and other 'spiritual recipe guides' as failure to let go of the 'I'—the ego (Fox 1981, p. 231).
7. See also Flinders' discussion of Gandhi's non-violence, 1998, bk 1, ch. 3 and bk 2, ch. 2.
8. Details of individual women's stories used in this chapter have been altered or combined to prevent identification and protect the anonymity of women and agencies.
9. See also Thompson 1997, p. 141.
10. See Flinders, op cit; Freire 1975.
11. The Holy Bible, Jerusalem Edition, *The Book of Isaiah*, chapter 49.

References

Bell, H., Busch, N.B. and Fowler, D., 2005, 'Spirituality and Domestic Violence Work', *Critical Social Work*, vol. 6, no. 2.

Flinders, C. 1993, *Enduring Grace*, HarperCollins, San Francisco.

Flinders, C. 1998, *At The Root of This Longing*, Harper, San Francisco.

Fox, M. 1979, *A Spirituality Named Compassion*, Winston Press, Minneapolis.

Fox, M. 1981, 'Introduction', and 'Meister Eckhart's Spiritual Journey' in M. Fox, (ed.), *Western Spirituality*, Bear & Co., Santa Fe.

Freire, P. 1975, *Pedagogy of the Oppressed*, Penguin, Harmondsworth.

Freire, P., Freire, A. and Araujo, M. 1996, *Pedagogy of Hope*, Continuum, New York.

Gutierrez, G. 1988, *A Theology of Liberation: History, Politics and Salvation*, Orbis Books, Maryknoll.

The Holy Bible, Jerusalem Edition

Kobia, S. 2005, 'Overcoming Violence: An Ecumenical Christian Task', paper presented at the Violence and Christian Spirituality Conference, World Council of Churches, Boston, 27 October.

McDonough, E. 2003, *Glory Be . . . for Dappled Things*, International Public
    Lecture, 23 October 2003, University of Melbourne, <http://www.unimelb.
    edu.au/speeches/emcdonough22oct03.html>
Sider, R. 1993, *Evangelism & Social Action*, Hodder & Stoughton, London.
Thompson, N. 1997, *Anti-Discrimination Practice*, Macmillan, Basingstoke.

13

Violence

Darri Adamson

... the teachings of the Buddha equate, on the one hand, an un-disciplined state of mind with suffering and unenlightened existence and, on the other hand, a disciplined state of mind with happiness, enlightenment, or spiritual freedom (Tenzin Gyatso, *Training the Mind*)[1]

My life used to be full of drama and pain. I was angry when I didn't get what I wanted and angry when I got what I didn't want. At times I was physically or verbally violent. My co-workers and patients used to be on the receiving end of my sarcasm, gossip, irritability and resentments. I went into nursing because I wanted to help people, but I thought that helping meant 'fixing' (in other words, controlling) them. Suffering from chronic envy, I found it difficult to rejoice in the happiness or good fortune of others. I was an angry participant in political movements, believing that the end we were fighting for justified our inconsiderate tactics.

Aware that I was not living up to my aspirations for myself, I tried to fix things. I changed countries, jobs, boyfriends, universities, used drugs and alcohol and acquired possessions, always with the deluded idea that these external fixes would make me feel better. But the relief never lasted. Eventually I would find myself in pain again, focusing on something external as the cause of my problems, and so the cycle would start anew.

When I look back, I have a great deal of compassion for myself. I was trying to be good and kind, to function in an appropriate way, but I didn't have the tools to do so. I wasn't bad; I was just ignorant of certain things.

Today I live very differently, with self-respect and dignity. I am able to make better choices about what I do and say, practising courtesy and respect for others and their choices. My mind is relatively calm and I can usually cope appropriately with anger and violence. I'm still concerned about social and political issues, but with a less angry attitude. Approaching things more calmly, I am able to be more effective.

So what changed? One thing is certain. Although I blamed my misery on external circumstances, the world and its people didn't change to suit me. The health-care system is still run down, work is busier than ever, patients and my co-workers can still be angry or violent. The only thing that can possibly have changed is my own mind. The reasons I needed to make this change and how Tibetan Buddhism helped me to do it are the subjects of this chapter.

Violence at work

I work as a registered nurse in a large, very busy coronary care unit. Our patients are at a major turning point, often confronting their mortality and the big questions of life for the first time. Sometimes they are from marginalised areas of society, without much understanding of the system or good coping mechanisms.

Stuck there, wired up to a monitor, they are apparently at the mercy of strangers (us, operating comfortably in our own environment). Some of them respond angrily or violently to this situation, especially if they also suffer from some degree of organic brain disease or are experiencing alcohol or drug withdrawal. We as health-care staff also respond in different ways to stressful situations and can be angry and violent ourselves.

Suppressed or denied anger often comes out sideways, as bitterness, negativity, addictive behaviour or depression. Expressed anger can take the form of verbal or physical violence. Most definitions of violence include the word 'uncontrolled'. Even violence that appears to be calculated is based on a mental delusion such as anger or fear. It is still the physical or verbal manifestation of a disturbed, uncontrolled mind which wishes to harm.

People sometimes think that anger can be a good thing, enabling people to empower themselves in an abusive situation. But why should it be necessary to harm another in order to empower ourselves?[2]

In the past I lacked wise and compassionate ways of containing anger and violence. Buddhism specialises in teaching ways of dealing with such problems.

A word of warning

I must stress that you need to be realistic. Contemplating Buddhist sol-utions does not mean you will never be confronted by violence again, or that if you are you will always be able to handle it. In such cases, it is important to follow your workplace safety protocols.

If you or others find yourselves in danger, you must remove yourselves from the situation and get help, from security or the police if necessary.

So are Buddhist techniques are a waste of time? No, because if you use them you should find that you are confronted with violence less often; and even if you are confronted with violence, it will probably be minimised. You should also find that the stress resulting from being around violence is greatly reduced.

The Buddhist approach to problems

Buddhism, a philosophy or psychology rather than a religion, is based on the teachings of Shakyamuni Buddha (Prince Siddhartha), who lived around 500 BCE—and as one of my teachers used to say, Buddhism isn't some groovy, hippy love trip.[3]

Certainly, Buddhists try to be compassionate, but their compassion is based on using logic and reason rather than blind faith in teachers or tradition testing fearlessly what the teachings say. Whether we are Buddhist or not, if the teachings make sense and are useful to us in our everyday lives, we are welcome to use them: if not, we are welcome to discard them. The early Tibetan Buddhist teachers developed very effective forms of training the mind to focus on valid thoughts and emotions, which correspond to reality and happiness, rather than invalid ones, which are contrary to the way things really are and lead to ignorance and suffering.[4]

To illustrate this they used a story about a king who was dissatisfied with the thorniness of the ground. Everywhere he walked his feet were hurt. So he ordered that the whole of the world be covered with leather. But someone spoke up, saying: 'Sire, wouldn't it be easier and better (not to mention cheaper) if you just covered your feet with leather?'

It is the same with our minds. Like the king, we are deluded, dissatisfied with much of what is going on around us and blaming external circumstances for our misery. But just as the king learned that what really was needed was to put shoes on his feet, so we can learn that if we protect our own minds we do not have to change the rest of the world.

In the health-care setting, delusional means 'out of touch with reality'. Buddhism says that in a sense we are all delusional: 'we are all out of touch with reality, it is just a matter of degree'.[5] We may be offended by this idea, thinking, 'I'm not hallucinating!' But think about it. Don't we keep going to extraordinarily painful lengths, as the king wanted to do, in our attempts to change external circumstances to make ourselves happy? Does it work?

We may see the deluded behaviour of others more clearly than our own, as they keep gambling or overeating, choosing inappropriate partners or expecting new possessions to make them happy. If our friends were in touch with reality they would not go near the casino or violent boyfriends. As relatively objective onlookers, it is obvious to us that the cause of their problems is not external: it is coming from their minds, which keep leading them to do the same thing over and over, expecting a different result. And if we are honest about our own behaviour, can we not see that we create pain for ourselves in the same way?

Since delusions cause our suffering, it must be possible to rid ourselves of suffering by ridding ourselves of the delusions. The good news is that we can do this: the Buddha said that the true nature of our mind is clear and unstained, like the sky, and that our delusions are like clouds. Clouds do not change the nature of the sky, and delusions do not change the basic pure nature of the mind.

Initially I found it difficult to come to terms with the idea that I should take responsibility for *my* anger and change *my* mind. Why should I, when *they* were the ones being violent? But what was the alternative? I could not ignore violence—people would get hurt—but responding angrily only meant that I had two problems instead of one; sedating or restraining the patient was distressing for everyone, and running away more quickly or learning martial arts would not help.

There are other reasons why I wanted to reduce my own anger and therefore my wish to harm. For a start, if I harm others I harm myself, because we are all interdependent. Without parents and teachers, farmers, truck drivers, the sun and the rain and the forests of the Amazon, I would not survive. Because of this I try to treat others with respect, no matter what their condition or behaviour. The bonus is that this in itself can dramatically lessen their tendency to violence.

Secondly, in Buddhism, all beings are seen as being equal in that they all want happiness and do not want suffering. When I realise this, I really begin to feel compassion for others. They suffer just as I do! So how can I treat them any less compassionately than I would want to be treated myself?

On top of that, while there is no sense of a system of reward and punishment in Buddhism, there is the law of cause and effect, or karma, which says that we cannot get a good result from a badly motivated action and we cannot get a bad result from a well-motivated action. Even from a selfish point of view, I want to avoid behaviour which will create future negative results for myself.

Case study

Mr K,* a 56-year-old farmer, became aggressive and verbally abusive when he was told that he would need to wait a week in hospital for surgery. The mental processes I went through, as the nurse in charge dealing with the situation, was something like this:

'Are we all physically safe? . . . his body language is aggressive . . . send less experienced nurse to call security . . . two nurses in the room is enough, more just increases everyone's level of mental agitation . . . when I met this man earlier I didn't like him much and I may not have acknowledged him with enough respect . . . how would

my spiritual teachers behave in this situation? . . . I can practise gratitude for his work as a farmer and focus on his value as a human
being . . . I choose not to let my dislike interfere with my care for
him . . . he is just like me in that he wants happiness, doesn't want
suffering . . . he has just been told he needs open heart surgery and
he is shouting about having to get back to his farm, but his biggest
worry is probably that he may die . . . he is being irrational, but I
choose not to get agitated myself and escalate the situation . . . Mr K
is creating suffering for himself; how can I help to defuse the situation
so that he doesn't create more?'

This is a complex process to be going through in a couple of
minutes, but the crucial thing is that I wasn't trying to do this for the
first time in the middle of a crisis. These patterns of thinking and
reacting had been laid down over a long period of time.

Speaking quietly and courteously to Mr K, I eventually got him to
focus his scattered attention, asking him what was going on and how
we could help. Listening to him with respect, his real concerns became
apparent: he was afraid of the surgery, which had not been explained
to him in detail yet, and he was 'worried sick' about what would
happen to his wife and children if he died. I spent time with him
explaining the surgery, and arranged to have our social worker come
and see him. In the end, we did not need the help of the security
guard.

Although I never really warmed to Mr K, we treated each other with
respect from then on, and he thanked the staff sincerely when he left
coronary care.

* The details of this case history have been changed, to protect patient
confidentiality.

Changing the mind through contemplation and meditation
Buddhism is like a martial art for the mind, and with a martial art we
cannot begin our practice in the middle of a tournament. Likewise, it is
no good trying to change our minds for the first time in the middle of
a violent confrontation. We need to practise so that our mental reflexes
become developed and we automatically respond more effectively to
difficult situations. If we can change our minds, behaviour that is more
skilful will follow.

One of the main Buddhist ways of doing such practice is to begin observing, transforming and protecting the mind through contemplation and meditation. This gives us the opportunity to practise valid ways of thinking before difficult situations arise.

You are welcome to try the basic meditation practice which follows. Understand that there is nothing spaced out or mysterious about meditation. We are alert, familiarising ourselves with our minds, cultivating the positive and trying to let go of the negative.[6] If you have never meditated before, remember that you are embarking on a voyage of discovery of your mind and the fewer expectations you have the better. In this way you will develop the patience and courage to continue.

It is helpful to meditate in a quiet place: many people meditate in the quiet of morning, before the cares of the day arise.

So that the flow of energy through your body is not blocked, it is best to sit with a straight spine, on the floor with a cushion under your buttocks and your legs crossed, or on a chair. If you have physical limitations, it is better to meditate in another position than not to meditate at all. Rest your hands in your lap, palms up, the right hand cupped in the left. Relax your shoulders, place your tongue just behind your upper teeth, let your head tilt slightly forward and have your eyes lightly closed or just slightly open.

At the beginning it is important to set yourself a good motivation, so that your mind is in the best state for meditating. The usual Tibetan Buddhist motivation is to think that we will meditate to try and improve our minds so that we can help all beings, but you could say any prayer along these lines that is meaningful for you.

If you have a belief in something greater and wiser than yourself, imagine that spiritual friend or energy supporting you as you meditate, helping you to tame your mind.

The central part of this style of meditation is an analysis of a topic, but to settle your mind, without trying to breathe in any special way, just become aware of the breath as it enters and leaves your nostrils. Count ten breaths in and out, and do this several times. We cannot empty our minds: thoughts will arise, but just acknowledge that they are there and try not to follow them. Let them pass, like waves rolling in to shore and out again.

Choose a topic of meditation from the following section of the chapter or invent your own, holding it gently in your mind, expanding and examining it as much as you like. As other thoughts arise, gently let them go.

Spend whatever length of time is comfortable, maybe ten minutes to begin with. Do not overdo it—you should feel like coming back for more, not so drained that you never want to meditate again.

As you finish, if you like, you can visualise your spiritual friend or energy dissolving into golden light which streams down into you from the top of your head, blessing you and purifying your body, speech and mind.

Then cultivate the aspiration to practise acting on this contemplation throughout the day.

Lastly, remind yourself that your ultimate goal is to help others and dedicate what you have done to their wellbeing—perhaps to someone you know who is suffering, perhaps just to beings in general.

When you are ready, gently open your eyes.

This is a very brief introduction to meditation: if you want to find out more try the Internet or your local library or go to some classes. If you have a religion you may find that it has teachings on how to meditate.

Topics for contemplation or meditation

All these topics can be used at any time, not just in formal meditation. Contemplate them whenever you have the chance—while walking, sitting on a bus, working, washing up or whenever life becomes a bit uncomfortable. In this way, they become integrated into every part of your life. The first one is given in some detail, and the idea is that you pause and contemplate at the end of each line. With the rest, the basis of a topic is given and you can expand on it yourself.

1 All beings are equal

Think of how you feel when you have problems, and of how you try to avoid this suffering and to replace it with happiness. (pause)

Now think of someone close to you and how they are just like you, in that they also try to avoid suffering. (pause)

Then expand this understanding out to someone you hardly know, a neutral acquaintance. (pause)

Lastly, imagine someone who arouses strong negative feelings in you and say to yourself: 'This person is just like me. They want happiness and do not want suffering, but at the moment they are suffering because of their uncontrolled mind. How painful it must be to live with such a mind twenty-four hours a day. At least I'm not in there with them.' (pause)

'Because I can see how they suffer, I will try to cultivate compassion for them.' (pause)

2 Changing the mind

'May I examine my mind in all actions / and as soon as a negative state occurs / since it endangers myself and others / may I firmly face and avert it.'[7]

3 Subduing anger

'How could you find enough leather to cover the ground? / Having leather on the soles of your sandals is the same as covering the whole earth.' Likewise, you could never subdue all your enemies, '. . . but if you subdue your anger you will not make a single enemy and it will be the same as subduing all your enemies'.[8]

4 Watching the mind and choosing not to act on negative thoughts

'No matter how wild my mind is, if I can observe what is happening I can choose not to act on my angry thoughts. I am watching my mind and choosing to behave well in this situation.' Observe how things change in your life as you practise this.

5 Working with disturbed patients

Imagine that you are at work, modelling good behaviour, creating an environment where patients feel safe and where they are treated with courtesy and respect. Picture yourself minimising chaos, both in the physical environment and by being calm yourself.

6 Gratitude to our enemies

'Annoying people are my personal patience trainers. I am grateful to them for the opportunity to develop a mind which will not be so easily disturbed. I practise being patient with them before I get angry, because once I am angry it is much more difficult to contain my behaviour.'

7 Compassion
'Those who seem to be harming us are certainly creating suffering for themselves. I wish to help them stop their behaviour out of compassion for them, rather than because I am angry.'

8 Taking responsibility
'When I experience others' bad behaviour, I suffer. I can break the cycle of anger if I cultivate strong regret for times in the past when I myself have behaved unskilfully. I will cultivate the resolve to try not to repeat that behaviour myself.'

As I said above, it is not necessary to be a Buddhist to use these practices—if any of these ways of thinking seem helpful, please feel free to explore and use them. Be patient with yourself, taking the time to see if they help you become a more effective professional.

Good luck in the practise of your profession and in the practise of these techniques, should you choose to try them.

Endnotes
1. Tenzin Gyatso, the Fourteenth Dalai Lama, *Training the Mind*, Wisdom Publications, Boston, 1999, p. 6.
2. Venerable Robina Courtin asked students to think about this, in a teaching at Vajrasattva Mountain Centre, Katoomba, 2000.
3. Lama Thubten Yeshe often said words to this effect in his teachings.
4. Tenzin Gyatso, op cit, pp. 7–8.
5. Venerable Robina Courtin, in a teaching at Balmain Town Hall, Sydney, May 2005.
6. This is a summary of part of the teaching given by Venerable Robina Courtin at Balmain Town Hall.
7. Tenzin Gyatso, op cit, p. 17.
8. Pabongka Rinpoche, *Liberation in the Palm of Your Hand*, Wisdom Publications, Boston, 1991, p. 637.

References

Dondrub, Thubten (ed.) 2001, *Spiritual Friends: Meditations by Monks and Nuns of the International Mahayana Institute*, Wisdom Publications, Boston.

Thubten Zopa Rinpoche 1993, *Transforming Problems into Happiness*, Wisdom Publications, Boston.

Yeshe, Lama Thubten 1998, *Becoming Your Own Therapist*, Lama Yeshe Wisdom Archive, Boston.

Yeshe, Lama Thubten 1999, *Make Your Mind an Ocean*, Lama Yeshe Wisdom Archive, Boston.

Acknowledgments

This chapter is based, with respect and gratitude, on the publications and teachings of the authors mentioned above and on teachings by Geshe Thubten Dawo (Sydney) and many other teachers in the Tibetan Buddhist tradition. Links to information about these teachers and publications can be found at <http://www.fpmt.org>

14
Islamic faith-based counselling

Hanan Dover

There is a well-known tradition in Islam that every child is born in a state of *fitra* (purity) with an intuitive inclination towards faith.

In counselling Muslims, one must understand the Islamic notion of human nature. Human nature is not void of religion and God. Spirituality in Islam is a core component of the self.

The spiritual dimension is one of the central tenants of the human psyche and yet is missing from both the Western and Islamic views of behaviour and human nature. Malik Badri (1978) has long worked to introduce the spiritual dimension to the disciplines of psychology and psychotherapy. He argues that the failure to include the spiritual element of human beings in the study of psychology is anchored to a society blinded by materialism.

I have found that the most successful way to counsel Muslims in Australia is to introduce Islamic concepts, beliefs and practices into the therapy room. I disagree with current Western practices of psychology that exclude the notions of religion and spirituality, keeping them separate from the problems of the individual. I've found in my practice that religion and spirituality have transformative capacity for change and growth.

Whether the individual you are working with is a Muslim, or identifies with another faith, it is crucial to know how their beliefs influence and shape their thoughts and behaviour (Haque 2001). Often these thoughts and actions are derived from the world-view the client holds. Ignoring these influential elements only serves to reduce the problematic issues for the client to parts, as opposed to the whole. Religion and spirituality form the basis of the self for many people. Islam recognises this and offers guiding principles which encourage psycho-spiritual growth and development, of which any practitioner working with a client of Islamic faith needs to be cognisant.

This chapter explores the concepts of *guilt* and *shame* to show how they are regarded as essential for the progress of psycho-spiritual growth and development in Islamic belief and counselling. Islam's equivalent concept to convey shame is the word *haya*, which is a term to denote life and living (Yusuf 2004). Prophet Muhammad, peace and blessing be upon him (pbuh), said: 'Every religion has a quality that is characteristic of that religion. And the characteristic of the Islamic religion is haya' (Bukhari, vol. 1, book 2, no. 8), an internalised state of shame which includes self-respect, scruples, bashfulness and modesty. Islam honours the concept of shame and takes it to a spiritual level where it is a feeling of a sense of shame before God: if a person decides to engage in acts that are contrary to the teaching and beliefs of Islam, the shame factor allows the individual to be conscious that even if no individual or society is aware of their actions, that God is an all-seeing, all-knowing reality they cannot escape. This realisation is taught to children to ensure that acts of disobedience are discouraged and the concept of the 'unseen' and an active awareness of God is nurtured. God-consciousness instils the character of shame. This discourages a person to act on sinful promptings. The stronger the sense of shame, the better equipped one is to deal with self-control.

The Western concept of shame, however, is defined in the negative sense and carries with it negative connotations. Shame is viewed by most psychological theorists, including psychoanalysts such as Erikson (1950), Freud (1914) and Kohut (1977), as a primitive emotion that impacts on one's basic sense of self. Guilt, on the other hand, is developed later in the maturation of the self. It is the development of guilt that develops real social consciousness, which in turn builds a high degree of self-consciousness.

In the therapeutic setting, if a Muslim commits the tiniest of sins, the guilt that results from such actions can develop into an excessive preoccupation so that more negative emotions are generated, felt and entertained, which may lead to unwarranted behaviours and thoughts inhibiting normal day-to-day functioning. Hence, when the guilt cannot be transformed into the appropriate channel for repentance and positive change, as suggested in Islam, mental health issues set in.

From an Islamic perspective, indulging in repetitive thoughts that are negative to one's reality, such as hopelessness or destructive thinking, is harmful to one's self and wellbeing. Individuals are encouraged to actively seek ways to protect themselves from conditions such as negative and destructive thinking that are detrimental to positive change. Loss of hope ultimately leads to loss of faith. What Muslims generally are not aware of is that negative thinking becomes a problem for us when we forget that God has given us a set of experiences that teach and remind people to have faith in God and trust Him in every situation that He created.

The Qur'an encourages the importance of directing attention to the positives in life, even when situations are bad, and also to maintain steadfastness in faith with courage:

Have We not opened up your breast [heart]?
And lifted from you your burden
That had weighed so heavily on your back?
And have We not raised for you your dignity?
And behold, with hardship [difficulty] there is ease [relief]!
Verily, with hardship there is ease!
Hence, when you are freed [from distress], remain steadfast.
And unto your Sustainer turn [all your attention] with loving devotion
(Qur'an: 94).

The example of a painful divorce can illustrate how Islamic principles may be integrated in counselling practice. Often during psychotherapy, time is spent with the client where the therapist re-educates the client about his or her religion, with information from the Scriptures about how God Allah is Loving and All-Merciful. Once this is done, it is easier to instil hope over despair for the client. The following case study illustrates how this may be accomplished.

Case study: Adjusting to life after divorce

A Palestinian woman came to me seeking help, describing her problems as domestic violence issues. She explained how in going through a difficult divorce she had lost so many things. The woman described herself as previously optimistic but worn down by constant abuse and the battles she had to wage during her divorce. Her trust was damaged and she feared having to make decisions, doubting her own ability to think clearly. The woman had been advised to document the abuse she was experiencing and the dealings she had with her husband in the time leading up to the divorce hearing. In great need, she turned to a friend.

This friend began by listening to the woman, hearing her concerns and acting as one would hope of a friend. However, as time passed it became apparent that the friend was not offering help or guidance. This was unfortunate, as the woman really felt the need for someone else to help her, for assistance in thinking through what was happening and how she should act in response to what was occurring to her. The friend then began to avoid the woman, leaving her even more confused, distressed and alone.

The pretence of a friendship then disappeared and the so-called 'friend' became openly hostile to the woman, criticising her for trying to involve the friend in matters which were none of her business. The friend expressed very judgmental attitudes and appeared to blame the woman for not being able to resolve her own marital problems, which were seen as being part of any marriage. The woman tried to establish what had gone wrong, asking whether there was anything left of the friendship or had the relationship only been about pity.

The woman felt she had lost everything, her marriage, her friend and even her trust in herself. She was desperate for assistance in how to move forward and overcome the guilt she felt over the divorce and the confusion she felt over her so-called friend's behaviour.

My reply to her was thus:

First, sister, the fact that you have experienced optimism puts you one step closer to knowing that it does exist. This can help to motivate you to think of this experience as a first step.

You cannot keep reliving history, worrying about history, dwelling on history and so on. This only serves to deepen your already deep emotional wounds and carve up more distress. You do not need any more emotional distress and you should not have any.

I have met many women who have come out of abusive relationships and divorce in a positive manner, where they are empowered to see their lives differently.

Guilt and shame about divorce that wasn't your fault will not help, as that serves only to weaken your hidden inner strength. Allah Most High wants you to be in a strong state because He has equipped us with the inner faculties and tools to overcome and deal with daily life challenges and difficulties. Remember that Allah the Most Compassionate tells us in the Qur'an that He will not place a burden more than you can actually bear.

Also, it serves to motivate us to know that Allah will not change the condition of a person until they change themselves. So I ask you, are you keeping yourself busy, picking up new skills by attending religious classes, women's support groups, taking your children out and so on? You know what it means to be optimistic, you are aware that it is within you, but you need to re-ignite it.

You need to initiate a healthy distracting alternative to the emotional turmoil you are engaging in because of what others around you have committed against you. Currently you have mentioned two people who have hurt you. These are two people among the billions who live on this earth. They seem insignificant compared with the number of people there are who you can learn to trust as friends in order to continue on the journey of healing and change.

Because you have children from your ex-husband, you will have to deal with him throughout your life because of the common link you share of having to look after your offspring. You must remain firm and gain mental strength so that you can handle his taunts and deal strongly with his comments. Most importantly, you cannot reach a stage where the thought of revenge comes into play, as you must seek justice through the courts of religious mediation, but avoid reactionary revenge tactics at all costs as this is not Islamic behaviour.

Stand firm, observe your rights and make sure your rights as a mother are given to you as well. Have some control over your mental health with the help of Allah the Most High and strengthen your well-being. Through taking care of your mental strength you will gain emotional strength that will also lead to positive physical strength enabling you to tackle the day-to-day stress of living.

Healthy people lose the mental capacity for wellbeing if they constantly absorb themselves in excessive unnecessary worry and immerse themselves in the negatives that surround them. Prophet Muhammad said: 'If Allah wants to do good to somebody, He afflicts him with trials' (Bukhari 7: 70 #548).

Take a look at what you have lost: an abusive husband and a friend not worth having. Hence, experience the solace you do have and accept your current circumstance as 'relief' from burdening relationships that could have made things worse, but Allah the Most Merciful has relieved you of such effects. Take this result as a gift of freedom.

Domestic violence hurts both physically and emotionally, but it is not a lifelong prison term. You have come out of one now so make the most of your time and inner energy. Constant and repetitive negative thoughts only defeat the purpose of your newfound relief.

You are responsible for yourself, not your ex-husband, not your former friend, but yourself. So, *inshaallah*, pull yourself together, make *dua*, take doses of positive thinking and splashes of optimism, with constructive activity, along with your reliance and dependence on Allah—in this way you have a recipe for success, *inshaallah*.

> Verily, I have created men in the best of forms—given him the best constitution (Qur'an 95: 4–5).

Staying focused and positive, maintaining faith with patience and courage
The Qur'an recognises human weakness:

> For when affliction befalls man, he cries out unto Us, whether he be lying on his side or sitting or standing, but as soon as We have freed him of his affliction, he goes on as though he had never invoked Us to save him

from the affliction that befell him! Thus do their own doings seem goodly unto those who waste their own selves (Qur'an 10: 12).

All is yet to be lost as Allah instructs us to change ourselves. We can do this if we sincerely make the effort to change our own state or condition.

Truly, God does not change the condition of a people until they change what is in themselves (Qur'an 13: 11).

These verses indicate that humans have the power to influence change and effort must be made to do so internally. They relate to changing negative states and conditions that bring about human downfall. It is through conscious internal effort that Allah will assist us to bring about positive change.

For within everyone is the potential of reaching the 'highest of high' because humans have been made with the best faculties and form.

An Islamic perspective on solutions to stigma

Educating the individual in therapy that repentance is a turning point of behaviour, an ideological shift, brings a positive change in the life of an individual. Repentance gives the individual hope to transform their thoughts and behaviours for the better.

There are five conditions of repentance in Islam: (1) sincerity; (2) regret for what one has done; (3) giving it up immediately; (4) determination not to repeat it in future; and (5) repenting during the time when repentance will be accepted.

Repentance in Islam is always possible and is always accepted if one feels guilty. It must be performed with inner sincerity. This applies whether one has an incurable disease such as AIDS or one has committed murder or performed sexual activity outside marriage. The repentance is valid, because Allah accepts the repentance of a person so long as repentance has taken place before their death. Allah says:

Allah accepts only the repentance of those who do evil in ignorance and foolishness and repent soon afterwards; it is they to whom Allah will forgive and Allah is Ever All-Knowing, All-Wise (Qur'an 4: 17).

Islamic scriptures open the doors of hope and returning to good. This is essential for psychological change. Islam in general deals with those who deviate from the laws of religion with references to how individuals could be directed and guided through their faculties of reasoning towards reform. Allah, the Most High, says:

> And whoever does evil or wrongs himself and then seeks forgiveness from Allah, he shall find Allah All-Forgiving, All-Merciful (Qur'an 4: 110).

The necessity of repentance

Islam considers repentance among its main pillars; the Holy Qur'an and the Prophet's traditions (sunnah) focus on the necessity of repentance and the return to Allah, opening a new page in a person's record, turning away from the detestable past which corrupted the beautiful life with the stamp of shame. Conscious awareness is vital.

Knowledge is the source of human psychological and ideological motivation. It is through knowledge that one:

- realises how to fear and love Allah;
- creates an internal sense of hope and desire to meet Allah;
- realises the light of the loving Allah shines internally;
- conscience is awakened and one's consciousness returns.

The psycho-social impacts of repentance

Repentance, with all its external consequences like giving up sin, in-dicates an external psychological behaviour which starts to grow in one's self and which extends out in the form of behavioural change and upright human manners.

The repentant also finds, in Islamic Shari'ah, the encouragement towards repentance such as is found in the saying of the Messenger of Allah (s.a.w.): 'Indeed a man who commits sins enters Paradise, when he repents'.

People asked him: 'O Messenger of Allah, how that could be?'

He (s.a.w.) replied: 'The sin will be before his eyes and, repenting from it, he will run away till he enters Paradise.'

It is vital that we should not give up life and hope.

The Prophet (peace and blessings of Allah be upon him) said: 'For Allah has not sent down any disease without also sending down cure.'

One's trust can be put in Allah; handing over all one's affairs to Him; recognising that 'one's forelock' is in His hand.

Muslims are generally religious and spiritual people, so that using their Scriptures, with modern psychological strategies in therapy, is appropriate for instigating change in thought and subsequent behaviour. The goal is not only to rationally convince them that excessive preoccupation with guilty thoughts is destructive to their health and wellbeing but to accommodate their spiritual hearts as well as their minds.

For Muslims these two areas—the heart and mind—need to work in synergy for the most effective response to treatment for mental health issues.

References

Badri, M. 1978, *The Dilemma of Muslim Psychologists*, M.W.H. Publishers, London.

Bukhari   <http://www.usc.edu/dept/MSA/fundamentals/hadithsunnah/bukhari/> (accessed May 2006).

Erikson, E.H. 1950, *Childhood and Society*, Norton, New York.

Freud, S. 1914, *On Narcissism: An Introduction*, Standard Edition, 14: 67–102, Hogarth Press, London.

Haque, A. 2001, 'Interface of psychology and religion: trends and developments', *Counselling Psychology Quarterly*, vol. 14, no. 3, pp. 241–53.

The Holy Qur'an (English translation Abdullah Yusif 'Ali, 1934), Islamic Propagation Centre International, Durban.

Kohut, H. 1977, *The Restoration of the Self*, International Universities Press, New York.

Yusuf, H. 2004, *Purification of the Heart: Signs, Symptoms and Cures of the Spiritual Diseases of the Heart*, Starlach Press, Chicago.

Stigma/discrimination

15

A hidden dimension of Indigenous health

Yvonne Orley

My spiritual lands are of the K/Gamilaroi in northern New South Wales. My birth place is Brisbane, Queensland.

How do you explain life force energy? We can see when people possess it: they are energetic, they have vitality, they are 'alive', they glow! If you are low in life force energy you are depressed, you are 'down'.

The island of Australia and its people remained untouched by the outside world for thousands of years. Only 200 years ago was the country and its people subjected to the process of colonisation and invasion—but since that time many Aboriginal people have been conditioned like a young elephant who is shackled with heavy chains to a stake in the ground when he is young and in his maturity still thinks he cannot break free (Belasco 1990).

The Dreaming is the central aspect of Indigenous Australians' experience of spirituality. Unfortunately we have just come through 200 years of disconnection from the source of our teachings.

Modern Aboriginal people have to reclaim their roots and the values of the way of life that supported the development of their peoples.

The Dreaming: the higher truth

What is the Dreaming? What is so special to our people about it and how does it affect them?

Our people describe their spirituality, as do many first nations peoples, as a special 'connectedness' with the land and environment in which they live.

Territorial boundaries—not understood by white colonists—contained the Indigenous persons' resources for daily living as dictated by their totems. Within these territorial boundaries they had a nomadic existence based on necessity in response to seasonal changes and animal movement. They had kinship laws and social mores based on tribal law, they had a culture that was based on the collective and sharing.

An excellent description is housed in the introduction written by Melva Jean Roberts to the beautiful artworks of Ainslie Roberts in the book *Dreamtime Heritage: Australian Aboriginal Myths in Paintings* (1979). It highlights how distanced our people are from that existence which is no longer, one that they have lost. It speaks of how the Dreaming for each Aboriginal Australian is concerned with everything since the 'dawn of consciousness', and follows on from the Dreamtime. The Dreaming includes physical and spiritual aspects which are inter-twined and at the core of Aboriginal being, it explains the laws of nature and survival and of social relations, the ways of being within your tribe and of relations between tribes. It was from the Dreaming that art, songs, dances and rites of worship sprang.

The Aboriginal people had a sense of security: they knew who they were, they had ownership and connection to the land and they knew what to expect. Their needs were met, they had the love of family and friends, they had the boundaries of laws to live by and they had a strong spiritual identity. They were very close to the land and the elements of nature, they were in touch and in tune with life energies.

The physical impact of Western civilisation reverberated through the whole psyche of the Aboriginal peoples.

Trauma

I have seen the 'missionising' process at first hand on the mission stations. Many white colonists taught the Aboriginal people to doubt themselves: that the Aboriginal people were inferior; that Indigenous people living an ancient culture didn't have the 'modern' answers. This was further reinforced by the colonists' perception that all those who did not subscribe to a Christian faith were of a lesser value, inferior, unforgiven sinners and pagans.

There has been a dissonance for Indigenous peoples. This has left many not knowing where they are, who they are. If you leave behind your cultural way of life you have left a big part of you: you have no tradition and no platform for your children to grow from, to celebrate who they are as a people.

Professor Mick Dodson, of the ANU Institute for Indigenous Australia, recently made an impassioned plea for the issue of extreme violence in our communities to be immediately and urgently addressed. Professor Dodson also reminds us that we have no Aboriginal cultural traditions based on humiliation, degradation and violation: 'It is occurring principally because of marginalisation of Aboriginal people, the economic and welfare dependency, continuing high levels of unemployment, the dissolution of our culture' (Roberts 1979: 9). Indigenous clients also suffer a heavy load of grief and loss.

I have a background in health care and health promotion. For the past ten years I have been investigating the aspect of spirituality and its implication for our human wholeness. I learned a lot as I completed one of the first Aboriginal Reconciliation Learning Circles. I have sought to assist the Indigenous community to holistic health.

If you don't believe in yourself and/or have no access to personal understanding of spirituality and no cultural bank to address life's crises, then you don't regard such crises as challenges but as problems and blockages—and they accumulate.

It is my belief that people tend to feelings of depression, despair and suicidal ideation and attempts when they have a combination of, or a large representation of, the following in their psyche: vague identity (who they are, how they relate to others); an overload of grief and suffering and lack of spiritual clarity (energies are low, they are not able to source an inner or an outer reserve of strength to deal with situations at hand; feel alone, not part of a greater energy system).

The 1999 Declaration on the Health and Survival of Indigenous Peoples proposed a definition of Indigenous health:

Indigenous peoples' concept of health and survival is both a collective
and an individual inter-generational continuum encompassing a holistic
perspective incorporating four distinct shared dimensions of life. These
dimensions are the *spiritual*, the intellectual, physical and emotional
(World Health Organisation 1999).

This Declaration says that improvement to Indigenous health requires
a 'broad approach covering a wide spectrum of intervention'. Durie
(2003) states that while people advocate self-determination and
autonomy they also have to put a priority on skilling an Indigenous
workforce with both professional and cultural competence. This would
include the adoption of Indigenous health perspectives, including
spirituality and traditional healing as part of primary health care, in
collaboration with health professionals.

Reconnection to knowledge of the ancestors

We realise the suffering of our people and the need for the reconciliation process, but it is also time to acknowledge and give respect to our
ancestors from whom we hold our legacy. Our Dreaming, parables and
history inform us that where energy, loving energy, doesn't flow
and aspects of our being, our community, do not get nourishment, then
we wilt, we die.

Spirituality, for Indigenous people, has been a missing dimension to
our being; we have tried to fill it with religion's overcoats and with
mind-altering substances to make us feel good—a temporary panacea,
never making a good fit.

Eastwell (1988) reviewed the recorded deaths of the Yolngu group
of Aborigines over a 30-year period—it showed only two cases of
suicide. In his summary he postulates that this confirms the findings
of a low incidence of suicide, noted in other Aboriginal communities
where, similarly, spiritual and traditional values remain strong.

Indigenous Australian people's spiritual identity is tied up with a
sense of place, a sense of belonging to the land where they are born.
Such a sense is connected with knowing who you are and having a sense
of your background and relationship with kinfolk. One's place in a

bigger interconnected world is intrinsic to an acknowledgment of one's value as a person. It is also the means by which others come to know who you are and where you 'fit'.

The cultural bank of Indigenous spirituality and being able to operate from a traditional value system provide Aboriginal people with respect and the ability to honour both themselves and others. The importance of acknowledging your past is vital in having a belief in your future.

The connection between spirituality and everyday life is evident in the centrality of those things which give meaning and purpose to our lives—having meaningful work, a sense of value, a sense that our presence has evidence of impact on the world around us. This is linked to a sense of fulfilment and of adequacy; of being capable of successfully completing a life goal and task and benefiting from it; of being able to adequately provide for family and not having to be provided for, so that you feel less than others; of being able to cope with the challenges in the family and seeing a positive future for one's children. These activities of living are essential to the respect and self-honouring which is so much a part of Indigenous spirituality. Moreover, all of these are pivotal in our ability to fulfil our spiritual custodial responsibility for the land of our birth (Australia).

Honouring that we are all part of this energy flow, part of each other and all that there is, we are being called to touch our spiritual being, realise who we are and enact our spiritual custodianship; to love and care about each other; love and nurture our land—the energy being who is our Mother Earth.

A crucial dimension: the nature of the helping process in restoring and maintaining our spirituality

The way service providers relate to Indigenous service users is the critical success factor. In every episode of care the service provider needs to move from a helping mentality to a *reversal of the missionising approach*. Service providers in the helping professions often see people who are in crisis—that is how they present. They are confused, lack clarity, decision-making skills and so on. The Indigenous reality is that a whole group of people are in crisis and display these symptoms.

Service providers to Indigenous people need to consider approaches that are different from those of the usual service provider; they need, in a reversal of the missionising approach, to actively engage with processes which lead to personal and community empowerment.

This empowerment process would assist people to transcend the atrocities of their past and present, redefine themselves and express issues of unresolved grief and loss. Aboriginal people have a traditional way of life that can show others how to get in touch with life and all its beauty. It would assist them to value who they are—as a person and as an authentic ethnic group, to clarify their capabilities, and enable them to access resources—be those resources physical, human or spiritual.

An approach to loss, grief and suicide prevention, for example, cannot be effective if it is only a single strategy in isolation. The whole context in which a person lives must resonate at a vibration that supports the life force energy of those involved: both individuals and groups.

I would advocate that people in helping professions who wish to work with clients of the Indigenous Australian community complete one of the Aboriginal Reconciliation Learning Circles to be able to fully understand the impact of colonisation on the Indigenous community.

An exemplary program which addresses the issue of Indigenous holistic health is the We Al-li Program. This is a training program for non-Indigenous service providers who work with Indigenous clients; it particularly addresses the issue of the load of grief and loss that Indigenous clients suffer.

Helpers, look at your personal and professional practices: how are you honouring and respecting yourself and assisting others who come to you to honour and respect themselves? Those in the helping professions now need to move up and touch their own 'being-ness'—when you do this then you can assist others moving to theirs, to their wholeness.

Leaders and structures are currently all showing visible signs of stress fractures. Where is there evidence of adherence to spiritual principles? Take the example of our environment—we cannot keep taking and depleting for ever. People, society and the environment are left wanting. We are all one.

It is the time to touch our own spiritual strength—and assist others to make a stand in theirs. Cynthia Smith-Schuhmacher (2003) encourages us to tune into our Indigenous form of spirituality and sing our own song:

Come along and sing my song, let me dream my dreamtime on.
I went along and sang my song and I dreamt my dreaming on.

References

Belasco, J.A. 1990, *Teaching an Elephant to Dance*, Hutchinson Business Books, London.

Dodson, M. 2003, 'Violence dysfunction Aboriginality', press release, National Press Club, 11 June 2003, <http://www.law.anu.edu.au/anuiia/dodson.pdf>

Durie, M. 2003, 'The health of Indigenous peoples', *British Medical Journal*, vol. 326, pp. 510–11.

Eastwell, H.D. 1988, 'The low risk of suicide among the Yolngu of the Northern Territory: The traditional Aboriginal pattern', *Medical Journal of Australia*, vol. 148, no. 7, pp. 338–40.

Roberts, M. (paintings by Roberts, A.) 1979, *Dreamtime Heritage: Australian Aboriginal Myths in Paintings*, Rigby, Adelaide.

Smith-Schuhmacher C. 2003, 'The angels walked in front of me', *Aboriginal and Islander Health Worker Journal*, vol. 27, no. 2, pp. 20–2.

World Health Organisation 1999, Geneva Declaration on the Health and Survival of Indigenous Peoples, <http://www.faira.org.au/lrq/archives/199912/stories/geneva-declaration.html>

16
Social work group practice
Diana Coholic

Some years ago, when I was at the beginning of conceptualising how spirituality could be integrated into my practice, a client gave me a card with the inscription: 'I thank you for the very professional guidance which has challenged me constantly. I can see a spiritual future which has been inspired by our sessions'. This feedback left me somewhat puzzled at the time, because although we had talked about spiritual beliefs as these related to the client's fear of death, I was not sure how our work together had fostered a shift in her spiritual viewpoints as it had not been my intention.

In my own clinical work, spirituality and spiritually influenced issues were increasingly becoming more of a focus for discussion, but relying on literature and research in this area was of little assistance because it was so sparse.

I had also noticed that there was a shift occurring on a broader societal level in terms of an increasing interest in spirituality. Several popular books had been published and there seemed to be more interest in alternative healing methods such as therapeutic touch and reiki.

As with most practitioners who are interested in spiritually sensitive practice, within my own life a broad understanding of spirituality was becoming increasingly important to me in helping to make meaning of life events, in coping, and in healing. My own sense of spirituality was evolving.

I lacked like-minded colleagues with whom to discuss spiritually influenced helping, yet I was keenly interested in learning how others made sense of spirituality and included it in their work. Hence, a combination of these factors formed the impetus behind my eventual decision to investigate how feminist social workers conceptualised spirituality and incorporated it into their practices (Coholic 2001).

Compared to the late 1990s, we can now argue that there has indeed been a shift, within academic communities and societally, towards considering and embracing a more holistic perspective on human health and development (Ai 2002). Within social work there is a burgeoning literature that examines the transformative potential of spirituality in personal, community and societal change (see, for example, Canda & Smith 2001; Coates 2003). Even medical researchers (Edmondson et al 2005) and the business community (Zsolnai 2004) have begun to study spirituality and human health and functioning. However, this is still an emergent field with a developing knowledge base. We know little from research about how spiritually influenced helping actually assists people and contributes to client change, despite the fact that many believe in the effectiveness of spiritually influenced practices (Coholic 2003; Leight 2001).

Thus, the focus of my current work is exploring how spiritually influenced group social work practice occurs and is perceived as helpful (or not) by group participants. Group practice was a feasible way to begin work in this area because there are few social workers who identify themselves as working with a spiritually sensitive practice. This chapter discusses some of the outcomes and challenges of a group work study funded by the Iris Addiction Recovery for Women (formerly called Northern Regional Recovery Continuum or NRRC), a Canadian community agency that works with women and substance abuse.

The overall goal of our six-week group program (co-developed and facilitated by Julie LeBreton) was to help participants improve their self-awareness and self-esteem. The group focused on utilising various experiential and arts-based exercises that are integral to many spiritually sensitive approaches (France 2002). While trying to improve clients' self-awareness and self-esteem is a basic aspect of most helping approaches, our group was unique in its incorporation of spirituality. The eight women involved were diverse in terms of their ages and religious/spiritual beliefs, but they shared a substance abuse history and a desire to improve their self-esteem.

This was a group of women who had experienced stigma and oppression in various forms throughout their lives

What worked

Overall, the participants reported that the group was helpful to them in increasing and further developing their self-esteem and self-awareness. For some the group was the missing link in their recovery. For others it enabled them to expand their healing to another level or helped them understand and amalgamate previous work they had completed. The group also served as a useful adjunct to other therapeutic work they were already engaged in.

The six sessions were organised around the themes of: fostering a sense of connectedness to each other and the group and emphasising process as opposed to product; stream of consciousness writing and learning non-judgment; meditative exercises and mindfulness practice; the shadow self; and dream analysis. The group exercises (such as dream analysis) did not have to be conceptualised as spiritual processes, but spirituality did permeate most of the participants' narratives of this and other group exercises.

We found that most of the participants talked about their spiritual beliefs as a way of helping them to make meaning of their life circumstances—for example, why they were struggling with an addiction problem and what they had to do to recover. This is interesting and important to contemplate in regard to social work practice in general, which often involves helping people make sense of life events. For this group of women (and, we suspect, many others) spirituality was an integral part of this process. For instance, one participant explained her belief that people have different troubles in their lives for certain reasons that they need to figure out. With regard to herself she said:

Maybe this is the disease that I'm supposed to be getting through . . .
I know about my disease but now I have to find what else I was put on this
earth [for] . . . right now it's to learn about myself . . . because I've always
had a hard time with that . . . That's the way I see it in a spiritual way.

Another participant argued that the stream of consciousness writing
exercise allowed God to speak to her: 'It continued to flow and I know
it was from within me and it wasn't me. And how God, in my writing,
came out.'

Prior to beginning the group program, we did not realise how
different this program would be for most of the participants. Although
a few did have previous experience with meditation and experiential
therapeutic tools such as journal keeping, for most of the participants
the processes used in the group constituted a very different experience,
particularly in relation to building self-awareness and self-esteem. One
woman stated:

I was longing for a group where I [could] deal with my issues in a positive
way . . . I think in the first two sessions I was thinking . . . if I'm not
sitting there and having a hard time and crying, I am not dealing with
anything . . . But this group . . . allowed me that connection with my
inner child . . . it's brought up a lot of past issues, stuff that I didn't want
to remember but gave me the opportunity to deal with it.

While various aspects of the group were successful, I will focus here on
two processes that were identified as particularly helpful by the participants: dream analysis and the meditations/mindfulness practice.

Working with dreams

The exploration of dreams constitutes an important part of the therapeutic work in spiritually influenced practice (France 2002). Also, in
group counselling, the analysis of dreams has been reported to help with
understanding other group members, promoting group cohesiveness
and stimulating therapeutic group interactions (Clark 1994).

France (2002: 129) makes the point that since the beginning of time
all cultures have regarded dreams as having some special power that

transcends the past, present and future and that many (especially Aboriginal cultures) believe that the messages of the dream are the vehicles through which God can speak. One participant in particular reported that she found a lot of her dreams manifested in her life, stating, for example, that 'God was letting me know this all along, that my addiction had to quit, so I went into rehab after [having the dream]'.

Another participant described her belief that a recurring dream was actually representative of a past-life experience. She used the dream to make meaning of her current life situation and family dynamics. For another, further reading about dreams elicited a spiritual experience (she borrowed a book from the facilitator). She said:

> It [understanding] came to me . . . it popped out of the book. That doesn't usually happen, so for me that's more of a spiritual thing because usually if I start reading, I'll ask my higher power to let me grasp what I really need to grasp. So that means . . . if I don't understand, it's not made for me to actually get it today . . . So when I get it, well everything was just popping out, so it was my time to do it.

Meditations and mindfulness practice

The facilitator introduced the participants to a variety of meditative exercises because different people generally prefer different approaches. We decided to begin each session with a meditation or to incorporate meditative exercises in the group, even if they were brief, in order to help ground and connect the participants to the work of the group. Also, meditating before engaging in experiential exercises and other psychotherapeutic work can help to calm the mind and open up the possibility for a stronger connection with feelings and/or unconscious processes.

For some, the meditations and mindfulness practice felt spiritual because they were 'taking the time to connect with myself', while for others it was an opportunity to 'feel their energy and other people's energy', or to connect with a higher power. For some of the women the meditations were difficult in that this was a new experience for them and one's ability to meditate generally becomes easier and more effective with practice (Kabat-Zinn 1990).

Mindfulness practice is a specific form of meditation. Jon Kabat-Zinn explains that the key to mindfulness meditation is an appreciation of the present moment and the cultivation of an intimate relationship with it through a continual attending to it with care and discernment. While mindfulness lies at the root of Buddhism, Taoism and yoga, it is also found in the works of Emerson, Thoreau and Whitman, and in Native American wisdom (Kabat-Zinn 1994). A mindful walking exercise was a new experience for most of the participants. One woman reported:

> The awareness is great, when it overcomes you, when you become very aware how big the world is. I know that sounds weird but I'm thinking of myself and feeling like my body walking, and then I'm seeing everything around me and it's like, 'wow, it's just me here walking on this huge big world'.

For another participant, mindfulness was identified as the 'missing link' in her recovery. She (along with others) identified that learning about and being more mindful facilitated feelings of gratefulness. She explained that she can now appreciate more the 'small details that we all take for granted and that it's making things more worthwhile . . . it fills my day with healthy things . . . I don't feel like I'm wasting my time', which in turn encouraged her to feel better about herself. Specifically, the participants found that the meditations helped them become more self-aware by helping them to visualise therapeutic processes or by helping them connect more with their thoughts and feelings by providing focus.

Mindfulness practice helped some women shift their self-perceptions; moreover, they learned that healing can be 'fun' and creative, and that creativity could help them build relationships with their children, others and themselves. Mindfulness practice is being increasingly studied in various fields and with a myriad client populations, with research results indicating its effectiveness (Sagula & Rice 2004). Mindfulness is a good example of a helpful process that is rooted in spirituality but which can be learned by many people with both diverse spiritual beliefs or even no spiritual standpoints. Perhaps this accounts in part for the current interest in mindfulness across helping disciplines.

Nonetheless, we should contemplate the complexities involved in divorcing mindfulness from its spiritual roots. As Kabat-Zinn argues, it is important that we recognise the unique qualities of mindfulness meditation practice so that it is not 'simply seized upon as the next promising cognitive behavioral technique or exercise, decontextualized, and plugged into a behaviorist paradigm with the aim of driving desirable change, or of fixing what is broken' (Kabat-Zinn 2003: 145).

Self-awareness and insight arise from an ability to pay attention to and experience one's anxieties, fears and other feelings, which often reside in the unconscious mind. Frattaroli (2001: 194) contends that you can think of this process as simply getting in touch with a feeling or, more profoundly, as listening to the soul.

If we, as practitioners, ignore the spiritual dimension of people's lives, our ability to assist them may be impaired. Thus, we need to address our own reluctance to engage in these discussions with clients. To address our inhibitions in examining spirituality with clients we need to explore our hesitancies, which may stem from various factors. These include lack of clear definitions and distinctions between religion and spirituality; the connections that are made between personal values and spirituality; fears of imposing personal beliefs onto clients; the process of professionalisation that divorces personal and professional values, and that puts stress on social workers to be accepted by other professionals; a lack of awareness of the substantial literature in the area of spiritually influenced helping, some of which is empirically derived; the continued marginalisation of this knowledge within the helping professions; and the absence of spirituality from social work and other helping professions' pedagogical processes.

Once one makes the room for spirituality to enter into healing spaces, clients will find and experience spirituality differently according to their own preferences. For instance, for a couple of the participants in our six-week program the whole group process felt spiritual. For other women the meditations were the most spiritual experience, while for others the dream-work and/or mindfulness elicited spiritual connections. The important point here is that in a group that incorporates the spiritual, participants are encouraged to bring their spirituality to the process and to make sense of their experiences in a holistic manner, if they so wish and if they deem this to be important for them. One woman explained how through using meditation and guided imagery in the group she was able to visualise rescuing her 'inner child' and so felt for the first time in 20 years that she could protect herself from abuse. She said that for her, 'meditation is a gift, is like wow, it really is and I just can't get over what I've accomplished, what I've achieved through meditation . . . I found my heart . . . It's like I found my soul-mate, and it's in me!'

References

Ai, A. 2002, 'Integrating spirituality into professional education: A challenging but feasible task', *Journal of Teaching in Social Work*, vol. 22, issue 1/2, pp. 103–30.

Canda, E.R. and Smith, E. (eds) 2001, *Transpersonal Perspectives on Spirituality in Social Work*, The Haworth Press, New York.

Clark, A. 1994, 'Working with dreams in group counseling: Advantages and challenges', *Journal of Counseling and Development*, vol. 73, no. 2, pp. 141–4.

Coates, J. 2003, *Ecology and Social Work: Toward a New Paradigm*, Fernwood Publishing, Halifax.

Coholic, D. 2001, 'Exploring Spirituality in Feminist Practices—Emerging Knowledge for Social Work', unpublished doctoral thesis, University of New South Wales, Sydney.

Coholic, D. 2003, 'Student and educator viewpoints on incorporating spirituality in social work pedagogy—an overview and discussion of research findings', *Currents: New Scholarship in the Human Services*, vol. 2, no. 2, pp. 35–48.

Edmondson, K., Lawler, K., Jobe, R., Younger, J., Piferi, R. and Jones, W. 2005, 'Spirituality predicts health and cardiovascular responses to stress in young adult women', *Journal of Religion & Health*, vol. 44, no. 2, pp. 161–72.

France, H. 2002, *Nexus: Transpersonal Approach to Groups*, Detselig Enterprises Ltd, Calgary.

Frattaroli, E. 2001, *Healing the Soul in the Age of the Brain: Becoming Conscious in an Unconscious World*, Viking, USA.

Kabat-Zinn, J. 1990, *Full Catastrophe Living: Using the Wisdom of Your Body and Mind to Face Stress, Pain, and Illness*, Delta, USA.

Kabat-Zinn, J. 1994, *Wherever You Go, There You Are: Mindfulness Meditation in Everyday Life*, Hyperion, New York.

Kabat-Zinn, J. 2003, 'Mindfulness-based interventions in context: Past, present, and future', *Clinical Psychology: Science and Practice*, vol. 10, no. 2, pp. 144–56.

Leight, A. 2001, 'Transpersonalism and social work practice: Awakening to new dimensions for client self-determination, empowerment, and growth', *Social Thought*, vol. 20, no. 1/2, pp. 63–76.

Sagula, D. and Rice, K.G. 2004, 'The effectiveness of mindfulness training on the grieving process and emotional well-being of chronic pain patients', *Journal of Clinical Psychology in Medical Settings*, vol. 11, no. 4, pp. 333–43.

Zsolnai, L. 2004, *Spirituality and Ethics in Management*, Kluwer Academic, Netherlands.

Cycle of hopelessness/
hope

17

A spiritual and political practice for reconciliation

Julie Foster Smith and Hilary Byrne-Armstrong

Naming the unnameable

Aboriginal spirituality has significant cultural and social capital when portrayed as a counter-narrative to the wastelands of modern capitalism. At base is the idealisation of the Aboriginal spiritual sense of belonging to place and country as creating a cultural identity that white Australians, caught up in the alienation of the twenty-first century, sorely lack.

At first glance, using Aboriginal spirituality to heal the disease of white culture might seem to be a positive move: it is a reversal of the usual starting point of Aboriginal relations. But the issue is more subtle than this. The content has changed, but the process has not. A dualistic framework is still in place, totalising peoples' experiences under simplistic stereotypes that maintain the division between the powerful and the disempowered. Pile (1994: 25) wrote, 'If we accept these dualisms then we collude in the reproduction of the power-ridden values they help to sustain'. Unfortunately this has been the basis for much work with Indigenous Australians.

Our issue with this approach is that it belongs to interiorised constructions of racism that assume that the problem lies within individual human beings and their attitudes and socialisation, without acknowledging societal systems and structures. As long as we remain convinced that it is an individual problem, opportunities to notice

Aboriginal culture in its own right or, more practically, to address the
appalling social conditions of many Aboriginal people are lost. This is
because we do not address the subtle social practices woven into the
fabric of our everyday lives—its language and social practices—which
are the roots of racism as well as its means of dissemination.

Breaching the norm

We introduce an alternative approach to exploring Aboriginal spirituality, which we call 'breaching the norm'. We describe it through two
events that were aimed at unravelling many of the taken-for-granted
and invisible language and social practices that are institutionalised and
systematised in our culture. The first is framed by an 'externalising
conversation' (White 1990) and the second by a 'definitional ceremony'
(Meyerhoff 1982).

Our approach starts with the premise that the world we inhabit has
been in the making for thousands of years. Discrimination is not a
recent aberration, but has been woven into the social fabric throughout
history. It will not diminish until it is unpacked and ways found to
destroy its deeply embedded roots. Both black and white should drive
this process because ultimately both black and white will benefit from a
world in which discrimination is minimal. Therefore discrimination
must be seen as collective rather than individual, and usefully positioned
within communitarian discourses to involve the performative and cere-
monial dimensions of life, because it is through these dimensions that
the social fabric is rewoven (Braithewaite 1989). It involves putting a
mirror up to our language and practices in order to reveal how we are
shaped by it as well as shaping it.

Externalising conversations: opening the middle space

We were commissioned to co-facilitate one session of a three-day
program at a large girls' school, to introduce Aboriginal spirituality to
Year 9 staff and students as part of a 'Women in Leadership' camp.
(This camp had been running for four years, with guidance and wisdom
from Aboriginal elders and educators.) The first session was to be an

information session for teachers in the school hall. Julie, the Aboriginal woman and project coordinator, was to facilitate this. The idea was to give the teachers a short synopsis of Aboriginal spirituality so they could follow it up in their teaching. As representatives of black and white Australia, conversations seem inevitably to drift back to connections (or lack of them) between spirituality and politics. Both of us wanted to position the workshop to embrace both spirituality and politics.

We were interested in practices that assisted people to understand the meanings they made of their experience. Experience may seem personal, but the meanings we make of it occur through language. With language we build meaning frameworks through our culture filter. An 'externalising conversation' (White 1990) is a way of bringing attention to this process. It examines the cultural narratives or discourses that shape our meaning making, and in this way politicises experience. Through an externalising conversation, people come to recognise that language is shaping them as much as they shape it, the meanings we make of the events of our lives are revealed as a social and political process rather than individual events. Furthermore, because different accounts are produced in the exploration, the externalising conversation opens the space for multiple ways of seeing things, taking participants beyond simplistic dualisms and into a middle space of ambiguity and uncertainly, and offering the freedom to choose and the possibility of empowerment.

We started with the idea of a 'definitional ceremony', a communitarian performance that progresses from the 'breach of a norm, to crisis, and resolution, with displays of common, powerful, binding symbols' (Meyerhoff 1982: 268). It serves to move an issue (in this case, reconciliation) from practices that encourage self-reflective interiorisation to practices that encourage collective and communal performances; we used this framework to create the externalising conversation. Julie asked the teachers to board a train at the school and travel to a suburb with a high Aboriginal population some 20 minutes away. They arranged to meet in the park in this inner-city housing area. Initially the teachers were wary, but agreed to go.

Julie's story[1]

They arrived in a fearful clump in their city clothing and hesitated when asked to sit among mounds of rubbish in the park and among people whom society had all but abandoned. Some newspapers were found, they arranged themselves carefully upon them. There, among the local drunks, drug addicts and the sad individuals who struggle with life on the streets, they began a conversation about Aboriginal spirituality. Some local characters sitting in the park intermittently joined the circle but most moved away and refused contact. One 'sister girl' spoke to us: 'What you mob doing here?' I replied that they were 'yarning about who they were and wanting to know more about us'. The 'sister girl' shook each hand around the circle. The teachers assumed she must be a friend of mine and were surprised to hear that we had not met before. I then asked the teachers to walk around the block and to talk to people, to knock on doors and to ask about the Dreamtime[2] and about reconciliation.

We met up at a local preschool an hour later. The teachers were visibly shaken and upset. Few had made contact. Some had been met with hostility. The teachers had tasted what racism and marginality are really like. They found themselves the 'other', a position that was virtually unknown to most of them as white middle class people. I asked if their experience had them thinking any differently. Someone commented that Aboriginal life had taken on a different dimension. This person talked about coming with a romantic notion about Aboriginal spirituality that she realised had nothing to do with Aboriginal life. I asked what the romantic versions of the Dreamtime had had her believing. What was she thinking now after this experience? How were these thoughts different from previous thoughts? What did this say about the value of romantic versions of Aboriginal spirituality to Aboriginal people, to white people?

Resolution and learning

By constructing the questions in this way Julie was asking people to think in other ways about Aboriginal spirituality. Sitting in a hall learning about Aboriginal spirituality is inadequate and conceals another reality that needs acknowledgment. After the event a teacher reflected that the romantic ideas she had held had blinded her to the reality of Aboriginal life and, more significantly, had blinded her to the privileged reality of her own. She had never thought about her life in these terms before—an awakening that would change her views for good.

Other participants in the group commented not only on their dismay at the conditions people were living in, but about the suspicion and hostility they had experienced. They were asked: 'Do you think there might be a link between your identity, the conditions and the hostility?' and 'What sorts of relationships and identities might be formed under the conditions you've seen?'

The externalising conversation is oriented towards 'outsight'. Some teachers talked about having their first face-to-face conversation with an Aboriginal Australian. They were astonished at the range of responses they encountered that had little to do with 'who' they were— especially when they were subjects of suspicion, hostility, irrelevance and/or disregard. This process of reversing the orientation of a negated 'other' was fraught with hazards but very powerful. Teachers found themselves stared at, glared at, whispered about and called names. This gave them direct experience of the power of small, everyday, subtle discriminatory practices. Their response ranged from acceptance to extreme discomfort, blaming Julie: 'If I had known I wouldn't have worn a suit.' Outrage: 'A door was slammed in my face!' Anger: 'We should have been warned.'

However, one teacher had 'even found common ground', spending time chatting about children and schools, pleased because he had chosen a door that had a reconciliation sticker on it. This gave him entrance to the house, where he had happily bought a jar of 'reconciliation jam'.

The most important message, however, and perhaps the resolution of this event was the teachers' insights after the experience of asking people about their spirituality. What they concluded was that if they were called upon to talk about their own spirituality they would feel that their privacy was being invaded. By organising the activity in this way we were positioning it in the notion of 'catch[ing] ourselves in the act of constituting ourselves . . . inside the very categories that we want to move beyond' (Davies 1994: 2). Through the power of breaching the norm, the externalising conversation was able to take people beyond their normal perceptions about the world. They began, from an Aboriginal perspective, to perhaps understand the basis of Aboriginal spirituality, the interconnectedness of *all* things.

Definitional ceremony: reconciliation in the moment

The second part of the event was to work directly with the Year 9 girls (aged around 15) to introduce them to Aboriginal spirituality. The workshop (after consultation with Aboriginal elders) was planned as a definitional ceremony, this time to search for an experience that would help the young women understand racism, marginality and discrimination as happening within the fabric of their own lives.

From a very early age, children stage rituals and performances in which they try on different social roles (police officer, nurse, teacher, judge) to give meaning to the sense they have of themselves (Mead 1934). The central idea of this is that life is not a text, but the 'performance of a text'.[3] We perform to someone, an audience, who reads and witnesses 'not only what people think they are but what they should have been or may yet be' (Meyerhoff 1982: 262). In other words, the performance defines and produces our sense of ourselves.

In a definitional ceremony, people practise different ways of defining themselves in order to become part of the group. The process of belonging occurs through self-narratives being proclaimed, witnessed and often re-told by the group. The shared experience is one of making explicit how we weave and are woven into self and identities through collective ways of thinking and doing.

Stage one: breaching the norm

Arrangements were made for a small theatre troupe from another school to relive the occupation of Australia. They were to occupy and pretend to rehearse a play before we and the participants arrived at the workshop space that we had booked to use for the day.

When we walked in, the scene went something like this:

STAFF AND STUDENTS: 'Excuse me, when will you be finished?'
PLAYERS: 'I don't know.'
STAFF AND STUDENTS: 'What are you doing in this space?'
PLAYERS: 'It is our space, we are rehearsing in here, and we have booked it.'
STAFF AND STUDENTS: 'There must be a mistake.'

The troupe continued rehearsing, saying we could watch for a while. The students were encouraged to continue filing into the room. The theatre troupe then expressed annoyance. 'Will you stop staring and get out of our space!' Nobody moved. The energy was high. The theatre troupe had begun to parry with ownership. There was agitation and anger. A war of words ensued. The theatre troupe melted out of the room. We were left.

Stage two: the crisis
The noise in the room was deafening. Everyone was talking at once, yet no one could be heard. Hilary suggested that the students sit down in groups and talk about what happened. This they did. Some parts of the room started to settle, but then the energy rose again because a group that was later identified by teachers as the 'troublemakers' spoke their outrage. One of their members burst into tears. She had been called an unforgivable name in the theatre piece and we were to blame. Hilary remembered Meyerhoff's statement that when groups feel particularly unheard, 'audiences may be hard to find'. She decided to create an audience. She searched around for some symbolic holding mechanism[4] and spied a pair of Aboriginal clapsticks (musical instruments) on the table next to the Aboriginal elder who was a co-facilitator. She shouted across the room, 'Uncle, is that a talking stick?', indicating one of the clapsticks.[5]

Uncle had the presence of mind to agree immediately that it was, and sent it across the room. Hilary asked the girls to use it, saying they could speak only when they had the talking stick, and everyone else would listen. This ploy worked well. The students waited their turn to speak and be heard by the group. They spoke about the event in terms of 'cruelty', 'deceit', 'treating people properly', 'betrayal' and experimentation. One asked to speak to, and hear from, the leader of the theatre troupe. The leader was brought in and explained the activity, in terms of the history of Australia. We apologised to the students for the discomfort they had experienced. Things began to settle.

Stage three: the resolution
Julie had been sitting quietly watching the scene. Suddenly she was invisible no longer. 'What you experienced for ten minutes today is what I and my Aboriginal colleagues in this room experience every moment of our lives,' she said. There was a sudden hush. The participants, as one, gave her their attention.

Julie continued, 'My great-grandmother [Luisa] was in her home in the bush, alone with her children one day, when a troupe of white settlers visited her. They burst into her home. She quickly told the children to run outside to the bushes and hide. Luisa was raped and murdered. She was seven months pregnant. Her baby was stillborn when the children came back and found her. They washed the baby and buried it. The police came and took the children from their father and sent them into service, aged ten, twelve and four. They never saw their father again. The perpetrators were not sought out or charged.' (This story is documented by the eldest and youngest of the grand-daughters, Julia and Elizabeth Joyce, and the written and oral story shared with the author Julie by grandmother Luisa, aunties Julia and Joyce and her father.)

Julie paused, then spoke again. 'I understand your anger and acknowledge your pain and the feeling of betrayal. I wake up every morning knowing that I am going to have to negotiate situations like you went through today. It may not be as overt as in my great-grandmother's time, but the cruelty, lack of rights, negligence and name-calling are always present. It is present when all the Aboriginal elders and educators in this room go to the shops. It happens when we walk down the street. We are made to feel a stranger in our land.'

There was a silence in the room. Some were in tears. Then a student got to her feet. 'I am one of the group that was particularly angry today,' she said. 'But I also want you all to know that I am Lebanese. I know it is not as bad as the story we just heard or what happens to Aboriginals. I get called names too and I get excluded. The names hurt, they are cruel. I have also called others names and I want to say sorry. I want to say sorry to my three Aboriginal friends and elders here for how they are treated as Aboriginals. And I want to say sorry to the other people in the room that I have called names.'

This began an emotional and spiritually enriching process. Students spoke about their pain at being labelled 'wogs' in the playground.[6] Others talked about being isolated and excluded because they were different. One student spoke about being labelled and marginalised because she was fat, another for having big breasts. We left the space for anyone to speak and melted ourselves into the background. As each person talked about their struggles, they also spoke of their shame: shame at labelling others, shame at their ignorance, and shame at their self-indulgence at the beginning of the afternoon. They spoke of the cruelty of labelling each other and their recognition of their complicity in this, and of their need to support each other. Students were able to share their experiences of the pain of being 'othered'.

A song, a chant, an Aboriginal spiritual ritual closed the proceedings with a 'smoking'[7] to cleanse the group, which the elder organised. After it was completed the students were to return to their rooms. But they did something different. We went back to the venue to tidy up and found that the 90-odd students, led by a 'troublemaker', had filed back into the workroom and were sitting in the shape of the rainbow serpent,[8] silently waiting. They had been there for five minutes before we found them. Julie bowed silently to them and the gesture was solemnly returned. They then quietly got up and left.

Learning

Framing an event such as this as a definitional ceremony is useful because as a collective and symbolic performance it provided a space in which the students could construct and engage in the multiple narratives of their lives. There are several ways in which this happened.

First, the definitional ceremony was an opportunity to show alternative ways of thinking and doing. It is a strategy that provides opportunities to the marginalised to be seen 'in [their] own terms, garnering witnesses to [their] worth, vitality and being' (Meyerhoff 1982: 267).

In the performance by the theatre troupe, students displayed and dramatised themselves in various manifestations of self-definition: an emotional display, a political speech, planned action, a spontaneous expression of their private struggles, truculent stubbornness, shades of cooperation, shame and pain. As they shifted their subjectivities in relation to the facilitation team as well as to each other, the performance of these various versions of selfhood was witnessed by all of us and by themselves. The girls' spirits had grown.

Secondly, the metaphor of a definitional ceremony, as a guide to practice, is helpful when there is conflict and confrontation. While we do not want to reify this process, the framework of a definitional ceremony progressing from 'breach of a norm, to crisis, and resolution, with displays of common, powerful, binding symbols' (Meyerhoff 1982: 268) is helpful in the chaos of 90-odd voices all talking at once. Symbols such as the 'talking stick' do 'hold the space together' in order to keep the conversation alive and maintain connections. This practice re-inforces Indigenous 'ways of knowing', Indigenous epistemology.

Although it was not our aim to produce such chaos, our experience tells us that through chaos there is an enunciation of collective symbols. In this enunciation, membership is reiterated and a shared commitment to each other expressed. At a tea break later in the afternoon the students hung around and chatted together, reluctant to leave, telling each other stories and reiterating their connection with friends and classmates. By unravelling the drama of collective meaning-making, people can challenge the isolating and divisive forces of stereotypes and discover and re-discover similarities and connections.

We live proudly in a beautiful country with a negative legacy because of its treatment of Indigenous peoples. As concerned citizens and friends we challenge the idea that it is useful or politic to produce internalising accounts of racism by continuing to colonise Aboriginal culture in the name of the spiritual deliverance of Western culture. An authentic spiritual practice is made possible through providing a space for real encounter and an opportunity for generating collective meaning. Such a spiritual and political process, a process that breaches the norm, makes genuine reconciliation possible.

Endnotes

1. This account was narrated by Julie to Hilary, who wrote it.
2. The basis of Aboriginal spirituality is the Dreamtime, a mystical time out of which the creation stories arose.
3. Meyerhoff developed this idea from symbolic interactionists, who thought this was the way that people interacted as social beings. People develop a reflexive awareness of themselves acting in the world (see Mead 1934). The performance metaphor evokes this reflexive awareness.
4. Hilary was taking up the idea that in times of crisis groups find some collective symbolic images to hold them together to ride the crisis.
5. Hilary comments: I realise that it is ironic that in looking for a symbol I chose a native American symbol used in conflict situations. This may be because my culture (Anglo-Australian) is lacking in symbolic collective mechanisms outside the dominant legal discourse symbols.
6. Australian slang term for person born of other than British stock.
7. An Aboriginal spiritual cleansing ritual that was performed by the Aboriginal elder.
8. The sacred symbol of Aboriginal spirituality.

References

Braithewaite, J. 1989, *Crime, Shame and Reintegration*, Cambridge University Press, Cambridge.

Byrne-Armstrong, H. 1999, Dead Certainties and Local Knowledge: Post-structuralism, Conflict and Narrative Practices, unpublished PhD thesis, University of Western Sydney.

Davies, B. 1994, *Post-structuralist Theory and Classroom Practice*, Deakin University Press, Melbourne.

Mead, G.H. 1934, *Mind, Self and Society*, University of Chicago Press, Chicago.

Meyerhoff, B. 1982, 'Life not death in Venice: Its second life', in V. Turner and E. Bruner (eds), *The Anthropology of Experience*, University of Illinois Press, Chicago.

Pile, S. 1994, 'Masculinism, the use of dualistic epistemologies and third spaces', *Antipode*, vol. 26, no. 3, pp. 255–77.
White, M. 1990, *Narrative Means to Therapeutic Ends*, Norton, New York.

Julie Foster Smith is a descendant of the Kalkadoon Nation. She acknowledges the teachings and wisdom of the current elders, who have graciously passed on to her their wisdom from the past and the present. She is mindful that this collective wisdom is inclusive of the many Indigenous peoples across Australia and beyond, including the many ancestors of these lands whose generosity of spirit is a testament to the continuous Indigenous ways of knowing expressed throughout this paper.

Acknowledgment is also extended to the non-Indigenous peoples who are significantly responsible for the continuing support of this school's Indigenous program. Without their efforts since the inaugural program to the present, their knowledge, commitment and passion to creating ways of working and learning together with spiritual strong hearts and minds, this 'practice of reconciliation with strong spirit' would not be taking place.

18
Engaging the client through connecting

Elizabeth Benson-Stott
(with the kind assistance of James Stott)

Why are suicide and mental health issues on the rise? Why is it that we spend many millions of dollars each year on intervention and prevention, yet the incidence of suicide and mental illnesses continues to rise? Perhaps we have not looked far enough, or are not seeking the right answers to intervention and treatment. Every psychiatric and psychological school has a different answer, yet still they concern themselves with merely treating symptoms.

I believe that suicide intervention requires more than just counselling, psychology or psychiatry—it needs to be spiritually rooted. When the spiritual nature is ignored, clinicians never get to the root of the problem—they are merely treating the symptom/s. Suicide and mental health issues grow from the soul struggling to connect, disconnect and reconnect. Treatment of a suicidal person is successful through a holistic management approach including an acute assessment, intervention and support. The attitude of the therapist also affects the overall effectiveness of treatment. Therapists who tend to treat clients as mere numbers or objects rather than as individuals need to start to take accountability for people's lives.

I identify as an Indigenous Australian. My spirituality is of significant importance to me, but what is of greater importance is my connection with God. How can a person be an Aboriginal and at the same time a Christian, you may ask. Over time, there has been an increase in the number of Aboriginal and Torres Strait Islander people who are becoming Christians. I belong to a church with an Aboriginal and Torres Strait Islander pastor and in which a large number of the congregation are of Aboriginal and/or Torres Strait Islander descent. Back with the creation of Aboriginal missions and reserves in the 1800s came churches and Christian Aboriginals. This is where Aboriginals began to find ways to incorporate Christianity into their Aboriginal spirituality and to find comfort in the opportunity to once again have hope and faith.

To become an Indigenous Christian you do not need to leave your culture behind. When I became a Christian I re-examined my lifestyle and rejected some aspects of Aboriginal symbolism which did not line up with biblical teachings in God. However, many of the traditions which have been passed down through the generations, such as how to care for the land and all living creatures through respect with the environment, are consistent with Christian faith. I am able to integrate my Christian faith with my culture and to incorporate these stories into my faith, so that I continue to have laws by which to live, and commandments by which to strive to obey, that were given by God.

Dreams have, throughout history and in cultures all over the world, served to connect people more closely and can allow healing. Dreams can break us away from our usual way of looking at things. The creative power of Indigenous dreaming depends on the interplay of making and breaking, connecting and disconnecting, creating and destroying. Dreaming, in Christianity, can allow an insight into our soul and to look at where strongholds may have formed.

It has been my role, as a Christian, a person of Indigenous heritage and a psychologist, to fulfil the purpose God has for me. I believe that psychology gives many tools with which we may look at the soul of a person, but ignores the spirit realm: our spirits, God's Holy Spirit, and demonic spirits. I allowed God to show me how He wanted to lead me in the area of counselling and healing people. I now briefly discuss how I am able to integrate the spiritual dimension into my work through my private practice with people who are suicidal and others in pain.

'The world is not here.' These four words profoundly changed my life. That afternoon Andrew (not his real name), a client of ours for four months, identified what had made our offices so different for him. Explaining further, he told of the overwhelming sense of peace he felt when he stepped through the front doors of our offices, as if a 'force of peace' met his worries at the door and refused them entry. For him, 'the world is not here' meant exactly that, that the chaos and troubles of the world could not follow him inside. My understanding of his words was slightly different. Darkness flees in the presence of light and evil cannot tolerate the awesome presence of God. Undoubtedly the 'force of peace' Andrew experienced was a Heavenly body, meeting him at the door and allowing him entry, brushing off the baggage he had been carrying.

So what is different about what we do? The biblical philosophy that our therapy is based on comes from several Scriptures. First, the acknowledgment of people being created as threefold beings is essential in understanding this approach. As physical beings our flesh (*soma*) is the part of us that experiences heat, cold, flavour, physical pleasure and pain, and receives sight, sound and smell. The psychological (*psyche*) aspect of our being defines our thoughts, emotions, conscience, memory and reason. However, many people misunderstand the spiritual (*pneuma*) aspect, the third of our being, which is the part of us that provides reverence, prayer and hope, and is the part of us that connects with God (Brown 1993). References to the threefold nature of people appear in many areas of the Bible.

The approaches to counselling and working with suicidal people are as varied as the number of practitioners working in the field. Of the 206 new referrals to our service in the twelve months to September 2005, 93 per cent had issues concerned to varying degrees with suicide. During the study period, in which from eight to twelve counselling sessions using Pneuma:Psyche:Soma (Spirit:Soul:Body:) Emotional Release Therapy (PPS-ERT) were conducted with each client, not one made a suicide attempt.

We have found our approach allows people to let go of negative emotions and 'strongholds' (strongly held positions) from the past like anger, sadness, fear, hurt, guilt and rejection. We focus on creating a balance in the person's threefold nature: body, soul, spirit. This approach, taking account of the spiritual, is based on the belief that thoughts and generational issues are stored on what we call a Spiritual Line. Using certain techniques, negative emotions (bad feelings), limiting decisions, anger and other conflicts we have within us are broken off from our past events (Campbell 1996). This results in dramatic improvements in personal growth and development. It is about replacing voids and 'strongholds' in a person's life with Jesus Christ.

A full history and mental state examination specifically considers significant incidents and traumatic events from the beginning of a person's life, and is taken in a safe and non-threatening environment. The client is made aware of the process to come, the aim being to break the strongholds from their life so that they can begin to 'connect' again and have freedom. As ERT commences, using the tapping of hands or listening to a clock, the scene is set with the person thinking of a peaceful, safe setting and picturing themselves there. They are reassured that if at any stage they feel stressed, they can return to the safe place, or focus on the sound of the clock or hand tapping. The person closes their eyes and is directed to this safe place. The person in their visualisation then walks from their safe place to a house that has one front door, but many inside doors. The person is encouraged to walk to the front door, where there is a suit of knight's armour, which the person puts on. It is described as weighing very little and making them feel safe and protected. The person is reminded that the armour comes with a sword—a sword that will cut the strongholds. After they enter the house, the person is directed to visualise a part of their history in a room—one that represents a stronghold in their life that is not allowing them to 'connect', which is keeping them from achieving things in life. The person is asked to describe what they see. As they describe what they see the clinician keeps reminding them that they have the armour on and are safe. As the person describes the scene in the room, the clinician directs them to an 'umbilical cord' or string attached from the person to the representation of the issue. This represents the spiritual bondages that form between the person and issue/s—and which, if not severed, can form into strongholds. The person visualises picking up the sword (Sword of the Spirit) and cutting the 'cord' through.

The clinician continues with the client until all the cord/s are cut completely. This allows the 'slicing' away of the stronghold or thing in the person's life that was creating a disconnection. The client is then asked to visualise the length of cord that is still connected to them, to connect it to 'love, peace, gentleness, and a sound mind' (Jesus Christ) and, as they do this, to feel a sense of warmth come over them. The client is then asked how they feel. If the client feels okay, then he or she is asked to walk with the 'love, peace, gentleness, and sound mind' out of the door. The client is then directed to close the door and bolt it. The client is then asked to visualise oil (the power of the Holy Spirit) pouring down over the door, sealing that stronghold completely. The person then may leave the house and return to their safe place, the therapist counting the client back from 10 to zero, with the message that they have overcome and gotten through this, and that they are free indeed.

The process is later repeated for every issue and life event that has been identified. The loose ends of all the cords are then tied to Peace, Joy, Love, Hope and the person visualises being washed with oil from head to toe. We don't provide the healing, God does through the Holy Spirit. The very clear point at which the person is reconnected to Jesus Christ concerns the process of breaking 'strongholds'.

As an Indigenous practitioner, I employ a Christian framework of healing while using this technique, but I also am aware of and adapt some principles of recent therapy for traumatic disorders, such as Affect Skills Management Training. PPS-ERT is not confined to Christian believers (though they may find it particularly compatible) and can be used regardless of the person's religious persuasion. It does require a trained and competent practitioner who has the discernment to deliver it. This technique should only be used by experienced practitioners and used with caution in areas of mental illness. It may not be regarded as suitable for all disorders. PPS-ERT is not a form of hypnosis. It is considered by some Christian Indigenous people who use it as a form of spiritual prayer counselling and breakthrough.

While our emotions bring richness to our lives, many times they don't fully resolve on their own. When they don't, their residual charge can diminish our health, emotional capacity and psychological ability, and affect our relationships. Through counselling we can help locate unresolved emotions and help the person to finally emotionally release them. Since emotional patterns are stored in the body, long-standing negatively charged emotional patterns can often deplete or weaken affected tissues. The counselling we use helps to promote healing and return of balance to a person's life (Crabb 1997).

Sometimes there is an unspoken assumption that Aboriginal Christians are not authentic Aboriginal people. However, because of the long presence of missions in Australia, Christianity is an integral element of identity for many Aboriginal people. Indeed, Queensland, particularly in the Far North, is continuing to produce numbers of Indigenous pastors and personnel in administrative positions within various churches. Aboriginal Christians can have a greater awareness of the spiritual world than many non-Aboriginal Christians because of their heritage and culture.

Using PPS-ERT has been highly effective in enabling me to work to help people overcome adversities. It requires an understanding of the psychological, physical and spiritual worlds and is used effectively by some Indigenous Christians, who are very comfortable with, and committed to, acknowledging and recognising the spiritual in our lives.

References
Brown, R. 1993, *He Came to Set the Captives Free*, Whitaker House, New Kensington, USA.

Campbell, K. 1996, *Those Ugly Emotions*, Christian Focus Publications, Tain Ross-shire, Scotland.

Crabb, L. 1997, *Connecting Healing for Ourselves and Our Relationships*, World Publishing, Tennessee, USA.

19
Socially engaged Buddhism
Subhana Barzaghi and Gillian Coote

. . . how small and interdependent our world has become . . . If we are to overcome the problems we face, we need what I have called a sense of universal responsibility rooted in love and kindness for our human brothers and sisters. In our present state of affairs, the very survival of humankind depends on people developing concern for the whole of humanity, not just their own community or nation (Dalai Lama).

Problems have become global in scope and yet we fail as a community to cultivate a unified global response. Engaged Buddhist practice attempts to cultivate this sense of 'universal responsibility' by acknowledging feelings of hopelessness and despair and finding the courage and compassion to face the suffering in the world. The aim of this engaging practice is to transform our suffering and despair and empower one another to take positive action. Various practitioners have demonstrated how one may take Buddhist practices into the community in a socially engaged way.

Engaged Buddhist philosophy and social action
'There is no way to Peace, Peace is the Way', expressed Robert Aitken (2005) of the heart of engaged Buddhism. This implies that one must *be* peace, embody peace, starting right here and now, then the way opens up to peace in our wider community and world. To be peaceful we must practise meditation, mindfulness, and cultivate the practice

of non-violence to end the war within our own hearts and minds and thus heal the divisions between them and us, you and me. A peaceful heart and mind is a grace upon this world and naturally engenders a respect and reverence for all life.

The heart of engaged Buddhism is founded on some key concepts and practices: the action-based understanding of the core teachings of the Four Noble Truths;[1] approaching suffering from the place of compassion; the way of non-violence; and a deepening realisation of our interconnectedness and oneness with all of life. These teachings lay the foundation for a socially engaged Buddhist peace movement and social service and have far-reaching implications for our spiritual practice.

The 2002 'World as Self' Zen retreat in Sydney was largely inspired by Zen master Bernie Glassman's street *sesshins* and peace work (Glassman 1994) as well as Joanna Macy's despair and empowerment work (Macy & Brown 1988). Glassman takes his students into situations where they can experience problems at first hand, into circumstances which they may first experience as overwhelming. For instance, he conducts *sesshins* (traditional Zen retreats, normally held in a remote, quiet monastery) on the streets of poor New York neighbourhoods, so that the retreatants live and meditate for a week on the street among the homeless. Glassman also conducts peace *sesshins* in Auschwitz; he invites people from all over the world to live in that most infamous camp, where they meditate on the suffering and evil it encapsulates, but also dig deeply into their own communal spiritual resources to overcome its radical evil.

The ultimate aim of these deeply challenging, engaged Buddhist retreats is to encourage people to relinquish the comfort of their familiar world-view, to broaden their minds and open their hearts. Glassman's peacemakers are continually making peace with themselves, their addictions and their families, and at the same time they work for peace in inner cities, troubled communities and war-torn countries. Their efforts provide lessons that apply to us all, ones we can put into practice in our daily lives.

The realisation of such interconnectedness and principles of non-violence distil the core teachings of Buddhism: each one of us participates in sentient life that is one seamless totality. The Venerable Thich Nhat Hanh gave sublime expression to this truth in his poem, 'Please call me by my True Name', written in 1978 while he was trying to help the boat people on the South China Sea. It emphasises the common humanity of perpetrators and victims: 'I am the twelve-year-old girl, refugee on a small boat, who throws herself in the ocean after being raped by a sea pirate, I am the pirate, my heart not yet capable of seeing and loving' (Hanh 1991: 123). His poem invites us to see the great river of pain underneath the many faces of humanity and keep the door of compassion open. If we nurture that compassion for the common humanity, we are working to overcome the self-perpetuating polarisation that leads to repeated alienation and atrocities.

The Venerable Maha Ghosananda, one of the few great Buddhist elders of Cambodia left after the carnage of the Pol Pot regime, en-capsulated in a simple statement the whole philosophy of the inter-connected relationship between the micro level and the macro level in overcoming war and human destructiveness. He was invited to New York by the United Nations. During his visit to America he spoke at a large rally on the steps of the White House to protest against the devas-tating effects of the land-mines in Cambodia. He had only these few words to say to that huge mass of people: 'You must dig up the land-mines not only on the outside but also on the inside'. Then he sat down, leaving the audience and press speechless and wondering what he meant.

Disarmament on the micro level and the macro level is one and the same process. The land-mines were put there by human hands and minds, where the challenge must be taken up. Our spiritual practice is to look deeply inside to dismantle the land-mines of greed, hatred and delusion to create true peace of mind.

An ancient twelfth century Tibetan Buddhist prophecy, the Shambhala Warrior prophecy, speaks about the challenges we face in these harsh times and the inspirations, compassion and courage we need in order to take wise and considerate action.

There comes a time when all life on Earth is in danger and great bar-barian powers have arisen. Although these powers spend their wealth in preparations to annihilate one another, they have much in common: weapons of unfathomable destructive power and technologies that lay waste our world. In this era, when the future of sentient life hangs by the frailest of threads, the kingdom of Shambhala emerges. You cannot go there, for it is not a place, it is not a geopolitical entity. It exists in the hearts and minds of the Shambhala warriors . . . Nor can you recognise a Shambhala warrior when you see her or him, for they wear no uniforms or insignia, and they carry no banners. They have no barricades on which to climb to threaten the enemy, or behind which they can hide to rest or regroup. They do not even have any home turf. Always they must move on the terrain of the barbarians themselves.

Now the time comes when great courage, moral and physical courage, is required of the Shambhala warriors, for they must go into the very heart of the barbarian power, into the pits and pockets and citadels where the weapons are kept, to dismantle them. To dismantle weapons, in every sense of the word, they must go into the corridors of power where decisions are made. Shambhala warriors have the courage to do this because they know that these weapons are *manomaya*. They are 'mind-made'. Made by the human mind, they can be unmade by the human mind. The Shambhala warriors know that the dangers threatening life on Earth are not visited upon us by any . . . extraterrestrial power, satanic deities or preordained evil fate. They arise from our own decisions, our own lifestyles and our own relationships. So at this time, the Shambhala warrior goes into training . . . in the use of two weapons. The weapons are compassion and insight (Macy & Brown 1998: 60–1).

Our spiritual practice, like that of the Shambhala Warriors, is to cultivate the primary tools of wisdom and compassion. Both are necessary; one without the other is not enough. Compassion is the passion and willingness to embrace the suffering and pain of the one and many and respond to alleviate that suffering. Wisdom is to see into the nature of reality and realise this profound interdependence with all phenomena that breaks down the divisions between self and other.

When wisdom and compassion correctly correspond, they are good medicine for healing ourselves and our planet and can sustain us as agents of change. To extend an open hand, an open eye, to hear the voice of pain across the world rise out of your own throat and your own heart is to reach across the abyss of race, religion and difference and close the gap between self and other. This is the spirit of the Shambhala Warrior.

Joanna Macy suggests that our Western psychology tends to reduce our pain, depression or anger about the state of the world to the level of personal maladjustment:

> This leads people to suppose that feelings of personal despair must be resolved and eradicated before feelings of social despair and action can be considered legitimate. This notion that one must find enlightenment, undergo transformation, or get one's head straight first, before dealing with social despair, keeps many otherwise intelligent people in a state of moral infantilism (Macy & Brown 1998: 67).

The Truth Mandala

'Though the many beings are numberless, I vow to save them' is the first of the Four Great Vows of Mahayana Buddhism. It is the vow of Avalokitesvara, the Bodhisattva of Compassion, who hears the sounds of the world—the crying and the laughing—and who responds freely. We become Avalokitesvara, the embodiment of compassion, when we can listen to the sounds of the world with our heart-minds open.

Over the past years, we have seen cruelty meted out to asylum seekers, the slow build-up to war, the debate around its morality and legality and the subsequent bombing, looting and chaos that continues in Iraq. Afghanistan and Palestine are among many other sites of violence and oppression. The images of starving children confront us daily.

How do we clear our minds of their preconceptions so that we can respond, can take responsibility for what we have seen and heard? Truth mandalas arise in times of need. It is a Buddhist practice that enables us to name the many aspects of the suffering we have witnessed.

In our current times we need to bear witness and speak out against injustice or else suffer the destructive consequences of silence.

Joanna Macy, realising the need for a respectful group structure for owning and honouring suffering, provided a means for its expression with her Truth Mandalas. Macy's Truth Mandalas have been offered all over the world, both in engaged Buddhist retreats and as one-off events at times of crisis.

The guide sets the scene and explains the process. People form a circle, enclosing a sacred space divided into four quadrants each holding a symbolic object: a stone for fear; dry leaves for grief; a stick for anger; an empty bowl for the sense of hopelessness and empty despair. In the centre is a cushion for those feelings that don't fit any of these symbolic quadrants.

One by one, as the time feels right, people step into the Truth Mandala and speak from the heart, taking hold of whatever object resonates—holding the stick as they speak their anger, shuffling the dry leaves as they weep for the suffering of asylum seekers. Those seated in the circle practise deep listening to what is voiced, weeping with their friends for all those beings in need and suffering, feeling the fear being spoken. There is no obligation to enter the Truth Mandala but somehow, as people listen deeply to others, there is a connection with their own buried feelings, and their words rise up from their hearts and join the mandala of truth.

When everybody who wishes to has spoken, the guide explains that each symbol has its ground in profoundly humanitarian feelings: the grief that has been heard arises from compassion and love for what is being lost; the fear from the courage to act; the anger from a passion for social justice, and the empty bowl from the space with the potential for new growth. The guide acknowledges the sacredness of these feelings; they all arise from love for the world and its many beings.

The power of the Truth Mandala lies in our willingness to speak our pain, and our willingness to hear others' pain. This requires trust that we won't be belittled or discredited, that this is a safe place. Some of us are fortunate to belong to communities such as a community of Buddhist practitioners where vulnerability is possible. The Truth Mandala is a key that unlocks our hearts and shows us we are not alone, that we are inter-connected beings, paving the way for compassionate action, freeing us to respond to suffering wherever it arises.

Socially engaged Buddhist retreats harness wise and compassionate action in the world. The 'World as Self' retreat held at Sydney Zen Centre in 2002 emphasised taking one's meditation practice from the cushion to the streets. It focused on learning to apply and embody the teachings of peace, compassion and insight to the very activities of daily life. Morning meditation was followed by afternoon voluntary community-based activities. These ranged from visiting refugees at Villawood Detention Centre, bush regeneration work at the Field of Mars, gardening work for the local communal garden in Annandale, the citizen-willing-to-listen project at Martin Place, a despair and empowerment ritual.

Socially engaged Buddhism helps to dispel any notion of a separate (and therefore alienated) self and fosters care for our interconnected world. People were making powerful choices that will create a difference in their own lives and those of others. In the final analysis, the cycle of hopelessness can only be ended by changing our frames of reference, looking deeply into our own hearts and minds and making radically different choices for action.

Endnote

1. The Four Noble Truths: 1. There is suffering in this life; 2. The cause of suffering is desire, hatred and ignorance; 3. There is liberation from suffering; 4. The eightfold path leads to liberation and a wholesome life.

References

Aitken, Robert, <http://www.bpf.org/html/whats_now/2005/iraq> (accessed May 2006)

His Holiness the Dalai Lama, <http://www.purifymind.com/DalaiLama.html> (accessed May 2006)

Glassman, B. 1994, *Bearing Witness: A Zen Master's Lessons in Making Peace*, Bell Tower, New York.

Hanh, T.H. 1991, *Peace is Every Step: The Path of Mindfulness in Everyday Life*, Bantam Books, New York.

Hong Kingston, M. 1980, *China Men*, 1st edn, Knopf, New York, reissued Vintage Books, 1989.

Macy J. 1983, *Despair and Personal Power in the Nuclear Age*, New Society Publishers, British Columbia.

Macy J. and Brown, M. 1998, *Coming Back to Life: Practices to Reconnect our Lives, our World*, New Society Publishers, British Columbia.

20
Wiccan spiritual practice
Douglas Ezzy

In the passage of the seasons 'we see reflected our own lives, and the lives of our gods' (Phillips & Phillips 1994: 65).

Despite the historical suspicion and prejudice about Witchcraft there are a surprising number of practitioners of various forms of Witchcraft in Western countries. Given the strong tradition of secrecy in the craft, a client may be reluctant to self-identify as a Witchcraft/Wicca practitioner to a human services professional. Yet encouraging such clients to tap into the resources of their craft for support, solace and guidance at a time of need, in a non-judgmental fashion, can be enormously helpful to them. This chapter provides some general background to help dispel misunderstandings.

The primary aim of many people's practice of Witchcraft is self-development (Greenwood 2000). This is clear in the early popular books on Witchcraft (Ravenwolf 1993) and even more so in more recent books (Monaghan 2001). The spells in these books mostly use basic household items such as perfumes, essential oils, herbs, candles, string and paper. These are combined with various techniques for focusing the mind, visualisations and short incantations, typically of a few lines or so. They are often timed to the phases of the moon or day of the week and use a variety of sensual cues such as flower petals, burning candles, tying knots or planting seeds. The spell-books focus on providing techniques for managing emotions such as love, depression, disappointment, desire, fear and anxiety, and techniques for working with emotional and interpersonal issues (Ezzy 2003b).

During the 1990s Witchcraft exploded into mainstream culture with movies such as *The Craft*, television shows such as *Buffy* and *Charmed* and a plethora of mainstream books on Witchcraft aimed at a younger audience, such as those by Ravenwolf (1993). The growth of the Internet provided young people with easy access to information about Witchcraft and also provided Witches with ways of networking while still remaining relatively anonymous. The positive images of Witches in the mainstream media and in the books available in mainstream stores provided young people who were 'seeking' with the resources to begin to practise Witchcraft on their own (Berger & Ezzy 2004).

The most common stories of conversion to Witchcraft describe a young person looking for a spiritual practice (Berger & Ezzy 2004). They see a movie or a television show and begin to think about Witchcraft. They search for more information and begin to practise on their own, often without having ever met another Witch. Witches do not proselytise. Older Witches will often send away young people who approach them to learn about Witchcraft. In Australia there are various pagan organisations, such as the Pagan Alliance and the Pagan Awareness Network, and information about these can be easily found on the Internet. (Paganism is a general term referring to a variety of new religious traditions, including Witchcraft.) These Pagan organisations mainly facilitate networking and information exchange. They do not prescribe beliefs or practices, while membership is inexpensive and does not require any active participation.

Case study
Kaldera is an 18-year-old university student who lives in Sydney, Australia. She attended a Catholic school and became interested in Witchcraft when she was 15 years old.

Kaldera: 'Well, at that time [when I first became interested in Witchcraft] one of our friends died. There was a lot of searching for answers why it happened. I was having a lot of trouble at home as well and I felt as though I wanted something that I could express myself in. Because I was at a Catholic school I found going to classes that had to do with religion that I just wasn't ever satisfied with it. When I was just reading all the information that I found on the computer and in books about Paganism I was like—oh I understand it. Like I could relate to it and it helped me through, I guess, grieving for my friend. There are lots of different things [that helped, such as] meditation and letting people pass over. It was a way of relaxing myself. Just a way of settling myself. It was an explanation for me to understand everything that I was going through and I found it helped a lot.

I think really my friend's death was more a starting point for me as well . . . Because I was really depressed about it obviously. [I was thinking] 'Oh, what's the point of living really if you just end like that.' I wasn't suicidal or anything, it just really made me think—like question every single thing that happened. Like is there a reason behind that or did it just happen or is there a reason for that? Did something make that happen? I guess [my friend's death] was a starting point for me to realise that there aren't just those religions that you're always constantly hearing about. There are other names for what you already do.

Witchcraft, or Wicca (the terms are used interchangeably), is a contemporary religious tradition that began in the 1950s in England (Ezzy 2003a), when Gerald Gardner claimed to have been initiated into an ongoing coven and later began initiating others into his own coven (http://www.geraldgardner.com). From there Witchcraft spread by books and personal networks, but remained relatively small until the early 1990s.

The growth of Witchcraft in Australia is reflected in the rising popularity of the magazine *Witchcraft*, now a bi-monthly publication distributed in mainstream newsagencies. The first article in the first edition of *Witchcraft*, the introductory letter, begins like this: 'Blessed be. Welcome to *Witchcraft*, a magazine for all those interested in this way of life; a way that practises respect for nature, the belief in self-determination, the courage to use your will and the respect of womancraft' (Cavendish 1994: 4). These three characteristics, a focus on self-determination, nature and the celebration of femininity, are representative of the beliefs and practices of Witches.

The popularity of the spell-books that contain rituals such as the following mirror ritual suggested by Monaghan (2001) can be seen as a consequence of the many issues and challenges faced by young people in contemporary society:

> Set up a mirror so that you can look into it comfortably. Put a candle beneath or next to it and light it. Then look into your face in the mirror. Look into your own eyes. As you do so, imagine that you are giving yourself unconditional love. Do not let any negative or critical thoughts intrude on this sacred moment. When you have finished, blow out the candle while wishing yourself a good morning or evening (Monaghan 2001: 81).

As Eckersley (2004) has noted, there is an 'emergence of a sense of hopelessness among young people'; while some are thriving on the rapid change and uncertainty of our times, others 'are anxious and apprehensive' (Eckersley 2004: 150). While the spell-books of popular Witchcraft often focus on relationships, they also include rituals for dealing with self-image (such as the mirror ritual above), death and loss, depression and finding work. The stereotypical love spell, while popular as a trinket spell-box, actually appears to be quite rare among the more serious practitioners of Witchcraft that I have interviewed. Rather, the focus of most young Witches is on re-creating themselves, finding hope and a direction for their life.

In research with 90 teenage Witches in Australia, America and Britain (Berger & Ezzy, forthcoming), three important things emerged that are relevant here. First, Witchcraft provides a ritual way of coming to terms with a variety of often difficult and confronting issues such as the death of a friend, a significant illness, tensions with parents or a relationship break-up. The meditation techniques and magical spells young Witches learn from books and the Internet provide them with a way of processing the thoughts and feelings generated by these experiences. Second, the exploration of Witchcraft is typically motivated by a personal search for a better way of making sense of their life. While the mass media makes the resources available, most Witches come to Witchcraft through an active process of seeking. Finally, for many people, the Witchcraft rituals work. One of the reasons for the popularity of Witchcraft is that it provides a way of finding hope, of making sense of difficult situations and helpful in processing emotions. Leaving questions of the 'truth' of religious claims aside, it is clear that contemporary Witchcraft is assisting many young people to successfully address some of the challenging issues that confront them.

Interdependence of humanity and nature

'Wicca sees a profound relationship between humanity and the environment; for a Wiccan, all of nature is a manifestation of the divine and so we celebrate the turning seasons as the changing faces of our gods' (Phillips & Phillips 1994: 65). The centrality of nature to Witchcraft is perhaps best illustrated by the ritual calendar that most Witches follow. This is called the wheel of the year and involves eight festivals. This ritual calendar follows nature's cycle of life, death and rebirth as it celebrates the transitions in and out of the seasons of spring, summer, autumn and winter.

The two major festivals are those of Samhain, at the end of April in Australia, and Beltane, at the end of October (as the seasons are reversed in the northern and southern hemispheres, so are the ritual calendar dates). Samhain is a festival of the dead, when those who have died are remembered and people reflect on their own mortality. Beltane is a festival of fertility and new life. This is seen in the traditional Easter imagery (which occurs around about the same time as Beltane in the northern hemisphere) of bunnies and eggs, symbols of fertility that fit well with the season of spring in the northern hemisphere but do not really make much sense during autumn in Australia.

The rituals that celebrate the festivals vary considerably in structure. Some young Witches may simply light a candle and meditate for a few minutes on the changing of the seasons. At the other end of the spectrum are large organised festivals such as the well-established Beltane gathering in a country location near Melbourne. This ritual often attracts over a hundred people, who stay at a local campground for the festival. The main ritual involves casting a circle around which incense, salt and water and a consecrated knife are carried. The four directions of north, south, east and west are then acknowledged, and a ritual bonfire lit in the middle of the circle with much celebration. After this the ritual may involve reciting sacred poetry or the re-enactment of a Pagan myth. Toward the ritual's end wine and cakes are consecrated and shared around the circle and the ritual may be finished with a spiral dance. While there are serious moments, there is often much laughter and celebration. Afterwards it is customary for people to jump over the bonfire and everyone joins in a shared feast that lasts well into the small hours of the night. This ritual is an example of how Witchcraft affirms humans' profound connection with all life and change, including loss and death as well as flourishing, new beginnings and new life. The sense of spiritual connectedness with the cycles of nature is at the heart of Witchcraft practice.

Celebration of femininity

In a similar manner to the celebration of nature, the following account of a first menstruation ritual illustrates how Wiccan practitioners may deal with a transition. Menstruation is celebrated and affirmed. Bodies are valued and cherished as reflections of the Goddess.

In early 1990 six women gather around a small table in a suburban Australian home. They have been meeting regularly for a few months to celebrate the full moon as part of their desire to rediscover a feminist spirituality. At this particular meeting they decide to ritualise their monthly passing of blood. They begin by recounting their own stories of their first menstruation:

> Our experiences are tellingly perforated with memories of shame and guilt: of mothers exhorting young daughters to clean up after them-selves . . . Some women around the table, who are only in their early 30s, knew nothing of bleeding until the moment it began; some women thought they were bleeding from a wound; others were lucky enough to find out from school friends; others were so baffled they kept it a secret in case of punishment . . . As each woman shares her story, the effects of years of silence, of loss and grief, of profound cultural displacement, are overwhelming. Everyone is crying (McPhillips 2003: 71).

Six years later the same group of women, and a few others, gather in a
suburban house in an Australian city with five of their daughters, aged
between eleven and thirteen. They are there to celebrate the first
menstruation of one of the young girls (McPhillips 2003). The girls
wait outside as the women organise the ritual inside the house. They
decorate a room with poetry and stories about their own menstruation
experiences, then retreat to a nearby bedroom where they cast a Wiccan
circle and call on the Goddess to be present. The young girl enters the
first room and reads the texts, then opens the door into the bedroom
and joins in the ritual with her mother's generation for the first time.
The ritual is both a joyous celebration of her womanhood and a serious
moment to reflect on their own traumas in the past.

In contrast to the older women's experiences of fear and grief, the
first menstruation ritual encourages the young girl to see her body as
holy and sacred. The older women read her a story of a Goddess 'whose
monthly flow created rivers and oceans', and describe the blessings that
menstruation makes possible, such as having children and maturation
into womanhood (McPhillips 2003: 84). For these women Goddess
spirituality and Witchcraft provide a ritual spiritual practice that
celebrates their femininity and their bodies. They emphasise their
power and ability to 'flourish' and celebrate life-affirming identities
as women.

Not all Witchcraft is feminist and most Witches practise on their
own, but this story of a first menstruation ritual beautifully illustrates
the primary reason that many young, and older, people are seeking out
Witchcraft as a spiritual tradition. Witchcraft provides a set of ritual
techniques for transforming feelings and self-understanding. Relationships with boyfriends or girlfriends are understood as sacred
relationships, about which one can talk to the Goddess or God.
Feelings of loss or depression are addressed as part of life, with Witchcraft providing ritual techniques for making sense of these feelings.
These are but a few examples of how Witchcraft rituals are providing
techniques for many people to find hope and purpose.

In contemporary Western societies new religious movements
such as Witchcraft are often treated with suspicion. This suspicion is

typically unfounded (Ireland 1999). Illegal activities such as sexual abuse are no more or less common among Witches than in the Christian churches, or any other walk of life, for that matter. There is very little that is dangerous in the practice of contemporary Witchcraft; while some of the language and practice may be surprising, and sometimes strange, the vast majority of Witches, particularly young Witches, are engaged in a religious practice that is positive, life-affirming and provides them with a sense of hope and purpose in life.

This is beautifully illustrated by the opening of Fiona Horne's book *7 Days to a Magickal New You*:

> This book is a guide to giving yourself a magickal makeover . . . you can unveil your hidden powers, fire up your focus and launch into the rest of your life in an empowered and vibrant way (Horne 2001: 2).

References

Berger, H.A. and Ezzy, D. 2004, 'The Internet as virtual spiritual community: Teen witches in the United States and Australia', in L.L. Dawson and D.E. Cowan (eds), *Religion Online: Finding Faith on the Internet*, Routledge, New York.

Berger, H. and Ezzy, D. (forthcoming), *Teenage Witchcraft*, Rutgers University Press, New Brunswick.

Cavendish, L. 1994, 'Introduction to Witchcraft', *Witchcraft*, no. 1, pp. 4–5.

Eckersley, R. 2004, *Well and Good: How We Feel and Why it Matters*, Text Publishing, Melbourne.

Ezzy, D. 2003a, 'New Age Witchcraft?', *Culture and Religion*, vol. 4, no. 1, pp. 47–66.

Ezzy, D. 2003b, 'What is a Witch?', in D. Ezzy (ed.), *Practising the Witch's Craft*, Allen & Unwin, Sydney, pp. 1–22.

Gardner, G., <http://www.geraldgardner.com> (accessed May 2006)

Greenwood, S. 2000, *Magic, Witchcraft and the Otherworld*, Berg, Oxford.

Horne, F. 2001, *7 Days to a Magickal New You!*, Random House Australia, Sydney.

Ireland, R. 1999, 'Religious diversity in a new Australian democracy', *Australian Religion Studies Review*, vol. 12, no. 2, pp. 94–110.

McPhillips, K. 2003, 'Feminist spirituality and the power of ritual', in D. Ezzy (ed.), *Practising the Witch's Craft*, Allen & Unwin, Sydney, pp. 70–87.

Monaghan, P. 2001, *The Pagan of the Young Goddess: Wild Girls*, Llewellyn, St Paul, Minnesota.

Phillips, M. and Phillips, J. 1994, *The Witches of Oz*, Capall Bann Publishing, Chieveley, Berks.

Ravenwolf, S. 1993, *To Ride a Silver Broomstick*, Llewellyn, St Paul, Minnesota.

Transitions

21
Rituals as a support for the life journey

Dorothy McRae-McMahon

So, why would a ritual add to anyone's life? At its best, a ritual is a marking of a person's journey which tells them that it is significant, not something to be glossed over as though it doesn't matter. It can respect a hugely significant event which may otherwise take place as though nothing has happened. For example, donating an organ to another or receiving one—these momentous and ambiguous events are usually seen as a good thing for those concerned but not worthy of further attention. Again, very often when women miscarry, even at a late stage in a pregnancy, some people expect them to simply move on and forget it.

A ritual can be a gathering-up of a special life moment—about having someone to take you through a caring journey of reflection when much of the rest of the world does not seem to have noticed the significance of a particular time in your life. Sometimes it can be about daring to believe that others could love us as ordinary stumbling members of the human race—a laying down of long-held guilt or regret in a way which can be far more powerful than simply talking about it with another person.

A ritual can be about giving due respect to deep pain or grief, or marking a moment of celebration in a way which goes beyond simply having a party. It can be setting aside a special time to stop and reflect by ourselves on what is happening to us and how we are feeling.

Many people these days suffer from a lack of ritual in their lives. Sometimes this is because, in the past, religious institutions carried this part of their life and they have become alienated from that source. Often it is because the culture to which we belong has lost some of its old rituals or never had many. Of course, for some people rituals are not helpful at all, for they carry old and painful memories or are simply irrelevant.

You do not need to have a special role such as pastoral care work to use rituals. If you, in any sort of support role, feel that a ritual may add to someone's life journey then it is obviously critical to explore carefully what such an experience may mean to the person. I usually do this by telling a story of a ritual in which I have participated and waiting respectfully for any response before I venture any further. Sometimes you can share your thoughts about finding it hard to say what we would really like to say to a person when life is tough or sad, and how it is often helpful to do that in a ritual. If the person doesn't respond, no problem. If they seem interested, press on.

Sometimes people respond to the idea of a personal meditation on their situation—a bit like taking themselves through a ritual alone. You might offer them some ideas on which they might focus during the meditation. You can indicate that you have written down these thoughts as a sort of tribute to their journey.

People who have no connection with organised religion can still value significant and appropriate rituals, even though they find it hard to find words and symbols for themselves. It is my view that many people long to connect with their spirituality, even though they are alienated from organised religion, and I like to respect that.

One of the strengths of rituals lies in their structured style. We are given boundaries for the entry into our grief and pain and a special solemn joy in celebration. People who feel that if they begin to cry they may never stop are often given a sense of security by the formality and dignity of a ritual, and by the fact that someone else is in charge and will take them through certain processes with clarity and responsibility.

Some thoughts on using rituals

The use of symbols or symbolic acts is very powerful; they are often the part of a ritual which people long remember. However, more symbols and more symbolic acts do not necessarily add power to the occasion. Their overuse can become cluttered and gimmicky. It is critical to keep things clear and simple.

Don't force people to be more intimate than they find comfortable—for example, not everyone wants to hold hands or give hugs. If you want to give a sign that people are there supporting each other, it is wiser to suggest that they may touch each other's shoulders. It is better to err on the side of careful boundaries. On the other hand, be confident in naming with care and dignity the pain or grief that is present.

Anyone can be chosen to lead a ritual. Sometimes the ritual may be initiated by someone like a chaplain, counsellor or member of staff and that person may choose to lead. In other circumstances, a person or group may invite a friend or family member to lead.

Often, as with a funeral, it is good to have someone just a little distanced from the situation or person concerned as they are not so emotionally involved. Having said that, never under-estimate the surprising calm and strength that can be present when you are taking on a significant responsibility.

It is good to be warm in leading a ritual but also observe a certain formality which gives the occasion a special significance and dignity. This is not the occasion for 'chatting' in ways which draw attention to yourself, but for a respectful and deep invitation into spaces and moments for another's journeying.

Planning a ritual

Ask yourself, 'Who is the ritual really for?' Sometimes, as with a funeral, it is important to have this clear. A funeral rite is not only for the person who has died but is also for those who suffer loss. Even among those who suffer the loss, there may be different categories—the family who knew the person in a particular way, friends who had another experience and possibly others who knew the one who died in quite different ways. So it is with any ritual—there are different players in the situation.

Who will be there? Is this a private, semi-private or public moment in someone's life? The ritual will have more power if there are at least a few trusted people there as they act as both the 'witnesses' and the community which affirms this moment as significant and supports the person for their future.

Where will it be held? Imagine the spot and note its possibilities for creating the required atmosphere, to become what is a 'sacred space'. Is it a place which is loved by the person concerned or one with which there are special connections?

What are the elements you wish to include in the ritual?
I like to draw on the traditional liturgical patterns of the church as they contain the basic elements for any ritual, which can be adapted according to the circumstances. It is usually helpful to include something like the following:

- The welcome and stating of purpose: We are all here together to . . .
- Something which sets the scene and creates the atmosphere.
- A naming of the situation and expression of how that feels, including the doubts and fears and pain.
- Something which places that in a wider context, such as a reading, story, reflection, symbolic act.
- A naming of our hopes and affirmations about life in general and this life in particular.
- A refocusing on the central person which offers her/him a new possibility and is expressed in some clear way.
- A surrounding of the person with the community of that moment, symbols of shared humanity and possible giving of a memento. It is often good during the ritual to present the one or those who are the focus of the ritual with something to take away from the occasion as a reminder of the event, perhaps a candle, flask of sweet smelling oil, cloth, small glass or cup.
- Sending out or blessing. The sending out is an affirmation that we are always on a journey to somewhere and you can use your imagination in doing this.

What symbols, symbolic acts or enhancing of the environment would give power to this ceremony? A few clear simple things are more powerful than lots of bits and pieces. You really need no more than cloths, stones, wood, leaves, flowers, earth, water and candles, primal symbols that cover virtually everything.

It is often helpful to hold to a theme, such as:

- Water—which can express tears as well as healing, refreshing, the source of growth for newness.
- Seeds—which can die if unwatered, lie buried waiting to grow, be nurtured and cherished in order to bring forth new life or to blossom as flowers.
- Stones—which can be both the hard things we face, but can be held in the hand and warmed and become part of the pathway into the future.

Creating the wording 'structure' for the ritual

Take each section and put down ideas, images, phrases which seem important. If you do this, it is easier to avoid cliché-ridden phrases than if you initially write the sentences in full. If you are working with others in producing the ritual, ask them to offer words and phrases as you focus on each theme and bring those all together in a draft.

Don't forget a comfortable ending. A powerful event with no helpful exit can feel quite difficult. It has all been very moving and special, so what do you do at the end? That depends on the context, but the leader needs to make the move. Sometimes you can put on some gentle music and invite people to move away quietly or invite them to share coffee or a drink together.

Possible occasions for a ritual

- When a family needs a way to farewell someone before they slip into a coma.
- When a person wants to say sorry to someone who has died.
- When a space has become associated with grief and pain and needs to be 'healed'.

- When people are separated from others when a funeral is being held.
- When someone needs to be placed into care and people are feeling anxious or guilty about that.
- When someone has experienced a miscarriage; there is no funeral for this ending of a beginning of life.
- When someone is giving or receiving an organ donation.

Example of a ritual: *Disposal of ashes*

Preparation
- Discuss where you would like the ashes to be placed—in some spot which is special for you or for the one who has died.
- Decide who is to lead the brief ceremony and what you want to remember about the person who has died.
- Discuss whether you want to bury the ashes or disperse them somewhere.

Opening
> We have come here today
> to lay to rest the ashes of our friend and loved one (Name)
> We choose this place with loving care.
> It is a sacred place for us (or the person concerned) because . . .
> Here we will remember a life which is lost to us
> and which we will always remember.
> Here we will create a memory for cherishing
> and a place which will be like a loving hand
> beneath this life which has gone from us.

The remembering
> Before we dispose of these precious ashes,
> let us each say one word which reminds us
> of our family member and/or friend.
> *The ashes are held up and each person says their word.*

The sending out
> We now send/bury these ashes to join universal life.

For burial
(Either have a small hole prepared or carefully dig one as part of the ceremony.)
Here in the earth,
which is gentle with us at the time of our death,
these ashes will be cooled in the winter and warmed in the summer.
Here the earth will gather around in comfort and grateful receiving,
as the cycling of life and energy is renewed.
Here will lie in peace all that has gone before,
united with the dignity of all existence.
The ashes are placed and gently covered with earth and flowers.

For a dispersal in water
(Be careful about winds and plan for a sheltered spot or wait for a calm day.)
Here life joins life in the waters of the earth,
flowing on in creative energy,
sometimes peaceful and sometimes with the joy of movement
and following the calling of winds and tides.
Here our loved one is held in a gentle hand
which will carry her/him on,
moving into newness and journeying on into another future.
The ashes are scattered into the river or sea.

The sending
We send (Name) into universal life.
Go in peace and with our love surrounding you.
Stay here in memories for us,
but never bound by what has gone before,
for you are now free to be part of all that lives.
Your spirit will travel on with us
and we will greet you with delight in many moments.
Let us also leave here in peace,
believing that we have truly honoured (Name).
Amen.

Meditation
Sometimes a meditation is simpler and more helpful for a person—
something created and quietly read to the person concerned or offered

to them for their reading. Here is an example of that approach, remembering the donation of an organ by someone you love.

A meditation
I will remember you with love as you lived—
part of my life, part of my loving.
I see you now, whole and breathing,
your body carrying your mind and heart and soul,
uniquely with us,
all with us,
changing us because you were among us,
important to us.
Reflection.

For those who live with the decision of the donor
I will remember you with love
even as you decided to give this gift from yourself,
this gift of yourself.
My heart wonders whether you ever knew what it would mean?
My soul cries a little,
because sometimes it feels that we lost a part of you somewhere,
even as we honour your offering of life to another.
Sometimes the images of that gap in your body are painful to me.
Sometimes I wanted to say 'No!' and, 'Have you thought of us?'

On some days I wonder whether the one who now lives through
you is grateful enough.
I want that person and those who love that person to be very, very
grateful
and I will never know whether they are, or not.
But, deep down, I believe that they are grateful,
that your gift was received with tears of hope.

There are days when I look at people as they walk by me
and ask myself, 'Could it be that person?
Does that person look worthy of a special gift?
Is this person different because you lived and died?'
I am not sure that I want to know
because I would be tempted to see if I like them.
I remember your kindness of heart and the essence of you

which still lives on complete in some sure way,
the gap in your body filled by the grace of your soul.
I know you did it for yourself, your own completeness of living.
I try to hold to that.
I do try to hold to that as you call me to do.
Reflection.

For those who made the decision on behalf of the donor
Engrained in my heart and mind forever
will live the moment of decision to give part of you to another.
In our time of loss it eased us a little to know
that something of you had the power to survive and to bring life to
another.
And yet, in the deeps of the night the murky fears visit me still—
Were you really dead?
What if there was the possibility of some miracle
waiting around the next corner
and we denied you that deliverance?
What if your soul was still attached to your body
and felt a violation as part of you was taken,
and you knew we had asked that of you?
What if you live on in another place, another generation,
and will always long for what is no longer there for you?
What if you never forgive us for doing this to you,
because you would have chosen differently?
Sometimes this is added to my grieving for you,
the one I loved,
added like a weight.
And then I remember who you were
and who we were together
and I hold on to that
Because you lived with generosity,
you related to us with grace in life
I will trust that you will not have changed in death.
This I believe. This I will believe.
Reflection.

So, how will I hold you now?
How will I see you in my mind's eye?
How will I carry you on into the future?
Reflection.

I will remember you with love as you died—
still part of my life, part of my loving.
I see you now as I saw you then,
as you moved into the mystery of spaces beyond my reaching,
except as I remember you in my heart,
except as I feel the loss of you in life and the pain of you in death.
Reflection.

I will remember you with honour
as your body gives life to another,
life which cost you some of yourself,
life which gives a gracious gift in the face of death.
Reflection.

I will restore your wholeness on this day.
I will bring you into a healed place in my heart and soul,
holding you again with me, cradling your life in mine.
Your body is transformed in the universal creation
of giving new life from the earth, from the fire, from the waters,
from the mystery of the seed
which breaks open and gives as it dies to itself.
Reflection.

You are never lost to me.
You are never less than yourself to me.
You are the grace which offers to us all
a vision of the generosity, the loving kindness,
the faithful commitment to a human community
which is carried into eternity.
Reflection.

I will remember you.

Engaging in a care-giving ritual is in some senses an ultimate test of our
own faith, no matter what that faith rests on. Especially if it is any sort
of healing ritual—healing of grief, of fear, of guilt—or a ritual specifically designed to bring about change, we are likely to feel very
vulnerable. It is like being anxious about praying for healing in case
people feel betrayed when they can see nothing predictable happening

in response. It is good to own this. From my experience, I am absolutely convinced of the power and good which can flow from such an event; the ways it can join people and at the same time confirm their value. A ritual is almost always an occasion when someone or some people are gathered around our lives in a way which tells us that our life matters and that we are gathered into human community.

22
Psychotherapy

Lorraine Rose

When our life is not moving, when we stumble over and over and we see that we are stuck, how do we relate to this experience of feeling stuck? Looking at it this way is where psychotherapy can become a spiritual practice (LeCussans)

As a student at a Catholic convent school, I embraced that religion as a source of making sense of my life. After becoming a clinical psychologist I worked intensively with people who did not have such secure attachment. The following reflections arise from my experience as a therapist and a patient. The use of the word 'we' often signals the collaborative enterprise between the two that animates and reveals humanity in the most difficult terrains and potentially links to all people.

Spirituality and the territory of therapy: a personal view

Spirituality is not a set of beliefs or dogmas and is not institutionalized religion . . . [rather] . . . Spirituality is connecting deeply to one's own creative source/soul/spirit and removing the obstacles that prevent us from recognizing . . . the ultimate values and concerns that give our life meaning (LeCussans 2006).

Spirituality is part of being human, so my clients/patients present me with their spiritual as well as their emotional, physical and thinking selves. To understand their needs, it is as if I have to expand to meet all these levels in the person who walks through the door. While I need to know how the spiritual self influences their everyday lives, I am not a spiritual adviser.

Spirituality is generally associated with 'higher things' (in terms of connecting with the highest ethical standards, ultimate reality and all humanity) but it is my view that a healthy spirituality depends on core physical and psycho-social needs being well enough met, especially early in life. Only when those aspects of our wellbeing are attended to will our spiritual practice be most fruitful. Likewise, I assume that for spirituality to flourish in those with relationship and 'self' problems, there needs to be some 'working through' these issues and new emotional experience. Often, but not exclusively, therapy is an arena in which this occurs.

Brain research now supports the notion that in order to develop the capacity to be aware of our feelings and have a mind that can think and reflect, we need someone available to us, enough of the time, and sufficiently attuned to our feelings, thoughts and wishes to become a secure, loving attachment figure. With this person we can find acceptance and develop our capacity to recognise and handle feelings and think, reflect and relate to others.

My initial task as therapist is, through thorough history-taking, to assess where the patient/client has received support and help in discovering who they are, where development proceeded well and where there are gaps, blocks, deprivations or processes that actively destroy their developing selves. We revisit the latter with the goal of reviving the 'unlively', 'deadened' parts. These difficulties may be hard to access. Often the body carries these lost memories, along with associations and dreams. They may also be opened up when both the therapist and client parties articulate what it is like being together.

This painful and sometimes hazardous process may reactivate past traumas and difficulties. By attending to the wounds, hurts and lacks of childhood, we may repair but not always remove injuries. Overwhelming feelings cannot be understood and processed unless another human being meets and understands the experience. Without such a meeting the baby/child can only dissociate from what is 'too much'. These arenas are places where endurance and strength are required on both sides.

There needs to be a sufficiently quiet inner space in the client and the therapist to make contact with these 'lost' experiences and to assess their impact on the personality. Hypervigilance, suspicion, self-preoccupation and protectiveness, even lies, may surface and will need to be patiently held and contained by the therapist in order to work through the blocks to real connection within the client and between therapist and client. The quiet space allows the attuned therapist to connect with the depths of the client's emotional state. This may be obscured from the client, at the time, because of the pain or trauma involved.

Inexplicable events can occur for which psychology does not always have an explanation. With one of my patients, who had suffered considerable and ongoing abuse at the hands of his parents, we found that whenever he was experiencing a very difficult emotional moment a couple of birds would come and sit just outside the window of my office. This was something I simply noticed and remarked on at the time. A few years into the therapy I moved offices, and the same client reached another point of dealing with traumatic material—and we saw identical-looking birds sitting on the fence outside the window! This event was noted. At particular points in our journeys unusual events can occur, which may not have an obvious cause but appear meaningfully related and may be ascribed spiritual significance. Such events may awaken us to the existence of realms beyond those which are rationally understood.

Spiritual 'direction' and the ends of therapy

Holding some notion of where we are going and what territory is to be opened up through therapy is important for the client's wellbeing and their spirit.

While we strive for meaning we also have to coexist with meaninglessness. The universe is not there just to give us a hard time, it is 'itself'. Yet we also can find that this impersonal universe is profoundly 'there' for us. The sun rises every day despite ourselves, fish live in the sea and nourishing food grows in the ground. This 'providence' does not allow for omnipotence because it acknowledges being part of something larger than ourselves, with mystery and unknowingness.

'Spirituality includes an enormous scope of awareness from which to view oneself' (LeCussans 2006). The therapeutic process can help develop a sense of perspective. When required, we observe the workings of our inner self to understand who we are, our motivations, needs and available choices. We may perceive our destiny: where our capacities can best be utilised for the greater good.

Spirituality, observes LeCussans, embodies practices of raising awareness to our interconnectedness with one another and all things. It involves connecting deeply with others and removing the obstacles that prevent us from connection. In embracing the differences and connections between ourselves and others and ourselves and matter, we also embrace life's paradoxes. What may originally be experienced as irreconcilable opposites are in fact complementary aspects of one reality: being in touch with ourselves is inclusive of being in touch with others and with the world.

In this context we develop a capacity for presence. We can be beyond time by being completely absorbed in what we do and can experience a moment of eternity. These experiences, often lasting for short periods, result from sustained effort to be mindful and to discover who we are, in many varied situations.

Compassion is a natural outcome of an experience of being sufficiently met, understood, known by someone else. It relates to our capacity to understand and empathise with the position of another human being. In seeking the greater good, true compassion is not a 'soft' state of mind. It discerns whether there is a need for understanding, sharing the pain, or confrontation.

Relinquishing the barrier between self and others may not be easily done, since we have spent years establishing a sense of who we are in relation to others; a deep unity with others without this boundary can appear threatening. We face the illusion that we have a self in opposition to a sense of communion with another. Yet it is possible to traverse this territory. The sense of identity is not threatened but expanded.

Having a global perspective requires a particular kind of 'love'. At this point we do not love the other because they love us, affirm us, reflect or secure us in our illusion but because they are who they are. The good of the other is what we want, not what it can do for us. At this point love becomes less ambivalent, passing beyond being a means, becoming an end and delighting in the thing itself.

Having worked towards finding the quiet inner space inside myself and those with whom I work, and clearing the static that gets in the way of that inner peace, I accept that we reach a point where spirit can flourish. The pain, suffering, hurt and rage that has been endured ultimately connects us to the human experience of all other human beings and to the joy of living.

We are, then, not just looking at the world through our own eyes but through the eyes of the collective human spirit!

Reference

LeCussans, <http://www.centerforpsycheandspirit.com> (accessed 13 October 2006)

23
Buddhist and Christian paths to healing

Michael Wearing

Christ—like Buddha—is an embodiment of self, but in an altogether different sense. Both stood for an overcoming of the world: Buddha out of rational insight; Christ as a foredoomed sacrifice. In Christianity more is suffered, in Buddhism more is seen and done (Jung 1962: 309).

Each person can cultivate a psychological 'depth and wholeness' through grounded spiritual practices, argues Catholic psychotherapist Thomas Moore (1992). All human beings have a faith or set of values, beliefs and practices that can be said to deepen meaning in our lives and enhance our spiritual wellbeing. The wellbeing of people and communities can be grounded in the great wisdom and potential for healing available in long-standing religions such as Christianity and Buddhism. These religious traditions offer, I believe, intricate and sustainable frameworks on humanness and healing in society.

Multiple sources of Eastern and Western spiritual practices can be drawn upon to enhance a person's spiritual wellbeing and this should be encouraged in the helping professions. Both Buddha and Jesus lived out subversive stances to the dominant norms and morals of each era and their actions were often counter-intuitive to what was expected by society. The salient images of Jesus as a redeemer, as a teacher and as opposed to injustice and of Buddha as serene, peaceful, compassionate and wise are powerful qualities that we can follow in our own lives. We can also, in more complex ways, use such qualities both with the oppressed and with perpetrators of injustice.

This chapter briefly addresses spiritual issues and practice in both Christianity and Buddhism to assist the reader in understanding and acting upon some of the painful experiences that can occur in major life transitions and the spiritual crises that might accompany these transitions. Carl Jung's claim, quoted above, that Buddhism more completely understood the 'earthiness' of human experience than Christianity, is a useful initial distinction between the two traditions. In this chapter I compare some elements of Buddhist and Christian understandings of healing and suggest useful practices for the helping professions from each set of traditions. I suggest how spirituality in Buddhist and Christian traditions can help deal with personal crises and trauma, drawing on symbolic and spiritual dimensions as distinct from psychological, emotional or physiological approaches to healing. I am of the firm conviction that it is the symbolic power of spirituality working on our inner and outer worlds, in roughly that order, that enables our lives and practices to be transformed by new awakenings and new beginnings.

Key to the definition of spirituality I use here is a living spirituality that engages each person in the realities of their own and others' 'life worlds'. This definition moves beyond defining spiritual growth as 'an end', rather defining it as a lifelong process that spirals out to encourage less reduction or closed thinking about the world. This is in contrast to an overemphasis on rational knowledge.

Spiritual healing can describe a process of 'coming to terms with' some pain or suffered hurt of physical and mental kinds. I use the term 'healing' here to connote restoration to a wholeness of being, focusing on emotional pain and on loss in particular. Involvement in the processes of loss may mean some mental un-wellness, a physical illness, psychological deterioration or some other form of suffering that fractures selfhood. How can we develop practices in the helping professions that integrate psyche and being through intellectual, cognitive and emotional therapy and healing and thereby help to restore a holistic and wholesome psyche? This is a key concern of this chapter. I am suggesting as the end stage of this process of spiritual healing that the client should feel relatively free of some of the hurt and pain. Existential and Christian psychotherapists, such as May (1953) and Johnson (1991) respectively, emphasise the need to explore our fears and shadow nature in order to understand possibilities within ourselves. Spiritual learning is an education in these possibilities.

Using spiritual traditions for healing

> All religions share a common root, which is limitless compassion. They emphasise human improvement, love and respect for others, and compassion for the suffering of others (His Holiness the Dalai Lama 2002: 35).

Today the effects of religious conviction and practice can be cited as having scientific validity as well as being artistic and creative non-rational processes that contribute to our welfare. But how can spiritual healing and growth be facilitated? In order to reach a wide audience, careful thought needs to be given to the blending of old and new age spiritualities in managing life transitions and in sustaining helpful practices through spiritual growth. Buddhism is primarily associated with Eastern religions and Christianity with the West. Nonetheless, for both traditions the main entry point is via the telling of parables or sutras rich with life experience and insight. In both traditions the use of sacred texts or scriptures offers ways in which even today meaning and purpose can be made of often perplexing and difficult life circumstances that confront us. Furthermore, modes of contemplative endeavour and silence are used successfully in both traditions to calm the mind and body and seek deeper insight and understanding. Such methods are advocated as overcoming the 'inner noise' of our lives (Casey 1996: 91–7).

Prayer and meditation practices from within older traditions of Christianity and Buddhism are powerful tools. We can also use visual, creative and physical techniques such as guided meditations, art, music, drama, yoga and massage to enhance our spiritual awareness and to guide people to growth. Such opening up of spiritual awareness needs to be done in safe environments with trusted and specially trained leaders. A context of protection and safety is vital for these practices to nurture and render meaningful insights.

I have, over the years, relied on several key writers in my exploration of the teachings in different faiths. Daisetz Teitaro Suzuki (1979), for example, interprets the Christian mystic Meister Eckhart as having much in common with Buddhist forms of mysticism, notably Zen and Shin. Eckhart claims there is a transforming self-compassion from closeness to God in Christianity that is also encouraged in all forms of Buddhist thinking. In this closeness negatives become divine where 'shame becomes honour, bitterness becomes sweet and gross darkness, clear light. Everything takes its flavour from God and becomes divine' (Suzuki 1979: 103–4). This rather metaphysical idea has an earthy grounding in Buddhism. Buddhism encourages us to learn about and change ourselves from our own and others' experiences of suffering. Both religious traditions encourage similar reflexive thought.

Buddhism

Buddhism is a set of traditions, as other chapters in this volume testify, with many schools of thought. In a general way the main schools I rely upon here are Mahayana (Indian), Tibetan and Zen (Japanese) Buddhism. Most schools maintain a focus and balance between wisdom and compassion to attain inner enlightenment. Buddhist devotions can include verbal prayers, mantra repetition, analytic and visual meditations and a variety of other meditative practices. Further, there is a strong emphasis on healing, especially in the Indian Mahayana movements of the last two thousand years or so. Buddhist devotees have taken these practices of compassion and wisdom further afield so that today these core elements are synonymous with much activity in the many variants of Buddhism (Amore & Ching 2002). There is a variety of Buddhist spiritual texts. The key text in the traditions of the Buddhist healing deities is the Lotus Sutra. In sum, we can say there are at least four areas of practice expressed in the Lotus Sutra that facilitate healing processes.

1 *Meditative practice*

Meditative practices encourage reflection, relaxation and, crucially, 'mindfulness'. Mindfulness is a broad term used in relation to the way that, through listening to our breathing and the waking sounds around us, we are alerted to the present and this also calms us. Usually this involves relaxation and reciting or understanding instructions or sutras as reflective material, such as the chant 'Nam-Myoho-Renge-Kyo'. This chant has no literal English language translation but invites us to become one with the Buddha in meditative practice and visualisation. Other examples of reflective meditative practice in this tradition are through instructions and the chanting of prayers and sutras. For example, a Tibetan Meditation instruction invites us to 'leave the body at rest . . . leave the speech at rest . . . leave the mind at rest . . .' (quoted in Das 2000: 84). This calming and relaxing of the mind enables entry into spiritual realms in the present. Without such calming and slowing down of the nervous energies of our thoughts it is difficult to undertake psychic healing and nurturing.

2 *The need for skilful work*

Tact and discretion as skilful means to solving issues or problems of deeply personal kinds are very important to Buddhist devotees. Becoming aware of the ways these skills can enhance one's own and others' spiritual wellbeing is a feature of Buddhist reflection and meditation.

3 *Transforming self, multiple selves and constant change*

Another key precept is that change is always occurring; nothing remains static or fixed. Such a view enables less worry and anxiety about the unknown future events and keeps our being subtle and flexible in the present, that is, ready to change. This may require meditation on the truth of impermanence and is an important part of the loss and bereavement process of Buddhist spirituality. There are also traditional reflections, prayers and chants associated with these of processes of loss.

4 *Non-attachment to desired objects*

This is an application of Buddhist teaching and meditation to encourage not so much de-tachment (as used in psychology) but non-attachment to material reality, including to other people. By strengthening our inner world we are able to move beyond such attachments in a spiritual sense. Non-attachment is perhaps the central concern of Buddhist healing in that it is in our attachment to things and people, in emotional forms and otherwise, that leads to unhealthy and negative feelings such as resentment, obsessive desire and loneliness. Space does not permit a full explanation of this concept in Buddhism and the reader is encouraged to study the idea more fully (see Das 2000).

The concept of non-attachment helps us to appreciate how Buddhism can assist in relationships. It is useful in distancing ourselves from unhelpful, strong, binding and often negative emotional states. This core idea in Buddhism gives a strong frame for accessing spiritual or symbolic power in people's lives, particularly in highly stressful periods where anxiety about change or hurt and sorrow can keep people frozen and unable to act. Key to all this is the central idea of non-attachment to others and an emptying-out of our emotional noise, remembering that in effect we are attached by what these others symbolise to us.

Christianity

Christianity also offers useful guides to spiritual healing and growth. Christian spirituality is varied in its effect on wellbeing, depending on denominational and regional variants across the world, with various and diverse approaches to Christian iconography, prayer, interpretations of scripture and so on. However, there are some central tenets that assist in healing psychological, emotional and even physical un-wellness. In continuing the insights of Jung (1962), we can use spiritual understand-ings to enhance our positive side, and to emphasise virtues and qualities in ourselves that encourage us to explore our lives.

Various forms of Christianity today offer new understandings and reflective insights on consciousness and behaviour in healing processes. Features of two main approaches are discussed here.

1 Redemption and respect for (different) others

The central spiritual text for Christians, the Bible, can be read in a variety of ways, moving from historical document to a spiritual guide and inspirational text. I believe several of the well-known Gospel passages can be read for insight as healing or redemptive narratives. I was recently with a group of young people aged 16–19 years in a discussion on the Bible parable of the 'Woman at the Well'. For these young people it was about a worldly kindness and respect for difference shared between Jesus and the woman, not about evangelism or promoting a message, although it is clearly a passage that can be used in that way. To start with, a basic tenet of the more liberal and open forms of Christianity posits that every person is forgiven and loved, especially by the rather worldly but extraordinary figure of Jesus Christ. With a strong framework of self-forgiveness and compassion for others, Christianity, through its redemptive nature, enables growth and healing. This is captured well in Quaker and Catholic traditions that see God and/or Jesus in all people, especially the vulnerable, as emphasised in the Catholic social teachings of preferential options for the poor (see Di Nicola 2004).

2 A sense of forgiveness as a whole
Excessive guilt is a common problem to be confronted in developing spiritual awareness in Judeo-Christian traditions, particularly because of their emphasis on morality and human conduct. Guilt, however, is not the answer to our excesses in behaviour. In exercising self-compassion and self-healing, our own emotional lives and those of others are supported and sometimes healed. It seems a paradox that modern Christianity engenders various forms of guilt and even excessive guilt in the individual as well as openly offering avenues for becoming free of such guilt. Guilt itself can be a helpful encouragement for remorse, but excessive guilt can bind in rigid ways and fix peoples' attitudes in very unhelpful and stereotypical ways. The Christian spirituality I want to encourage for the helping professions is one that expresses unreserved and wholehearted forgiveness for perceived wrongs or hurtful actions without denying duty or responsibility.

In Protestant traditions there are several avenues for understanding how 'the Kingdom of God' can offer forgiveness of others and of ourselves.

Dorothy McRae-McMahon gives a positive example of how spiritual friendship can be enhanced by affirmation and support of self-forgiveness:

> We, your friends, announce to you that you are forgiven
> We will remind you of that when you forget it
> We will help you to remember
> That you are as vulnerably human as we are
> And that binds us together with all people
> We will walk with you . . . (McRae-McMahon 2003: 74).

Often in processes of loss, emotions become extreme and people act in uncharacteristic ways for which they may later be embarrassed or regretful. This very practical prayer encourages an understanding of people as not alone, as having family and friends around them who affirm, respect and forgive whatever hurt or ill-will the person believes they have perpetrated on others or themselves.

Prayer and ritual, group discussion and reflection
One further aspect of Christian fellowship worthy of note is the communal and collective sense in which followers become aware of spiritually being in the world. In such 'community', there is a strong sense of interconnection and of sharing which encourages service to others. Such explicit and deliberate practices have similarities in their awareness in both Buddhist and Christian belief.

Professional practice and training implications
Spiritual awareness can assist in the caring professions. Increasing clients' stocks of inner knowledge and awareness can help both individuals and groups. For example, the suffering brought about by loss may be only a temporary event for some people, but for others may require either brief or longer sessions of counselling and assistance. Various losses can involve strong emotional changes that need ongoing support and counselling with central regard for the spiritual wellbeing of a person.

Clients who suffer prolonged stress, such as caring for relatives, or distress suffered as a result of abusive relationships, may benefit from

ongoing support and attention to spiritual wellbeing to aid psychological and emotional wellbeing. Appropriate spiritual counselling and
links to caring communities can offer some safe ways of dealing with
such trauma.

In the health fields in particular, where issues of death, serious
illness and associated psychological and emotional suffering are
encountered, spiritual awareness can be a great asset. Other writers
emphasise these effects in areas such as stress management and in
dealing with cancer (Garret 2005). I have been particularly interested
in how, in moving through life transitions, say, in mid-life or as a young
person coming into adulthood, we can be confronted with a myriad
possible traumas and life-changing events. The calming effects of
contemplative and meditative practice within both Christianity and
Buddhism can only create conditions of less harm and less hurt.
Furthermore, these practices can encourage inner healing for those who
suffer crisis as a result of ill health or mental ill health.

The skilful and experienced health and human service practitioner,
through careful nurturing of 'the soul', can become equipped with,
among other qualities, an ever-replenishing depth of awareness, understanding and warmth. The kind of spiritual consciousness and being
that such frameworks encourage make for a creative dimension to
helping practice. I suggest that in our spiritual being we can develop
insights about a person's qualities and help people make some new
beginnings in their lives. Qualities of discernment, discretion,
judgment, truth and positive intuitive understanding are encouraged,
especially via contemplative practices such as meditation and other
healing reflective rituals and practice.

Interpersonally, spiritual practices and their effects need both light-
heartedness and an integrity of personal ethics that builds trusting
relationships based on respect for the self-worth and empowerment of
others. Tried and true spiritual practice based within the long-standing
religious traditions of Buddhism and Christianity (despite their differences) can be seen as having both active and passive dimensions that
enable an engagement with others in the world today. Role-modelling

spiritual appreciation, spiritual healing and listening to the spirituality of clients can encourage people to live less fragmented lives. This new awareness of spirituality in helping roles can also be a dimension of social programs. This is not to forget that we and our clients live in an unjust and often 'cruel' world in which spiritual growth will (must) also be about change and justice.

Acknowledgments
I am grateful to a number of people for recent conversations on Christian and Buddhist aspects of spirituality. They have made this journey a lot easier for me. I would specifically like to thank Nara and Malcolm Pearce, Robert and Julie Urquhart and Mauro di Nicola for their conversations on and ongoing commitment to spiritual awareness.

References
Amore, R.C. and Ching, J. 2002, 'The Buddhist tradition', in W.G. Oxtoby (ed.), *World Religions: Eastern Traditions*, Oxford University Press, Oxford, pp. 198–315.
Casey, M. 1996, *Sacred Reading*, Liguori Books, Missouri.
His Holiness the Dalai Lama 2002, *The Dalai Lama's Little Book of Inner Peace*, Element, London.
Das, S. 2000, *Awakening the Buddhist Heart*, Bantam Books, Sydney.
Di Nicola, M. 2004, 'Faith seeking justice', in R. Lennan (ed.), *The Possibility of Belief*, St Pauls, Sydney, pp. 192–3.
Garret, C. 2005, *Gut Feeling: Chronic Illness and the Search for Healing*, Rodopi, Amsterdam.
Johnson, R.A. 1991, *The Shadow Shelf*, Harper Row, New York.
Jung, C.G. 1962, *Memories, Dreams, Reflections*, Collins, London.
McRae-McMahon, D. 2003, *Rituals for Life, Love and Loss*, Jane Curry Publishing, Sydney.
May, R. 1953, *Man's Search for Himself*, Norton, New York.
Moore, T. 1992, *Care of the Soul*, HarperCollins, New York.
Suzuki, D.T. 1979, *Mysticism: Christian and Buddhist*, Unwin Paperbacks, London.

24
Working with prisoners
Mark Carroll

With this chapter I'd like to acknowledge the incredible bravery and commitment of people who are willing to trust and open themselves up to involvement in a program which attempts to balance and de-toxify the mind, body and spirit of those who have custodial and non-custodial sentences. Sometimes this means a courageous departure from a drug lifestyle and facing the transitional pain of living in a drug-free uncertain existence.

BACE (Balancing Awareness Community and Empowerment) works with people who are in the probation and parole system to assist them in identifying the choices they have in the lives they lead. It attempts to work not only from a cognitive approach but from the heart and at a spiritual level too. It is a home-grown, largely participant response-driven program. By combining a cognitive and spiritual approach, BACE appears to fill a void in the treatment programs that are available for Corrective Services' clientele. While BACE does not push a particular religion or faith, it works to encourage clients to take full responsibility for their behaviour and actions.

Using principles common to many spiritual traditions and cognitive behavioural techniques, the program attempts to increase awareness, respect and discipline, capacity for good and service to others. It aims to assist participants to break free from old patterns of behaviour to re-claim their inner strength and re-connect to their potential, from which they may have separated. The participants often articulate the spiritual dimension of the program as being of great importance.

> Before I did the program I felt I had a dirty spirit. My spirit feels clean now . . . I have a will of my own now, stronger than it was before. I know what decisions to make. I never rush into anything . . . I haven't had a drink since the day I got in trouble . . . it has kept me strong in the mind and strong in the heart (B, previous inmate, long-term alcoholic and violent offender).

We have based the program on universal principles of morality that emphasise 'higher-level action' consistent with principles underpinning many of the world's great faiths, principles such as helping others, respecting oneself and others, connection, compassion, remorse, non-violence, forgiveness and individual responsibility.

Aspects of the BACE approach which set this program apart from others and which acknowledge a spirituality of participants include its voluntary nature, providing options and encouraging clients to keep their minds open and to choose strategies that have resonance for them. We wish to stress that it is not only the content of the program that is important but also the manner in which the program is conducted. An environment that is safe and supportive is paramount in creating an atmosphere of trust, where people can give themselves over to change. A holistic approach with each person and an atmosphere that is nurturing on a range of levels is created. We have found it helpful to have appropriate music, healthy food such as fruit and nuts, herbal teas and candles available during sessions of the program.

A key element of the program is the belief in a core of goodness within each person and an acknowledgment that people can grow, change and develop. There is constant recognition of the positive traits exhibited by participants. We encourage participants to focus on the present, rather than dwell on past behaviours, to focus on what they can do now and on where they want to get to. Through the development of an awareness of the consequences of their actions and the disempowering impact of problematic behaviour, the law of cause and effect, participants begin to comprehend that they may not escape their negative actions and hence a new sense of accountability is found. Karma is explored from both a spiritual and scientific perspective.

> I believe in karma. I call it right way (A, 20 years in prison, agoraphobic, heroin background).

As part of the respect for self we explore a focus on what are termed 'heart characteristics', such as self-acceptance, respect, unconditional love, honour, integrity, enthusiasm, forgiveness and compassion. We use a Buddhist meditation technique to release past negative experiences, letting these experiences go, forgiving ourselves and others, as a tool to help one be more present. We use various contemplation techniques to develop empathy and compassion for the victims of our past behaviours and to increase awareness of how to avoid recurrence of such behaviours. We introduce techniques to assist the release of anger, tension, emotional blocks and negative thoughts. These include introductory emotional release techniques, related meditations, breathwork, affirmations and visualisation. As such, we attempt to increase participants' awareness of how the mind can take control over emotion, especially with the assistance of the breath, so that negative emotions or thoughts can have less impact.

> I have developed a deep sense of self respect and inner peace . . . I regularly utilise the BACE exercises to control my anger and even depression (G).

A link is made between the importance of respect for self and for our own bodies. This is explored in the program through a focus on nutrition, the harmful effect of toxins and a particular emphasis on the adverse effects of drug use and addictions on the physical and mental body as well as the spirit. Participants are offered a yoga session as a way of facilitating physical relaxation and inner peace. Discussing and encouraging participants to engage in selfless service and compassion for others is part of a spiritual practice and acts as a bridging mechanism allowing for the possibility of a connection with other people on a deeper level. Participants are introduced to the concept that by hurting another we are not only causing a karmic consequence to ourselves, but we are also creating a ripple effect that may impact on others more widely as we are all connected.

> I think it [BACE] has cleaned my body out, not just of the toxic waste, but the negative thoughts. Now, through BACE, I think I have regained a lot of my dignity and integrity and I want to try to keep that intact (D).

There is open discussion of our purpose in life with reference to great spiritual teachers such as Gandhi, Jesus, Buddha and Mohammed, as well as reference to videos and stories of previous graduates. This discussion is put in the context of connecting participants to a greater universal energy and awareness through their positive behaviour and their exploration of a higher purpose.

> . . . 'cause it's a different way, or it's not the same old same old. It's about your inside and how you feel and stuff. It shows you different ways of dealing with stress . . . I liked some of the breathing exercises and how you could participate but you could just sit there and listen and take everything in and think about it (C).

A particularly important dimension of the work we do with our probation and parole clients is concerned with relationships, developing insight into the importance of respect in all relationships (person–person, person–society and person–police relationships). Exploring their higher purpose, participants are encouraged to participate in community projects. This can be illustrated by M's example. In July 2001, in week three of BACE, M was heavily addicted to heroin, was ostracised by his family, living in his car and thinking of committing suicide. After completing BACE, M said:

> I used to hurt people all the time. Now I enjoy helping them. Make up for my wrongs. When I first started I thought nothing of it. But, after I started, I started to learn new things . . . now I'm a million miles away from where I was before.

The police produced a 10-minute video on M and other BACE gradu-ates. Community integration is assisted by encouraging clients to try out, connect to and continue with community-related activities such as local relaxation centres, spiritual places, Alcoholics Anonymous, Narcotics Anonymous and being counsellors during and after the program.

> I no longer feel intimidated by them [Police and Department of Community Services]. I think that's based on coming to the realisation that we're all human beings and we all deserve respect (J).

At various times the program has invited spiritual practitioners from disciplines such as yoga, Christianity, Buddhism, Judaism, Islam, chi guong, kung fu and aikido to share their experiences, beliefs and philosophies with the group. The objective is not to have participants convert to any philosophy or belief, but rather for the practitioners to share information and experience that may be of benefit to participants.

> ... saved me from thinking obsessively about slashing up or committing suicide ... (D, 27 years old, three times in prison, heroin user nine years, violent background, periods of homelessness and suicidal thoughts).

I offer this chapter as testimony that the spiritual dimension is an important part of making amends and finding a path through life.

> Maybe if I can help other people on this path that I've been shown, maybe even one person, it will be worth it (D, 30-year heroin history).

Reference
All quotations are given with permission of the people involved, taken from transcripts.

Resistance

25
Eco-spirituality

Joanna Macy

Foreword

While some helping professionals have incorporated broader concep-
tions of environment into their practices (Coates 2003), the helping
professions as a whole have 'not yet appreciated the significant changes
that will occur in our personal and social relationships either in response
to environmental changes or in efforts to avoid its detrimental effects'
(Coates 2004).

Many helping professions focus on working with the 'person in
their (social) environment'. We are now challenged, however, to take a
broader perspective, in which 'environment' is not limited to the social
environment but includes the physical environment. The environmental
crisis is worsening (Coates 2004) and helping professionals are being
required to become more sensitive to links between environmental
problems and the kinds of issues with which they deal.

Western focus on the primacy of the individual and individual independence has led to exploitation of the Earth in the pursuit of
progress, growth and profit. These pressures to exploit the Earth are the
same pressures that result in social injustice (Coates 2004).

One compelling example of the link between social injustice and
environmental exploitation, in Australia, is the experience of Indigenous
Australians (and, as Coates notes (2004), the experience of many
Indigenous peoples) who suffer disconnection, including spiritual

disconnection, due to displacement from their land. This has significant implications for their wellbeing (see for example Orley, also Armstrong and Smith in this book).

We know also, for example, that degradation of the physical environment contributes to many psycho-social concerns such as crime, suicide, apathy and mental illness (Brogan & James 1980; Moroney 1981; UN WCED 1987). Moreover, ethnic minority and rural communities are disproportionately affected by various types of environmental degradation: 'In many cases, environmental risks are inextricably linked to poverty and racism' (Truax 1990: 20).

In what might be termed an 'eco-spiritual' perspective, however, everything is *interdependent* and connected and, within an overarching and integrated whole, there are many overlapping and interlocking groups, for example families, villages, cultures, economies and ecologies. This broader eco-spiritual perspective does not give economic growth overriding priority, neither is it concerned only with human development, but rather with sustainable development. It emphasises that 'person and environment are engaged in constant circular exchanges in which each is reciprocally shaping and influencing the other over time' (Eckersley 2005: 5).

Quality of life, Eckersley argues, is 'the opportunity to experience the social, economic, cultural and environmental conditions that are conducive to total well-being—physical, mental, social, (and) spiritual' (Eckersley 2005: 8). One area in which the helping professions may be involved is in challenging those structures that block individual and communal wellbeing.

Humans are thus urged to put aside competitive individualism—what Macy (1989: 210) refers to as the 'false self-concept' and 'mistaken identity'—and recognise their 'intimate and essential connectedness' to Earth and people everywhere (Coates 2004).

Issues of spirituality will, thus, be increasingly important in helping professional practice because this challenge entails the process of questioning our identity, our ultimate values and sources of meaning and engages us in 'striving for personal integrity and wholeness in the context of relationships between oneself and nature, society and ultimate meaning' (Canda 1988: 31).

In this chapter, drawing on Socially Engaged Buddhism, Joanna Macy goes some distance towards addressing this challenge.

Adapted from Joanna's talk on 14 June 2006 for the Postcarbon Institute in Oakland, California, this piece also draws from her speech on 9 May 2006 in Oxford, England for the Climate Outreach Information Network.

Interdependence with all living things: Joanna Macy

In Buddhism, there are two mudras, or hand gestures, that I cherish. Statues and paintings of Buddhas and bodhisattvas often show them. One is the 'Fear Not' or *abhaya mudra*—right hand raised at chest level, palm outward. It says, 'I will not be afraid of the fear. I will not close down, I stay fully present.' It's strikingly similar to the gesture of greeting associated with Native Americans. 'How!' they said, as I saw in the movies, and later I learned the meaning of that raised empty hand: 'See, I carry no weapon, don't be afraid.'

The second hand gesture is the Earth-touching one, the *bhumis-parsa mudra*. Its other name is 'Calling the Earth to Witness', and it connects with the story of when Gautama, soon to become the Buddha, sat down under the bodhi tree. I picture him saying, in effect, 'I am not going to get up until I have broken through to the secret of the suffering we cause ourselves and others. Until I wake up to that, I am not going to move.' This infuriated Mara, the embodiment of sin and death. Mara sent demons to frighten Gautama and dancing girls to distract him, but the Buddha-to-be didn't waver. Finally, Mara challenged him outright. 'By what right and authority do you think you can solve the mystery of suffering? Just who do you think you are?'

And Gautama offered no personal credentials. No curriculum vitae. He didn't say, 'I'm the son of a king. I graduated summa cum laude from the Yoga Institute or went to Harvard Business School.' He said nothing at all about himself. He just touched the Earth. It was by the authority of Earth that he sought liberation from suffering.

We can make that gesture too. We can touch the Earth. That act, even if only mental, reminds us of who we are and what we are about, as we confront the collapse of our oil-based economy and our oil-damaged climate. We are here for the sake of life. By the authority of our belonging to Earth from the beginning of space and time, we are here.

These Buddhist mudras are mirrored in the protocol which the Haudenosaunee or Iroquois Six Nations Confederacy used when opening their treaty meetings. You can make the following gestures mentally or physically.

> We offer salutations and respect to all present at this meeting and to all who will be affected by it.
> We brush off the chairs on which we sit—
> to make a clear space for a meeting of minds.
> We brush off from our clothing any debris picked up on the way—
> to clear our minds of extraneous matters.
> We wipe the blood from our hands—
> to acknowledge and apologise for any hurt we have inflicted.
> We wipe the tears from our eyes—
> to acknowledge and forgive any hurt we have received.
> We take the lump out of our throats—
> to let go of any sadness or disappointment.
> We take the tightness out of our chests—
> to let go of any fear or resentment.
> We acknowledge and pray for guidance
> to the Great Creator Spirit of All Life.
> Ho. So be it.

The Six Nations Confederacy weighed every decision by its effects on the seventh generation. To adopt such a practice ourselves, we would need to let the future ones figure in our minds. To help me do that, I've been trying to imagine what storytellers of the seventh generation may recount about us. Maybe they'll say something like this:

> Once there was a mighty people. They possessed the greatest concentration of economic and military power the world had ever seen. And that vast power of theirs derived from ancient sunlight stored deep in the body of the living Earth. They felt entitled to that black gold—entitled

to use it all, leaving none for us who came after. They felt entitled to it even when it lay under other peoples' lands. They felt it was theirs, because they had come to depend upon it in every aspect of their lives— in food, clothing, shelter, in travel and transportation and communicating with each other. They had lost the ability to imagine any other way of life.

A few voices warned that the black gold would run out and that its end was soon approaching. But those voices were hard to hear. More warnings came: that the burning of the black gold was disrupting the seasons and weather patterns, bringing vast climatic changes in the very metabolism of Earth. But that seemed too huge and too remote to take seriously, until . . .

Until, faster than anyone had foreseen, it all began to happen. The black gold grew harder to find, costlier to pump. They called that point, when the decline began, Peak Oil. And at the same time, it was plain to see how melting Arctic ice was altering the ocean currents which had steadied the climate for thousands of years. Droughts and flooding increased, giving a hint of the suffering in store from hunger and rioting and mass migrations.

This much, we know the future storytellers can say. What will they go on to recount? What ensuing drama will they recall?

That is partly up to us, of course, because we are living it. We cannot make the realities of end of oil and climate change go away, but we *can* choose how we're going to respond.

It seems to me that there are two kinds of response to massive collective trauma. One is to contract—to close down in denial and fear, to tighten the heart and the fist. The other is to open up—open eyes, heart, hands, freeing the capacity to adapt and create. We know we're capable of that, because it is happening now all around our world.

A revolution is underway. You may not see it, if you don't know where to look, for in the words of Gil Scott Heron (1970), 'this revolution will not be televised'. But once we become aware of this tidal change, the end of oil appears not as some hopeless, ghastly fate, but as an adventure requiring all our wisdom and passion for life.

This adventure is what many of us call the 'Great Turning'. It is the epochal shift from the industrial growth society to a life-sustaining society. This is the context in which to view the end of oil and climate change. Those two major disrupters of normalcy weave through all our other environmental battles, and they are at play, as well, in our militarism and social inequality and abuses of political power. More clearly than other crises and calamities, they sound the death knell of our industrial growth society.

So those future storytellers, looking back at our time, may go on to speak of the Great Turning. I can imagine them saying:

> Our ancestors back then, bless them, they had no way of knowing if the Great Turning could succeed. No way of telling if a life-sustaining culture could emerge from the death throes of the industrial growth society. It probably looked hopeless at times. Their efforts must have often seemed isolated, paltry, and darkened by confusion. Yet they went ahead, they kept on doing what they could—and, because they persisted, the Great Turning happened.

For us alive today in the midst of it all, we can learn to see the Great Turning by bringing into focus its three dimensions. They co-arise and reinforce each other. The first dimension is holding actions in defence of life; they function to slow down the destruction caused by the industrial growth society and buy time for more fundamental changes. The second includes all the life-affirming structures emerging now, fresh social and economic experiments ranging from land trusts, eco-villages and local currencies to alternative forms of education and healing, many of them inspired by old, Indigenous ways. And the third dimension consists of a profound shift in our perception of reality. As the ecological and systems world-view takes hold our planet appears to us, not as supply house and sewer, but as a living web of relationships. And as ancient spiritual teachings resurface, we awaken to our essential identity with this web of life and accept our sacred responsibility to honour and serve it.

This multidimensional revolution holds such promise that I can't help thinking of it as comparable to the First Turning of the Wheel, when the Buddha Dharma broke forth upon the world. Once again the reality of our radical interconnectedness with each other, and all beings, through space and time becomes clear. And now our very survival depends on our waking up to that reality.

This Great Turning alters none of the facts about the end of oil and climate change. It cannot save us from the immense and painful challenges they bring upon us; but it does enable us to engage them wholeheartedly, with wisdom and courage. For, like those two mudras—Fear Not and Touch the Earth—it grounds us in our mutual belonging.

In that mutual belonging is our solidarity—with past and future generations and with each other. There is no end to it. That resource will never run out.

References

Brogan, D.R. and James, L.D. 1980, 'Physical environment correlates of psychosocial health among urban residents', *American Journal of Community Psychology*, vol. 8, pp. 507–22.

Canda, E.R. 1988, 'Conceptualizing spirituality for social work: Insights from diverse perspectives', *Social Thought*, vol. 14, no. 1, pp. 30–46.

Coates, J. 2003, *Ecology and Social Work: Toward a New Paradigm*, Fernwood, Halifax.

Coates, J. 2004, 'From Ecology to Spirituality and Social Justice', *Currents: New Scholarship in the Human Services*, 2004 [webapps2.ucalgary.ca/~socialwk/Currents/articles] (accessed May 2006).

Eckersley, R. 2005, 'The challenge of post-materialism', *The Weekend Australian Financial Review*, 24–28 March, pp. 5–10.

Macy, J. 1989, 'Awakening to the ecological self', in J. Plant (ed.), *Healing the Wounds: The Promise of Ecofeminism*, New Society, Santa Cruz, pp. 210–11.

Moroney, R.M. 1981, 'Policy analysis within a value theoretical framework', in R. Haskins and I.J. Gallagher (eds), *Models for Analysis of Social Policy*, Ablex, Norwood, New Jersey, pp. 78–101.

Scott Heron, G. 1970, <allpoetry.com/Poem> (accessed May 2006).

Swimme, B. and Berry, T. 1992, *The Universe Story*, Harper, San Francisco.

Truax, H. 1990, 'Minorities at risk', *Environmental Action*, January–February, pp. 19–21.

UN World Commission on Environment and Development 1987, *Our Common Future*, Oxford University Press, Oxford.

Conclusion
'The end is where we start . . .'[1]

Natalie Bolzan and Fran Gale

Developing a spiritual helping practice is not an easy or well-signposted development in professional helping practices. Many practitioners who daily struggle in their attempts to best assist the people who come to see them wrestle with issues of spirituality and how to connect with an aspect of existence which is not tangible or even acknowledged. The dominance of economic rationalist and managerialist thinking in human services over recent decades has meant that human services are under increasing pressure to function in certain often 'measurable' and standardised ways. This book raises a challenge to this perspective and asserts the significance of deeper, broader values. In the preceding chapters practitioners have revealed that it is not only legitimate but even 'mainstream' to be discussing larger questions around life's meaning with those seeking help. We have heard from practitioners who have not only struggled with these concerns but have endeavoured to put into practice ways of working in a manner which is spiritually sensitive.

From many faith traditions and newer spiritual understandings this book has explored how the spiritual can be part of professional practice. Practitioners spoke of their formal training as ignoring spirituality, a significant omission which then left them to negotiate this area on their own; consequently the pathway to their spiritually informed practice was often a private and ongoing journey. A diversity of paths to spirited practices emerges, with no one path as dominant. Spirituality emerges as multifaceted and something which is dynamic, with a power of its own. It may involve a personal relationship with the Deity or may be a 'losing of oneself' as in meditation, prayer or yoga. It may be a 'giving over' of oneself to a higher being, or a revelation and commitment to 'honouring the God within'.

Many of the preceding chapters provide clear endorsement of the belief that a spiritually informed practice provides insight and change, as manifested in wellbeing and a sense of 'wholeness'. This is consistent with an increasing body of literature which articulates the benefits of such practice. However, the process by which change occurs requires exploration. Our contributors describe a transformative experience that occurs beyond the helping relationship and which allows a new encounter within the helping relationship. Something is created that is more than the spirituality of the practitioner or the person seeking help, though both of these are significant. Spiritually sensitive practice introduces another dimension into the helping relationship, and offers a new layer of understanding and a very different way of responding.

'Spirited practice' is not without challenges, as the practices discussed throughout this book have revealed. Tensions may exist around expectations of one's own spirituality and the change which can be brought about by spiritually sensitive practice. As our contributors suggest, this is an issue which requires ongoing awareness and reflexive practice. For some the conflation of religious dogma with spirituality was of potential concern. While religion may offer the means for a spiritual practice, as our contributors have shown, proselytising practice is distinct from spiritual practice.

This volume has shown a relationship between spirituality and power. The political force of the collective associated with spirituality can be seen in many chapters, such as those dealing with Indigenous issues, domestic violence, asylum seekers and eco-spirituality. Making whole contains elements of responsibility for the self and also for others. Hence, the focus in some spiritual practices on attending to the self or preparing the self was described as a precursor to more honest and authentic dealings with others. The 'letting go of attachment to things in order to free oneself from unnecessary pain' was also seen as preparation for a fuller connection to others. In many of the accounts, helping involves an immediate social imperative, an interconnectivity and interrelatedness with all people and the life-world.

The individualistic nature of some understandings of spirituality has been challenged by the practitioners, who see that spirituality acts as a unifying force for social justice.

Spiritual practices appear in a variety of settings and present in a variety of modes, from very structured and planned, through to spontaneous and free flowing. In this work we have heard from those involved in the helping professions, generally at the level of the individual or small groups. The spiritual practices which occur in larger communities or organisations are of increasing interest and also worthy of exploration. The way in which spirituality informs health and welfare agencies is of particular interest, given the Australian trend toward the increasing provision of welfare services through non-government organisations, many of which are religiously based, and needs further attention.

None in this volume would put themselves forward as an expert or even as accomplished in a particular field of spiritual practice. Still, they have each found a path or a means by which to explore, with the people who seek their help, a spiritual dimension. A spiritually sensitive helping practice can be developed by all who have a concern for a holistic practice.

Merely being open to a spiritual dimension in one's helping practice enables the creation of something unique. Spirituality as a 'making whole' reveals our connection with each other and with ultimate meaning, and shows that whether at the level of the individual, the community or more broadly the Earth on which we live, spirited practices enable a new awakening.

When we come to the end, we find a new beginning . . . and 'know the place for the first time'.[2]

Endnotes
1. T.S. Eliot, *Four Quartets*, 'Little Gidding'.
2. ibid.

Reference
Traversi, D. 1976, *T.S. Eliot: The Longer Poems*, The Bodley Head, Sydney.

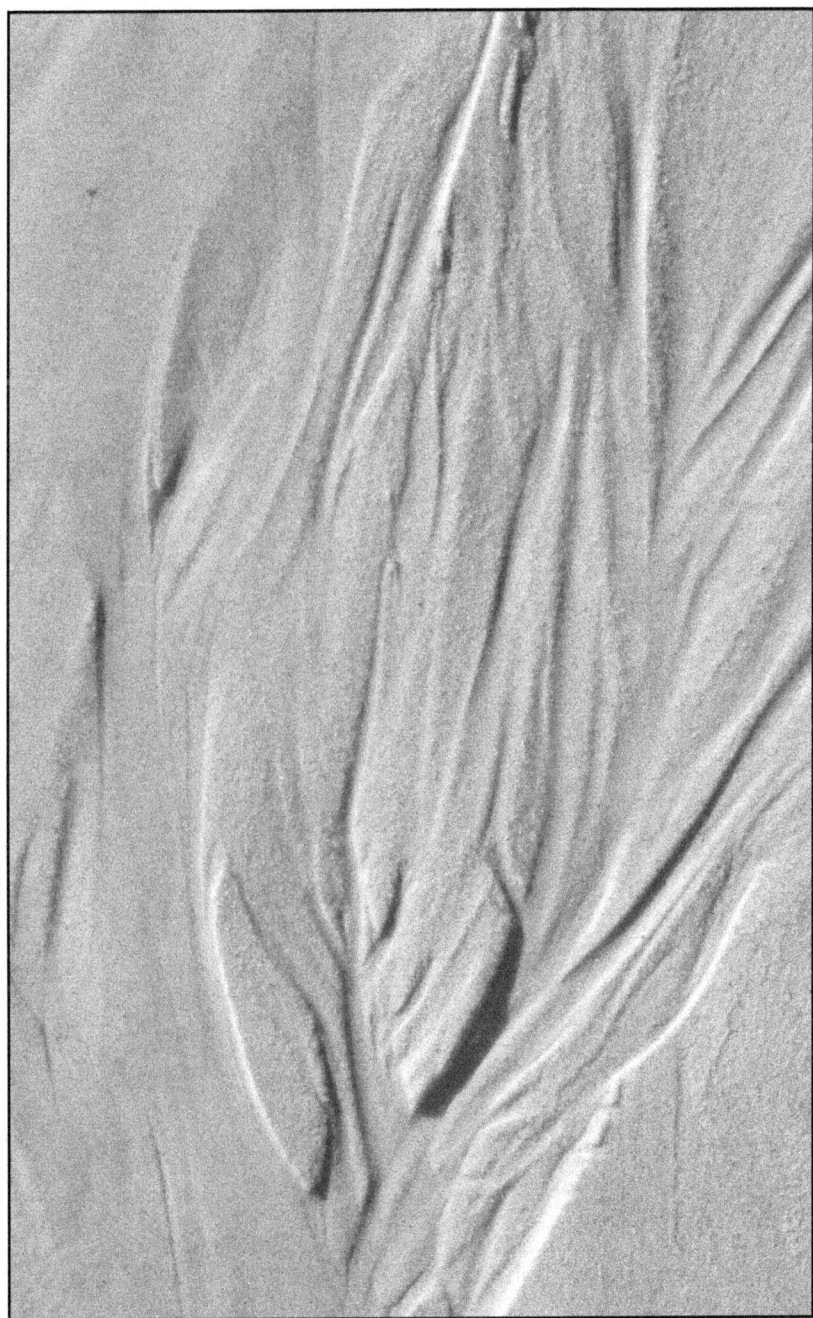

Index

For Product Safety Concerns and Information please contact our EU
representative GPSR@taylorandfrancis.com
Taylor & Francis Verlag GmbH, Kaufingerstraße 24, 80331 München, Germany